Aesthetics and Human Resource Development

The emergence of Human Resource Development (HRD) as a subject presents many opportunities for reviewing intellectual and practical boundaries. Many streams of contemporary thinking can be connected with it, to better illuminate the challenges of developing people in a time of flux and change. The aesthetic perspective can be as significant in that process as can political, psychological, social and economic perspectives. This is because it offers a way to contest the utilitarian economism which has a stranglehold on HRD and a theoretical, narrow, skills-based, quantitative and theoretical approach. This can be broken and a fresh era in HRD introduced, for the good of more people, if the dormant, silenced or absent voices, such as those associated with the aesthetic tradition, are heard.

The connections between HRD and aesthetics are not only intellectual and theoretical. They are intensely practical, too. Alongside the growth of the creative class, with cultural industries now forming a major sector of employment and wealth creation, creativity and imagination are becoming highly valued in the workplace. *Aesthetics and Human Resource Development* explores how this increasing importance of creativity impacts on the ways in which we understand HRD, and what its role is in the future for cultural industries to prosper. Part of this is to ask whether HRD is an area of theory and action whose professionals are, or can become, members of the creative class.

In exploring these intellectual traditions and practical issues around aesthetics Stephen Gibb identifies how the discourses of, and debates around, creativity, beauty and imagination have something to offer the world of HRD as it seeks to evolve beyond the utilitarian paradigms of human development and people management that prevailed in the twentieth century. Aesthetics and aesthetic values can be used to reconfigure how we might understand and practise HRD anew in the future.

Stephen Gibb is Senior Lecturer in Human Resource Management at the University of Strathclyde, Scotland. He researches and teaches in HRD with the aim of continuously testing the boundaries of the subject, keeping it alive and open to creative and imaginative theorising and practice.

Routledge Studies in Human Resource Development
Edited by Monica Lee, Lancaster University, UK

HRD theory is changing rapidly. Recent advances in theory and practice, how we conceive of organisations and of the world of knowledge, have led to the need to reinterpret the field. This series aims to reflect and foster the development of HRD as an emergent discipline.

Encompassing a range of different international, organisational, methodological and theoretical perspectives, the series promotes theoretical controversy and reflective practice.

Aesthetics and Human Resource Development
Connections, Concepts and Opportunities

Stephen Gibb

Routledge
Taylor & Francis Group

LONDON AND NEW YORK

First published 2006 by Routledge
2 Park Square, Milton Park, Abingdon, Oxfordshire, OX14 4RN

Simultaneously published in the USA and Canada
by Routledge
270 Madison Avenue, New York, NY 10016

Routledge is an imprint of the Taylor & Francis Group

© 2006 Stephen Gibb

Typeset in Garamond by
Taylor & Francis Books
Printed and bound in Great Britain by
Antony Rowe Ltd, Chippenham, Wiltshire

British Library Cataloguing in Publication Data
A catalogue record for this book is available from the British Library

Library of Congress Cataloging in Publication Data
A catalog record has been requested

ISBN10: 0-415-36097-8

ISBN13: 978-0-415-36097-5

Taylor & Francis Group is the Academic Division of T&F Informa plc.

For Jen, making the world beautiful beyond imagining

Contents

List of illustrations

Figures

Tables

Boxes

Foreword

Growing interest in Human Resource Development (HRD), the realisation of people's potential, reflects many hopes for the future, for change and progress in the twenty-first century. If HRD is to fulfil those hopes then the researchers and practitioners concerned with it need to keep abreast of the many opportunities that change and progress bring. This book is about a particular set of opportunities: those associated with the onset of an age of aesthetics, the rise to prominence of the creative class, and the reconceptualisation of cultural industries. These all share at their core concerns about people's potential: the people whose role it is to create new ideas, technologies and content, people involved in science, engineering, design, arts, education, music and entertainment. As well as these the concern is also with the potential development of creative professionals, people who engage in complex problem-solving requiring autonomy, flexibility, judgement and high levels of education. What these people are all deemed to share is an ethos; valuing creativity, individuality, difference and merit.

There are three particular opportunities for HRD that are identified here. First is the opportunity of meaning. If the age of aesthetics and the creative class, creativity and artfulness, are to be an integral part of much socio-economic activity, then how are we to make sense of HRD and its role in that kind of environment? The concern here is not to reproduce arguments about what class is and how to define the creative class closely. It is to accept the issue and move on to consider how that changes our thinking about HRD. It means that, as well as the conventional analytical frameworks of psychology, economics and systems thinking, there are constructs around creativity that need to be understood and articulated around HRD: aesthetics, beauty and imagination. Second, is HRD itself to be seen as an area of practice depending upon creativity, belonging to the creative class, or not? It will be argued here that HRD can belong to the creative class, and that this implies treating HRD in theory and practice more as an art and not primarily as a science. The implication is that being artful is intrinsic to effective HRD, and that there is fresh thinking about HRD processes to be gained from exploring the arts. The final opportunity is then to consider the role of HRD in helping to make the creative class and the artful organisation. In this regard, the concerns are then how to develop creativity, the nature of issues around the growth of the creative industries, and the consequences of aligning HRD strategies on cultural capital and artfulness.

Our current understanding of the interaction and effects of these three opportunities is limited. It is fragmented, and largely determined by theoretical developments originating in the USA. A more complete and thorough analysis of these opportunities around creativity and artfulness and their interaction with HRD is needed, historically, empirically and internationally. This is intended to be a UK-grounded but generally accessible introduction and overview. The general interaction and interdependence (see Figure P1) is of concern to those studying and teaching HRD, and those concerned with organisational and management change more broadly, wherever creativity is an issue.

The aesthetic opportunites of HRD require a reaffirmation of HRD itself, in the context of the forces that otherwise belittle and overshadow the human dramas of people realising their potential: that is, the context of successes through science and technology. These render culture, the arts, the aesthetic both more precarious and more precious. They are precarious because they appear to be of so little economic, social, political and theoretic

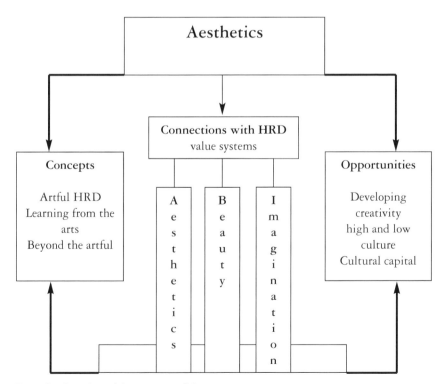

Figure P1 Overview of the structure of the text

value; they are mere entertainment. Yet the roles of culture, the arts and the aesthetic are more than mere entertainment and diversion. They are a source of making sense of, and valuing, the human condition and conduct. That is as important as ever. Exploring aesthetics and creativity is not an excuse to be diverted from appreciating the role and function of developing people's potential; it is an invitation to confront current and future dilemmas face on.

The following provides a chapter-by-chapter overview of the text. **Chapter 1** concerns defining creativity and HRD, and the significance of the creative class concept and debate. The creative class are meant to be the new leaders of dynamic economies and societies (Florida 2002). This represents a key context for rethinking HRD. The purpose, processes and practices of both HRD and creativity cannot be identified definitively and universally. Rather, they are interpreted and understood according to the values of the participants who constitute them. These participants act in circumstances, historical and cultural, which influence how they see and think about HRD and creativity. As those circumstances change, so do perceptions and thinking about HRD and creativity. This is illustrated by outlining four examples of concerns with creativity, artfulness, organisational analysis and exploring what art is. Taken together, the culmination of concerns around creativity in the rise of the creative class is argued to present three opportunities for HRD: the opportunities of meaning, of membership and of making.

Chapter 2 considers how these themes have been aired most explicitly, but in a fragmented way, in the context of the USA. It explores in more detail the idea of increasing interests in creativity, artfulness and the rise of the creative class. The major change is new thinking about creativity and the growth of the creative class. The rise of this class has the potential to remake commerce, culture and consciousness (Postrel 2003). It accompanies a change to 'artful making' displacing industrial organisation (Austin and Devin 2003). Artful creation is desired and sought by leading organisations (Darso 2004) who seek to change and grow through creativity at work (Kingdon 2002). Together, these examples of inquiry and analysis around creativity themes suggest a new context within which HRD needs to be considered: the age of creativity.

Chapters 3, 4 and 5 deal with the challenge of meaning around the constructs of the aesthetic, beauty and the imagination in HRD. **Chapter 3** considers how a theory of values, and one particular model of that with six value sets, foregrounds the aesthetic. The aesthetic value system is the equal of others in shaping instrumental and terminal values that underpin beliefs and behaviours alongside the social, economic, theoretical, political and spiritual (see Figure P2). HRD interpreted from an aesthetic value system is outlined. Alongside the utilitarian pursuit of practicality via HRD, the serious social campaigns for amelioration and justice via HRD, and the veritistic pursuit of theoretical truth about HRD, there is HRD motivated and structured by playfulness, artfulness and imaginative truth.

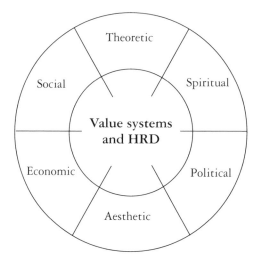

Figure P2 Modelling value systems, six factors

Chapter 4 explores imagination, a wellspring of creativity and focus for improving the capacity to engage with development effectively. An initial discussion of the imaginative worlds of young adults illustrates the relevance of examining imagination in HRD. Conceptual issues and connections with HRD are expanded upon by analysing how the playing of games can be integrated with learning – both physical games and computer games. Engaging with the HRD imagination presents opportunities for improvements but raises serious questions about the style and control of learning and development.

Chapter 5 considers how, accompanying the emergence of greater interest in aesthetic values and debates, the discourse of beauty has become more significant. The exploration of this concept proceeds by defining and critiquing four major theories of beauty: the metaphysical, the rationalist, the structure of feeling theory and the biological. The structure of feeling theory is considered further, and how it affects understanding and interpreting HRD. This is examined by looking at the importance of the structure of feeling to the Bohemian world view, and a direct textual treatment, derived from architecture. The structure of feeling of beauty is to be analysed as a part of social construction. Social construction is integral to connecting beauty with HRD, and includes inevitable contests and resistance as well as insight.

Chapters 6, 7 and 8 deal with the implications of HRD being seen to belong to the creative class, depending on creativity and artfulness. **Chapter** 6 extends analysis into the interplay of values and practical issues in HRD. The examples of Earl's ideas about creative training, Coleman's ideas about the artist's model of teaching and Darso's ideas about artfulness in business all lead to contrast: between an expert and an artful approach to learning and development. It may be that a creativity-oriented and artful framework is able to help give a more convincing and powerful account of the human experience of change, and the kinds of forces, other than economic, social, political, theoretic and spiritual, which can be harnessed to move and shape the course of human development in positive directions. This reveals underlying paradigm problems of discipline versus control, which need to be considered by individuals, organisations and policy-makers as they seek to develop more creative HRD.

Chapter 7 considers the use of arts-based HRD. In various ways the forms and mechanisms of the arts, from mythic storytelling to public sculptures, may be adapted to and integrated with HRD. The role of organisations like A&B, seeking to promote arts-based training, is reviewed. A case of an orchestra ensemble is discussed. The broader links with arts and organisational change are also reflected upon. If there are these possible benefits, there are also potential drawbacks. The use of form and harmony for shock and estrangement versus producing great art introduces concerns about the functions of art, and the roles that actors around arts are playing. With the former, the primary purpose of realising people's potential is an esoteric one, producing whole and harmonious people. With the latter, it is an exoteric one, proceeding by shock and dissonance to constantly break people away from their comfort zones.

Chapter 8 extends the analysis more broadly and more deeply, beyond a concern with artfulness to the interactions of the aesthetic with the shared and contested territory that the other neglected value system, the spiritual, occupies. Three different interpretations of this interaction are explored. First is that beyond artfulness there is a greater purpose fulfilled by artfulness than the merely aesthetic (De Bouton 2004). Second is that there is no greater purpose beyond artfulness, and indeed the aesthetic is a distraction from more serious purposes (Tillich 2000). Finally there is the modernist concern with critical theory, and the hope that aesthetic experiences themselves could play a role equivalent to the spiritual, either in the vacuum of such beliefs in advanced capitalist cultures or as an alternative to them. The affinities and contests between artfulness, aesthetic-based perspectives and spiritual theories and debates are considered a complex challenge.

The next section explores HRD and its role in making the creative class. **Chapter 9** explores HRD as a means to an end, supporting the economy of the imagination. When we seek to understand the task of developing people's potential, should we be motivated and guided in part by whatever it means to create a more beautiful and sublime person? When we think about HRD, should we be more or less in thrall to our imaginations, ceaselessly asking 'What if?' Would exploring HRD as a means to attaining harmonious resolutions compromise reasoning and argument? So that research determining what is true, and countering the delusions people may otherwise be prone to develop is turned away from pursuing practical goals?

Chapter 10 goes beyond the basics of nurturing creativity to consider how HRD becomes an integral part of sustaining the creative industries, the economic engines of the culture of beauty and the economy of the imagination.

HRD then needs to be oriented on supporting and developing these. As HRD itself is in transition around the creative and cultural industries, in the advanced economies and elsewhere, the state has had to respond to this. The UK history and context for this is described. This raises new question about the interface between the long-reigning force of financial capital and the organisational forms it favours, with the newer reconceptualisations of social capital. These cannot be analysed any longer without taking into account cultural capital as well.

In **Chapter** 11 the problem of double standards which exist about valuing the artful and the creative is outlined and explored. This involves considering how in the world view at the dominant conventional class, the middle class, the valuing of the aesthetic alongside the well-established frameworks of social, economic, theoretic and political ways of understanding HRD is problematic. The ultimate opportunity is how to rehabilitate what have been neglected paradigms, re-installing them as ways in which it becomes common and useful to have to understand and interpret HRD. For some time it is likely that the predominant value systems will resist the influence of those who are associated with an aesthetic value system in HRD. The aesthetic will continue to seem unusual, weird, odd and suspect. Yet alongside the reincarnation of ethics along with metaphysics, the nurturing of pleasure and sensibility could be a part of realising the potential of HRD more fully.

In conclusion some problems around seeking to understand the greater interaction of HRD and creativity in the context of meanings, membership of the creative class and its manufacture are explored with reference to the values system model. In **Chapter** 12 the issue is how to connect with the other participants in HRD – the sceptical economists, the committed social campaigners, the critical positivist scientists or the pragmatic politicians – and explores how aesthetics provides a new and useful value system for understanding and interpreting HRD. The opportunity is to make as clear a case as can be made that understanding the totality of realising people's potential is enriched by acknowledging that the aesthetic value system exists and matters. Such a gestalt can help to counterbalance the imbalances associated with other frameworks: with the utilitarian imbalances of impractical measurement ambitions, the social imbalances of seeking through HRD to remedy problems whose roots are elsewhere, the political imbalances of the right and the left in co-opting HRD to their causes, and the theoretic distortions of objectivism. There is also an imbalance, a shadow side of the aesthetic as a way of making sense of HRD. This can be understood via the imbalance it introduces with regard to each of the other value systems. These would include being anti-economic, valuing 'higher' things and art making HRD ineffectual; being anti-social, by accommodating mysticism, the irrational and the weird; being anti-truth, a refuge for fantasy, falsehood and ideology; being anti-political, an excuse to substitute personal creativity for collective action, living inside the belly of the whale; and being anti-spiritual, affording the sensual and the passionate precedence over the moral.

Part I
Connections

1 Pretty smart: aesthetics and HRD

Introduction

There is an opportunity to engage openly in new and experimental thinking. In HRD such as is possible around exploring aesthetic opportunities. This can be better understood and explored as a normal part of the study of HRD. There is an emerging interdependence between the two major arenas of aesthetics and HRD in theory and action. Definitions of these are outlined here. The questions this interaction raises are identified. How can delighting the senses, providing pleasure, being like an artist, be relevant to producing and consuming HRD? Why are the methods and forms of appreciation found in producing and consuming art relevant to producing and consuming HRD? What will it take to realise a future with more dynamic, innovative and creative workforces and organisations? The question is not whether aesthetics are relevant and significant for HRD, but how it is significant.

Why aesthetics?

Ambitions for the public image of Human Resource Development (HRD) are great. They are to be charismatic, powerful and accepted into the eche-lons of serious science, business and policy-making: possessing a combination of qualities something like psychology, something like economics, and something like the finance function. Any new contribution to the debates around the subject's identity, such as this is, will be explicitly or implicitly judged in that context. The problem with building such a public image and impression of HRD such that it means different things to different people, and may be manifest in diverse forms. One aspect of that is to consider HRD as an arena of discourse and practice influenced by aesthetics.

That is the opportunity, but the threat is that to the repute and credi-bility of HRD as a subject concerned with scientific theory and professional practice. These kinds of question have not been an essential or integral part of either of these (Phillips and Soltis 1998). Theory and professional practice were too serious to be entangled with the mess of aesthetics and associated matters like beauty and creativity. But even within such critical views, that perception is changing. This is because a consciousness that design permeates all aspects of human endeavour (Lawson 1997; Norman 2001) is being more widely accepted. HRD is not exempt from being thought about, like anything else, in terms of its debt to creativity and the associated aesthetic issues that raises (Strati and Guillet de Montoux 2002; Shani and Docherty 2003; Bredeson 2003).

What the terms HRD and creativity entail does need to be clarified, but that is something of a process to be achieved by the reader on working through the book rather than something that can just be stipulated at the outset. Examples of their interaction can be given initially, as glimpses. Beyond these glimpses there is a concern with the onset of an age of creativity and the growth of a creative class, and what that means for HRD. HRD needs to adapt to this changing environment, and this changing environment depends upon improved HRD.

This is the environment in which HRD consumers and producers exist and are adapting to each other anew. Some HRD producers are having difficulty adapting to the challenges and opportunities. Some simply insist on ignoring the need to make changes that they consider beneath them; to be concerned with creativity, with the look and feel of things, is anathema to them. They will not condescend to dignify such 'dumbing down'. Yet all the time they are disingenuously ignoring that what they actually do is defend their existing forms of creativity and aesthetic rather than deny that they do matter. If people are turned off HRD and do not participate – or if they suffer in sullen complicity where they have to join in but feel time and energy is wasted – tough on them; the consumers need to change. HRD producers are ready to level blame everywhere for the problems that exist, for the difficulties, gaps, resistances and failures of HRD. They will maybe attribute it to all sorts of factors; but close to home there is the extent to which they themselves may be the cause, through being ambivalent members of the creative class, and neglecting aesthetics failing to support the development of creativity.

Defining creativity

To be creative is to bring things into existence and to cause them to happen as a result of one's actions: to make things. The opposite of this ontological sense of creativity is to be destructive: to remove things from existence, to stop things from happening. The 'making' definition of creativity is only a part of the picture, though. For people may be making things but in a repetitive, replicating way. The absence of creativity is then not 'not making': it is to have no original ideas, but merely to follow and never produce anything new; to be static, repetitive, and thus dull and boring. Creativity is also about going beyond what exists. The desire to go beyond what exists is apparently intrinsic to the human condition, transcending what has been and is currently being made as it is imperfect, inadequate, unsatisfactory, shocking, dreadful – or just plain old. To be creative is to bring in the new and change, it is to want to dispense with the already existing, the established, the old.

Creativity is a complex concept. It is most often simply associated with having original ideas and making, especially in the production of an artistic work. For some it is revered as the highest-level cognitive capacity. It is perceived to be at the core of rare genius in the artistic, scientific, economic, social and political arenas. But it also exists within and informs the lives of many in the 'creative classes', people whose work requires them to bring things into existence, to cause things to happen. More than that, for others creativity is a basic human capability, not a talent reserved for artists or a special class; it is a universal and integral part of what it means to be human, and exercising creativity is as essential to health as is exercising the body. For the purposes of initial discussions, creativity will be defined as 'imaginative activity fashioned so as to produce outcomes that are both original and of value' (NACCE 1999).

Defining HRD

A first concern is that the significance, the culmination and purpose of this analysis depends on what is meant by HRD. HRD can be defined in multiple ways. In narrow terms it may be defined as being concerned with practice in and perceptions of the education, training and development of people in the employment context. Or it can be defined in broader terms as practice in and perceptions of a discipline which is the product of the union of organisational analysis and theory on the one hand and Human Resource Management (HRM) on the other. In the narrow sense, the concerns of HRD may be seen as theorising and practising around adult learning and development. In the broader sense, the concerns of HRD may be seen as an integral part of the organising and management of employment. In any case, HRD involves more than running training courses and vocational education for skills, though these are indeed matters of fundamental importance. It may stretch from the challenges of making the experience of prison one that reforms offenders to the challenges of facilitating the emergence of a new generation of leaders in major institutions.

A second concern is that HRD in either of these senses can be understood from various perspectives. The psychological, the economic, systems thinking and ethics are all understood to be and accepted as prominent perspectives (Swanson and Holton 2001). As HRD evolves as a subject, other possible perspectives which may be additional to these are encountered (McGoldrick *et al.* 2002). Is a concern with the 'strategic' or the 'international' or 'knowledge management' an additional perspective on HRD, or just a mixture of these primary perspectives in a special context? Should there be an anthropology perspective on HRD, a social psychological perspective on HRD, a 'critical' perspective on HRD? These seem to be the intellectual concerns which are being encountered as the subject evolves. They may be intellectual concerns which are welcomed as part of a burgeoning discipline, or treated with scepticism as intrusions upon the coherence, identity and boundaries of the subject (Gilley *et al.* 2003; Marquardt *et al.* 2004). To understand such empathy or antipathy to new perspectives it is possible to structure conceptualisations of HRD as representing two traditions, the naturalist conception of HRD and the positivist conception (see Table 1.1).

In the narrow and positivistic tradition the concern with subjects like creativity is then to be centred upon 'the selection, orchestration and delivery of stimulation (by means of these various sources) [which] comprises a large portion of the decisions the teacher must make every day' (Gagne and Perkins Driscoll 1988, p. 151). With the naturalistic conception of HRD the attention is more directed towards the case for exploring creativity using qualitative methods, for ethnographic sense-making and the methods that entails, and promoting dialogue rather than adopting the norms and methods of science. Here the concern is that there are multiple perspectives on the meaning and detail of creativity in HRD; no single, independent and objective version of the truth about an aspect of HRD is possible; what should be done, what works, what is of value is open to interpretation and contextually bound, not law-like and generalisable.

Defining the creative class

The economics of creativity, the demand and supply, the costs, benefits and wealth-generating functions of it, require HRD for creativity. Human creativity has always been an elementary economic force, with creative people and their works being an integral part of cultures and civilisations. Their creative impulse has always been present, but it now features more strongly and is something that advanced economies and thus the global economy are more dependent upon. The historical trend, following the rise and decline of the working class in manufacturing industries, then the rise and decline of the service sector, is the rise of the creative class (Florida 2002). This class, rather than an elite of entrepreneurs, comes to the fore as the foundation of economic vitality and success. A platform for reversing the decline of cities by

Table 1.1 Conceptions of HRD

Positivist conception of HRD	*Naturalist conception of HRD*
HRD is an ensemble of activities around learning and performance.	HRD is a changing synthesis of concerns, socio-economic forces and circumstances.
HRD in organisations seeks to control and direct people at work.	HRD in organisations seeks to offer insights that open options.
HRD theory prescribes what should be.	HRD theory is grounded in cases.
Good thinking about HRD shows premises and invites critique.	Good thinking about HRD helps escape limiting frames of mind.
HRD can be based on 'scientific' authorities.	HRD needs to encourage and participate in 'language' games, creating meaning through critique.

building a better people climate, not just a better business climate, produces the homage to the creative class.

New ideas, new technology and new content are needed from science and engineering, architecture and design, education, arts, music and entertainment. More creative professionals are needed, not more entrepreneurs. Florida does help situate this broad trend in the context of reciprocal interactions, between economic activity and social change, centred upon this creative class. The class prefers, and needs, certain social conditions to prevail; yet those conditions are ones which others oppose and challenge. The expanding creative class, to take over the reins from old entrepreneurs, needs to develop an awareness of itself, to be able to influence and lead in the broader society, accordingly in an enlightened way. This 'raising of consciousness' in pursuit of enlightened leadership is the task; researchers, policy-makers and others ought to orient themselves around that. That is the crux of the interaction of the economic and social analysis Florida proposes.

Florida's propositions

The economic proposition is that the right mix of features in a 'place', a location, is needed as the necessary foundation to be secured for the complex matrix of resources and people needed to operate in the high-value-added industries and sectors. And by 'place' Florida does not mean 'nation' or 'region', but rather specific zones: corridors, valleys, parts of cities. A prime example would be Silicon Valley. The social proposition that accompanies this is that part of this mix of features are social relations based on a preponderance of many 'weak tie' relations, contingent commitments and quasi-anonymity. Those are the desirable – indeed, essential – 'community' conditions for a creative class to exist. This contrasts with community conditions based on relations involving a few strong ties, abiding commitments and being well known and integrated. That latter recipe has come to be know as the nurturing of social capital. Florida is explicit: the cultivation of the creative class who underpin financial success is the goal, not the cultivation of social capital. Indeed, the cultivation of social capital, strong ties and commitments in tight networks is an obstacle to the growth of the creative class.

When identifying dimensions of creativity Florida makes it clearer what he is proposing. Creativity is the ability to synthesise, to produce new and useful combinations. It is a fragile capacity; history demonstrates that creativity can flourish and fade in people, organisations, places and entire civilisations. And creativity is a capacity which all people may possess, not just an elite. Creativity also requires a 'social process': relations in which contributors and collaborators can connect and be in open ferment. The conditions favouring this are then to be valued. Florida mentions specifically:

- valuing self-assurance and risk-taking; people who are subversive, disruptive, rebellious;
- valuing creative methods; preparation, incubation, illumination;
- valuing variety in interests and knowledge; all forms of creativity are deeply inter-related, and creators feed off one another;
- valuing creativity as work; discipline and focus can take a long time – 90 per cent perspiration;
- valuing those who do not form close ties, as these lead to 'distractions';
- valuing people driven by intrinsic rewards, not money.

Florida, 2002

In this recipe some significant points come together; the creative class is a hard-working, dedicated, tie-free, risk-taking, interacting set of people who will pursue new and useful ideas and products; and all for intrinsic rewards, not money. This of course reflects a capitalist's fantasy of a willing work-force, indulging their own desires to be creative while someone else banks all the money. This socio-economic analysis has its origins in identifying the existence and significance of the creative class in creating wealth, but then moves on to prescriptions for reshaping norms and values around these dominant stakeholders; the design of places should be structured to be creative-class friendly. Florida provides a series of indices which aim to capture what that means and to measure how creative-class friendly places are. These indices are about innovation, new technology and diversity. Places with a high proportion of 'creative-class' members are: innovative, measured by patents per capita; high technology; 'open to diversity', measured by the proportion of gay people in the population. These measures identify places in the USA like San Francisco, Austin, San Diego, Boston and Seattle as being the top spots, and role models for other aspiring cities. It identifies places in the USA like Louisville, Buffalo, Las Vegas, Norfolk, VA, and Memphis as the bottom spots, as the negative role models. The former places are role models for the leading edge of socio-economic change; the latter are struggling to adapt and find a place in this new order.

What Florida claims is that these 'top' places have in common a cultural environment with norms, attitudes and values supportive of cultural freedom, looseness, diversity and non-conformism. This, rather than the repressive conformity and constraints of old-style communities, with norms, attitudes and values that stifled difference and diversity, is essential for the creative class to thrive. The social conditions that accompany this, relations of weak ties and contingent commitments, are not to be fought but to be embraced, because they are rational and sensible. Lifestyles founded upon weak ties, mobility and living quasi-anonymously have advantages greater than their disadvantages for most people. The ultimate advantage is that these conditions allow a creative class to exist and thrive. The economic benefit is participation in the sunrise industries, the creative industries. As these social conditions are associated with such economic success, the reverse logic is attractive: adopting the freedom, looseness, diversity and non-conformism of that social mix can be a first step to attracting or germinating or expanding those kinds of organisations and economic sectors. Creating an environment valuing creativity, individuality, difference and merit, discarding an environment emphasising homogeneity, conformity and fitting in is the first step to possible economic success.

Creative communities and their companies will only develop where play-grounds for creative classes, the amenities they want, are constructed, and the impermanence and quasi-anonymity they desire is embraced. The places that do succeed in leading this era will be ones where the 'no-collar' work-place, places characterised by casual, fun and stimulating environments, will become the norm. In these places more and more people will experience patterns of intense work then relaxation, both in their everyday working patterns and across their whole lifespan. They will not be nine-to-five for each week of every year until they retire. Managing creativity for these people, personally and in their occupations, will present the critical chal-lenge. Expectations of life in general, not just leisure, will centre upon expectations of a richer experiential lifestyle and an acceptance of diversity.

A quartet of initiatives

Why then and how might creativity assume a role in understanding HRD? Here four different brief examples are outlined to offer insights into what this might mean. The first is a government initiative to establish Creative Partnerships between schools and arts organisations. The second is an anal-ysis of organisations as 'artful makers', whose management can learn from the process of rehearsing plays. The third is about a way of approaching organisational analysis adopting an aesthetic perspective. The final example is a consideration of debates about what is and is not art, about defining aesthetic value.

First there is the establishment of Creative Partnerships (CP). These are a government-funded initiative,[1] promoted by the Arts Council, established to develop schoolchildren's potential, ambition, creativity and imagination. They were launched with funding of £70 million from the Department of Culture, Media and Sports (DCMS) for projects in the first few years. The goal is to build sustainable partnerships that impact upon learning between schools, creative and cultural organisations and individuals. They are an opportunity to develop creativity in learning and for children to take part in cultural activities of the highest quality. The origins of these lie in a recent analysis which characterises the United Kingdom (UK) as a creative hotspot, producing some of the best designers, artists, musicians and creative thinkers in the world. The idea behind Creative Partnerships is to animate the national curriculum, the sciences as well as the arts, and to enrich school life by making best use of the UK's creative wealth. They should help schools to identify their individual needs and then enable them to develop long-term, sustainable partnerships with organisations and individuals including architects, theatre companies, museums, cinemas, historic buildings, dance studios, recording studios, orchestras, film-makers, website designers and many others. These projects should transform expectations, encouraging those involved – the children, the teachers, the partners – to continue learning and working creatively, and invoking shifts in thinking in the wider education system for the longer term.

In this context the creativity debate is one being explored across the world, as countries are reforming their systems of education to better prepare young people for the increasingly complex and challenging demands of the twenty-first century. In many countries creativity is being given priority as never before, as in the workplace, employees who can think and act creatively are expected to be more agile and flexible. Creative employees adapt proactively to challenge, ensuring business is ready for anything. Creative Partnerships (CP) responds in part to the widely held view that, in the UK, creativity has been squeezed out of teaching through the focus on the '3 Rs' (reading, writing and arithmetic). CP provides teachers with the time for planning, thinking and evaluation as well as activity, enabling them to develop creative approaches to teaching and learning as they address the standards agenda.

In a broader historical context this reprises a persistent concern about the use, function and role of 'high culture' and the arts in society as a whole. On the one hand, studies of 'play' which illustrate the role of the imagination (Lieberman 1977) reprise the points Schiller made centuries ago about the value of arts in human education and development. On the other hand, concerns about countering dumbing down, about the need to include people in learning and personal growth through absorption of high culture and the arts which represent that, lead to contests with the mass media and elements of the popular culture which more often engage the imagination.

A second example comes from research and developments about companies (Austin and Devin 2003), and contends that 'artful making' is an integral part of organisational performance, and considers what managers can learn from how artists work. Conventional corporate wisdom is that there have to be clear objectives before actions. Austin and Devin disagree: companies now compete in a world where they need to explore, adjust, improvise. Knowledge work in particular involves doing and trying, not planning then acting. When people are involved in a process of doing and trying without a blueprint to guide them, they are involved in artful making. It is artful in following the typical theory and practice of collaborative arts, in particular that of the theatre and rehearsal processes. Theatre is about making, forming something new, where the raw materials are not iron and charcoal being turned into steel but imagination and ideas. Artfulness is not something achieved by flaky and unreliable people. It is about putting on a play, a valuable innovative product, delivered to a deadline, with great precision, incorporating innovation. Organisations share structural similarities with this artful process rather than conventional rules-based processes.

The model of a business being like the theatre is only right in some cases. These are cases where the costs of iteration are low, where getting something wrong and improving it is not a problem. That is, it does not cost a lot to reconfigure the production process and run it again. If these costs are high then there is still the need to plan prior to acting. Auto assembly has high iteration costs, with a need to get it right first time; software development has low iteration costs. In the latter, the value of doing is greater than the value of thinking about how to do it. The only demand is to make it great before the deadline. If the principal technology in use is the brain and the principal material is ideas, then there are very low iteration costs. Detailed planning, tight objectives, creating a blueprint and then conforming is unnecessary and counter-productive. Instead of the rule being 'Don't do anything until you can do everything', the rule is to run iterative cycles and reform the product continuously.

Trying again and again, getting things wrong, is the way to high-quality choices. People need to be released from restraint, preconceptions, intense interdependence, to see wrong choices as advances not setbacks. They need to engage in artful making, which has four key qualities:

- release: accepting wide variations within known parameters, rather than restraining ideas; avoiding inhibition, enabling focus, returning time and again to improvements, not distracted by inputs as interruptions;
- collaboration: being released from vanity, egotism and preconceptions to seeing others' contributions as material to make with, not positions to argue with;
- ensemble: acting as a whole that is greater than the sum of its parts, relinquishing sovereignty over individual work, reconceiving together, not replicating individually;
- play: being playful in the iterations, game-like rather than rule-bound in interactions with each other.

In rehearsing plays, scripts are limited; they need new ideas and implementation from the basic material. The rehearsal structure is to prepare individually then convene daily and discuss and rehearse. In organisations other than theatrical ones, the challenge is to create a secure workplace where there is psychological safety for creative interchange, to develop a place where people 'work on their edges', seeking discomfort and being okay with that, developing greater self-knowledge. It is an environment in which it is possible to build up ego as self-esteem, and be a distinct person of value, but also to tear down vanities; the inner need to look to others as we think we ought to. And improvisation is valued; no one refuses to accommodate the others' work, but always includes what the others do. If that environment exists, then artful making will be possible and effective.

Third, in addition to material developments like Creative Partnerships and the parallels drawn between theatre and manufacturing, academics have been exploring intellectually an explicit role for creativity in researching organisations and HRD. One outline of what that might mean has been proposed by Strati and Guillet de Montoux (2002), who argue that aesthetics should be recognised as a legitimate perspective in organisation theory. They propose that there are three different kinds of approach that merit the term 'aesthetic'. There is first the 'archaeological' approach to organisational analysis, which entails identifying the values and symbols of organisational culture. These are identified not in neutral, objective terms, but in using aesthetic terms as part of the description of the culture: what is appreciated, what is found to be disgusting. There is, second, the possibility of an 'empathetic-logical' approach. This entails an analysis of these aesthetically rendered accounts of organisational culture using conventional logical and rational methods, exploring why what is appreciated or found to be disgusting is so, based on rational, objective interpretations of these phenomena. Finally, third, there is the 'empathetic-aesthetic' approach. This is perhaps the true aesthetic approach. Here the analysis is not confined to, or centred on, using conventional logical methods. Rather, each and every aspects of the aesthetic investigation of organisational life, everything from deciding a focus for research to the way the research is communicated, is determined and driven by a researcher's personal, active, aesthetic sense and faculties.

These approaches to aesthetics analysis are, in effect, variations on forms of ethnographic research, but concerned with apprehending, through the specifically aesthetic rather than the broadly anthropological, a community's beliefs, values, practices and artefacts. The aspiration is still strongly influenced by a utilitarian mindset, though. That is embodied in the hope that, by being attuned to what is appreciated as beautiful, what is repellent and ugly, what is seen as tragic and what is amusingly grotesque, an organisation and its functioning and its performance problems can be more clearly perceived and dealt with. The truly aesthetic value system, the purely aesthetic value system, would not accept that.

Finally, moving beyond the explicit consideration of aesthetics to the general dilemmas of understanding art, when is a pile of bricks a work of art, and how does that help to redefine and refocus HRD? There is a classic concern with the question 'What constitutes the personal and cultural tastes that shape and inform people's aesthetic valuing?' Answers to this pose concepts of Intrinsic Aesthetic Value (IAV) and Extrinsic Aesthetic Value (EAV) (Vickery 2003). IAV is concerned with the properties that an object, experience or person needs to have to be deemed of aesthetic value. Just as the beauty industry or the art world need to track, and create, changing fashions, so HRD theorists and practitioners may benefit from knowing more about the look and feel dynamics of imagination, creativity and beauty. In place of a scientifically grounded, gradually accumulated knowledge informing practice about settled and certain HRD, there is instead a need to keep up with changes in aesthetic value, in fashions. Are high-performance work organisations still fashionable, or has a newer concept appeared?

But many would contest the idea that a set of intrinsic qualities can be identified as describing what is to be deemed of aesthetic value, beautiful or otherwise, in any domain. Rather, what prevails is EAV: value attributed by things other than the inherent properties of an object or person. The determination, then, is of what controls the attribution of EAV; and that leads into concerns with the dynamics of the 'artworld'. EAV is a special area of concern among those who make up the artworld; they are the source of the 'extrinsic' valuing, as what they decide and say is art, and great art, goes. The artworld is a special world, made up of the artists, institutions, critics and consumers of art in the contemporary world. In Western culture, what counts as aesthetic value, and good art, is no longer plain and certain. These are the people concerned with defining what is and what is not art. For them, aesthetics provides a language for discussing art, and defining what is and what is not art. This is a specialised, and many would argue elitist, business and process. What makes one pile of bricks 'art' and another pile of bricks 'not art'? This raises questions about definitions of art and its function in the modern world.

Beyond the quartet

These four examples are intended to illustrate the fact that the concepts of creativity, from arts in school to aesthetic valuing, are diverse and can be connected with HRD directly, in its own right. Creative Partnerships illustrate some of the main themes that are considered in more detail throughout the book. First, there is the explicit return to creativity as a competence. Second, there is the interplay of institutions, schools, government departments and arts institutions. Third, there is the interplay of aesthetic values with other values, most evidently here with economic, social and political values. Austin and Devin make and explore the parallel between artful making in theatre and work organisations, offering ideas about organisation and management.

Strati and Guillet de Montoux reflect on the problems of extending the analysis even further. Primarily, they observe, organisation scholars and actors are not 'authorised' to develop discourse using aesthetic terms. They consider this to be so because the aesthetic is associated with the artistic, the light and the superfluous, whereas organisational actors and scholars seek to be associated with the scientific, the serious and essential. Even though social science, particularly in the organisational analysis field, has been a broad church and is not hard-science fixated, it is still not seen as entirely sensible, or legitimate, to adopt such a peculiar approach as the aesthetic. The ultimate connections between practice in and perceptions of modern art and HRD can be made, for what makes one form of management development valid HRD and another not-valid HRD is arguably not any intrinsic qualities but the esoteric views of the 'HRD world', and those who inhabit it.

The creative class

But a broader socio-economic justification for a creativity-oriented approach can be proposed. This is that the practice of HRD is embedded in the creative class. Florida (2002) identifies the growth of the creative class in the major cities of the world as the key to economic growth and productivity. This class of producers, the creative class, do not seek and value what the elites of the past have sought: the grand houses in the suburbs, with good local schools. They seek instead a mix of lively arts venues, culture and an embracing of diversity as the foundations of their brave new world. That is what appeals to them, and will attract them and their businesses. Establishing and sustaining localities with economic growth, which will attract the creative class, demands the development of that kind of environment.

This belief in itself is nothing new, representing an embracing of the bohemian ghetto in a way that past generations would not have forseen. But the explanation for this is grounded in part in status anxiety. The anxiety associated with having and maintaining the signs of status is greater than ever. The social status attached to having stylish looks, living and homes has become much more prominent (De Bouton 2004). In economics, the obsolescence of satisfaction with any product, the fleeting fulfilment through buying, is institutionalised in the constant and endless upgrading of technologies. In social terms, the management of an ever growing network of weak ties rather than the cultivation of a few strong ones, most strikingly in changes in the family, is central. In politics, it is cynically accepted that the manipulation of image and the evasive sound-bite, rather than honour and substance, has become the chief modus operandi. In academia, the value for scholars of brief celebrity in the mass media, or a CV that runs to pages but which represents hardly any work of substance, is preferred to lasting honour among the scholarly community based on a serious piece of major work. And even God, via the alternative religious movements, is 'made over' in ways that renders an absolute deity acceptable for a world that cannot upset the narcissistic, the soft and the easily distressed. The reign of sentimentality looks good, and it feels good. Put these strands together, converging on creative concerns, and there is an emerging picture of an age in which questions of style, matters of look and feel demanding creativity and artfulness are no longer the peripheral, specialist concerns of the few; they are integral to the central and general concerns of all kinds of people, professions and organisations. And the core of this is simple: you have to be both pretty and smart to make it.

Implications

The change embedded in seeing HRD as belonging to the creative class is not just about the producers, it is also about the consumers. First, organisational actors and learners, as consumers of HRD, are not exclusively logical-rational; they are sensory, and influenced by their aesthetic judgement. To fail to understand and engage with exploring these issuing in an organisation is to exclude much from the picture. HRD actors and learners also possess forms of personal knowledge; these can be explored and engaged with. Second, this knowledge can be accessed and studied, using various approaches. Rather than the collection of more and more quantitative data, the enactment of creativity can influence organisation actors and researchers. Being creative, making things, may help structure empirical fieldwork, direct theorising and influence the presentation of research. The subject of HRD can be thought of and studied, and includes fieldwork and theorising, which engages with the creative. Third, a 'dialogic style' needs to be adopted in doing this, which allows for different interpretations of creativity and making, rather than descriptions and analysis in terms of dichotomies where one interpretation is true/false, or where an organisational context is deemed entirely beautiful/ugly, and so on. The dialogic style can also be adopted for exploring HRD; the aim is not to define what is beautiful and what is ugly, but to see how these ideas allow an interpretation of what is going on, and how and why things work as they do (or fail).

Those three aspects of a creative approach, from the consumer's point of view, are variations on widely recognised themes. But to explore the creative is also a reorientation, aimed at understanding the novel and unusual confluence of two critical forces. First is the imperative to be both 'pretty and smart'. This has become the shorthand for an era in which look and feel, the creation of aesthetic value, influences economic, cultural and personal value and competition and conflicts. The reactions of the 'no logo' movement, with a campaigning agenda to oppose the power of the major multinational companies and their brands (Klein 2000), was one sign of this imperative emerging more strongly. Now there is an increasing acceptance, and beyond that a welcoming and embracing of the creation of aesthetic value (Postrel 2003). For some this is little more than hype over business as usual: organisations have always had to pay close attention to the look and feel of their products and services, and this concern with creativity is just a leaching of marketing and public relations jargon beyond the normal boundaries of branding. For others, though, like Postrel, it represents a real change: to an era where meaning and pleasure are embedded not in the function of an object but in its aesthetic value. Drinking a coffee has no particular meaning, as it is a functional experience, quenching thirst and getting a caffeine boost; but consuming coffee from a Starbucks is about meaning and pleasure, to be understood aesthetically. Aesthetics affords a differentiation strategy, using look and feel to create diversity and choice. Now more people have greater expectations of design. The payback is that, ultimately, people will pay more for the thing of greater aesthetic value. The phenomenon is that people care more about how stuff looks, including themselves, than they do about other dimensions of reality.

Now HRD cuts right across that, for HRD is caring about realising people's potential, not about how they look. But to fail to rethink HRD in creative class and aesthetic terms would be a mistake. We can be usefully challenged by the narcissism, by the interest for or against a concern with meaning and pleasure rather than functionality. This at least brings forth a defence of HRD as it is, or a transformation of how the experience of learning and development is conceived and managed. Contemplating how the evolution of HRD keeps up with the look and feel standards, the creation of aesthetic value, in the context of people's other experiences, from the environments in which people drink coffee or that they inhabit when playing computer games, must excite both empathy and disdain. It is not enough just to critique the superficial branding of products and services with images and impressions to make them look and feel attractive. It is necessary to look again at HRD activities, so that where there is a choice the fact that there is creativity will mean that people want to engage with HRD.

This creation of an aesthetic imperative needs to be defined, and needs to be done in a chapter of its own. It is, according to a range of observers, the heart of a new period where there is greater substance to what have been limited, but classic and abiding, concerns about style. Where an age shaped by an aesthetic imperative is going, and where it will culminate, is unclear; its positive and its negative impacts are abstract at the moment. What is clear is that it will not be confined to superficial changes in the look and feel of fashions, products and services and what people find sexually attractive; it is not just about rehabilitating logos and brands, about new universal standards for the perfect form. Indeed, the idea that there is a single ideal that can be defined for sexual attractiveness is consigned to history (Eco 2003). It is instead fragmented, polymorphous. What is systemic, and grounded in individuals', societies' and cultures' sense of identity is less a distinctive single ideal and more a distinctive, leading concern with the aesthetic. For some, there is then a belief, widely endorsed and adopted, that a fresh and strong concern with aesthetics is permeating and reforming all kinds of human activity: culture, commerce, consumption and, ultimately, consciousness. To fail to recognise and adapt to this is to risk losing contact and influence with the times and audiences for any product or service.

It can be agreed that there is a concern with creativity in HRD, but it is superficial, even false. This conceptualisation of the separation of package from content, of style from substance and appearance from essence, is a misleading case for limiting the role for aesthetics in HRD. It is misleading because the case for aesthetics is not that HRD has to look 'prettier' to be attractive and successful; it is that the aesthetic challenges are of substance, of the essence, in the 'real world' of HRD. Much more than better pack-aging is needed. Rather, mastering the very conditions in which HRD emerges links with aesthetics. For the conditions in which HRD emerges and is often practised are conditions where:

- there are uncertainties;
- problems cannot be comprehensively stated, and they require subjective interpretation;
- there are many different solutions, but there are no optimal solutions;
- initial solutions are often holistic responses, as the designer cannot map solutions to problems exactly;
- these solutions represent steps to progress, not the final outcome; solutions become parts of other problems.

These are conditions which require more than logical and rational analysis of objective data. These conditions combined place a premium on creativity and imagination, and effective creativity and imagination depends on having and applying a sense of the aesthetic and beautiful as well as a grasp of the functional. The need to consider issues with the meaning of HRD is repli-cated with the concept of an aesthetic imperative. Throughout the text, this issue will be revisited and reconsidered. At the outset it is useful to acknowledge that there are two ways in which the term 'aesthetics' is commonly defined and might then be considered to have an imperative impact. In a narrow sense, aesthetics has been concerned with matters of style and beauty, and the processes of delighting the senses (Beardsley 1966). This is most commonly associated with the creation and appreciation of art works and the creation of pleasing objects and environments, and, of course, with our creation and appreciation of ourselves as human beings. In a broader sense, aesthetics involves understanding and exploring the complex of mind, body and sensibility (Howard 1992; Mellander 2001) with which people encounter and make sense of reality. In this sense, analysing aesthetics is not confined to understanding the discrete and special experi-ences of appreciating art. It is an approach to understanding a part of the totality of human consciousness and behaviour. It contrasts with rational-logical approaches to understanding human consciousness and behaviour (Cazeaux 2000). In the narrow sense, then, to explore aesthetics is to consider the processes and challenges involved in delighting the senses: a concern primarily and previously most closely associated with art and design. In the broader sense, to explore aesthetics is to encounter debates and challenges about human nature, consciousness and morality, concerns primarily and previously closely associated with philosophy.

It is possible to think of HRD as satisfying or not satisfying, and ineffec-tive or effective, because of its aesthetic value. This does not have to be about absolute aesthetic standards. It may be more a matter of 'fit'. Where there is a fit between the aesthetics of a producer/designer and the users of

HRD, the HRD is more likely to be experienced as satisfying and effective. Where there is a mismatch between the aesthetics of a producer/designer and users of HRD, the HRD is more likely to be experienced as dissatisfying and ineffective. Even if, for example, the HRD designer is a subject expert who has sought to accommodate learning styles and has a clear map of needs, the HRD may fail.

Conclusion

A concern with creativity is generally evident, and a sense of important interconnections with HRD is growing. Practice in and perceptions of HRD have been free of much concern with creativity. For all that trainers and teachers may think of themselves as performers, or that organising may be viewed as like staging a performance, these are just fanciful ways of reflecting on what are essentially non-creative activities. HRD aimed to stand on an academic and professional foundation that was scientific. However, if the question is rephrased as 'Is HRD theory and practice free of concerns about aesthetics, beauty and imagination?' then the response may be different (Earl 1987). These concepts all have existing roles and a significance in the context of adult learning and organisation development. A concern with them in the context of the rise of the creative class is just a systematic and methodical way of considering the nature and role of aesthetics, beauty and imagination in HRD.

The concept of creativity has initially been defined in both a narrow and a broad sense. In its most basic sense, it is about producing new and valuable products, ideas, experiences. More broadly, it is about attending to the look and feel, the style and appearance of everyday objects, and the 'beauty' of works of art such as poetry, music or painting, and the perception of our selves. It may also refer more broadly to the experience, the feeling, of a unity and simultaneous engagement of mind, body and sensibility. Such structures of feelings might be elicited by many things in various circumstances, the natural and the man-made. These kinds of experience, as well as art appreciation, raise questions about the structures of feeling creativity originates from: why they are so powerful and how they might be harnessed. In this broader sense human experience is never free from creativity. Creative imperatives are an essential and integral part of human consciousness. We inhabit a created world that affords the opportunity to go beyond it. What matters is not that creativity exists, and that a creative class as such is growing in importance: it is that often there is a contest over judgements about creativity (Postrel 2003). These can concern, for example, the concept of beauty. On the one hand are those who seek to define and promote the creation of certain standards of beauty. The beauty industry embodies and reflects these concerns, the fixations, with such ideals. On the other hand there are those who seek to deconstruct 'myths' of beauty and challenge their ideological origins and consequences. If HRD is to be more enmeshed in an age of creative imperatives and aesthetic valuing these issues matter, whether as producers or consumers of HRD, as practitioners and as users.

Further, in connecting HRD and the aesthetic there is a wider context, HRD producers and consumers within a culture's whole system of creating, of making and going beyond what exists. The standards of value in use at large will shape what HRD can be and will be: that is to say that there is no independent aesthetic of HRD set apart from the standards of the general culture and its subcultures. The implication is that in addition to understanding rational analysis factors such as analysing needs, knowing learning styles, having functional expertise in a subject, and so on, there is an aesthetic factor.

HRD and aesthetics have been independent, increasingly important concerns in modern cultures. This introduction has sought to show that HRD and aesthetics now can, and should, join forces, with HRD practitioners being members of the creative class and managers of it at the same time. The producers and consumers of HRD have to adapt to the age of aesthetics imperatives affecting people's choices and lives in superficial and fundamental ways. There are several points of contact between them that can be explored further. These points of contact are, first, ideas about creativity, beauty and imagination. They are subsequently about being members of the creative class, and about the arts of learning and the role of arts in learning, and about managing the development of creativity. These are all consistent with seeing HRD as being secure only as it is identified with compassion, not as a player among the 'impression managers' of reflected glory and charisma from science, business and policy-making. HRD can best maintain its influence by being true to itself, not by adopting disguises. In extended analysis it is necessary to set out explicitly the particular framework of values analysis that helps to flesh out aesthetics, and the opportunities these presented to HRD.

2   Making it up

Constructing creativity

> People who are well behaved, agreeable, accommodating and cooperative are seldom creative ... creative people ... can be unpredictable, inconsiderate, arrogant and downright cantankerous ... [so I] caution people to be sure they know what they are doing when they introduce someone to the wonder, possibility, and magic of creativity.
>
> (Lyman 1989, p. 47)

> The development of scientific capacity is, generally speaking, a straight line upward; the lifeline of artistic development is punctuated by ups and downs.
>
> (Gardner 1982, p. 217)

Introduction

Attitudes to creativity produce the new divides between the good and bad, the vibrant and the stagnant; superseding the old divisions between left and right, or technocrats and greens. This is the world divided into stasists and dynamists, to use Postrel's (1999) terms. The stasists believe that regulation, planning and control are necessary to contain creativity. That belief leads them to be against the unbounded freedom, enterprise and progress that has enabled creativity until now. Because of this the stasists are the 'enemies of the future'. Dynamists are for continuing and greater freedom to playfully experiment, follow where enterprise leads to progress, and through creativity continue to bring about a better world. Dynamists, the creatives, are the future. The contrasting is clear: either a regulated, engineered, stable, controlled, predictable world or a world of constant creation, discovery and competition, evolution and learning, of surprise. Diversity and choice-driven systems are central. Postrel is for unstable messiness and fluidity of dynamism; creativity produces change. Others recoil, and rather seek to curb such unruly forces and change (see Table 2.1).

The examples Postrel cites include the expected, from the growth of the internet as an unruly, messy, diverse system to China's history as an innovator which became paralysed and is only now recovering. They also include the more unusual, such as the evolution of beach volleyball and other forms

Table 2.1 Stasist and dynamist world views

Stasist	*Dynamist*
Central organising principle	Many visions and competing dreams
Regulating	Exploring
Repressive	Playful
Explicit knowledge	Tacit knowledge
Majority rule	Minorities compete
Regimented; the herd	Undesigned order; the flock
Future closed and finite	Future open-ended

Source: After Postrel (1999)

of 'fun in the sun', the irrepressibly weird. This is a variation and restatement of essentially American beliefs about the open society, allied with broader perceptions of man derived from thinking along the lines suggested by Huizinga (1938/1971). He characterised man as being, in essence, a 'player', and argued that play was the source of all culture. The functions of play, and of those who seek new combinations and the inventive and feeling good about discovery even if it is useless, are an essential feature of a civilisation. The need is to keep a society 'young' and vitality oriented, to avoid the sterile. Stasists see this as entailing the unruly: they fear change, and can see only potential abysses ahead if the dynamists prevail. But to go ahead at all it is necessary for us to have vitality; let us head for Mars, seek to double the human lifespan. This striving, seeking, finding, not yielding, is the key to eternal youthfulness. The dynamist vision is a mix of the high and the low, the exalted and the mundane, and a relentless hostility to stasists seeking to undermine the party by insisting that such dynamism does not produce all the answers and indeed contributes to the problems. One immediate qualification is that this represents a typically brash, US-centric view. It enshrines the economic supremacy of an elite having a great time as the engine of growth and vitality. Why that should appeal to anyone other than members of that elite is curious; harnessing 'creativity' to the cause normally associated just with amassing great wealth is a new twist. But it does also draw attention to serious issues, and it shows that there are many paths to and from creativity.

The interest in creativity

As creative 'revolutions' at work are sought (Kingdon 2002), the nurturing of a creative class is seen to be the foundation of prosperity and civilisation, and analyses of creativity (Amabile 1998) draw attention, the stock of interest in creativity is going up. This is because, on the one hand, an interest in creativity is a matter of strategic concern, but also because it remains a poorly understood phenomenon that warrants closer investigation. Thus creativity may be a major policy around which many practices can be arranged and evaluated. Individuals, business leaders who want to enhance creativity in their organisations, should try to avoid or reduce the 'obstacles to creativity'. These obstacles are not difficult to identify: they are time pressures on task completion, political problems with trying and 'failing', harsh criticism of new ideas, and a dependence on the status quo despite espoused interests in change. Organisations ought to enhance the 'stimulants to creativity': freedom, positive challenge in the work, sufficient resources and work-group supports. They need to put together diversely skilled teams that communicate well, are mutually committed to the work, and constructively discuss ideas. Supervisory encouragement is necessary from team leaders who communicate effectively with the group, value individual contributions, protect the group within the organisation, set clear goals while allowing freedom in meeting the goals, and serve as good work models. Further encouragement, such as conversations about ideas across the organisation and a top management focus on rewarding and recognising good creative work, is also useful. Leaders and organisations who can attain creativity through managing all these processes around learning and organisation development will succeed. Upstream of all these corporate issues are the schools, and education. The move, in the UK, to invest in Creative Partnerships, mentioned in Chapter 1, has become a major policy initiative. Describing why that has happened can set the scene for considering creativity and HRD more generally.

Creative Partnerships for schools

A report prepared for the UK government about the importance of creativity in education (NACCE 1999) exemplifies this. Education is investment in human capital; the main focus of the report was on literacy and numeracy but there was a recognition of a need to also unlock all potential. And creative and cultural education is part of that. Creativity was defined as 'imaginative activity fashioned so as to produce outcomes that are both original and of value' (NACCE 1999, p. 29).

To enhance creative education would be to encourage forms of education that develop young people's capacities for original ideas and action. And there is creative potential in everybody; everyone has creative abilities. Indeed, finding one's creative strengths can have an enormous impact on self-esteem and overall achievement. And everyone has and can use imagination. That may mean a range of things, from generating something original to developing an alternative to the conventional, or just engaging in generative mental play. And everyone can do that while pursuing purposeful making in any area: as long as they are actively engaged in making something they can be imaginative. Being original is also possible for all. That may be judged against greater or lesser creativity in relation to their own previous output, their peers' output, or in a historic context in relation to everyone's output. The central hope is that by promoting lesser degrees of originality and creativity in relation to personal achievements among the many, this will help produce greater degrees of originality, in historic terms, by the few.

In promoting this an underlying concern is revealed about balancing freedom and control in education: serious creativity is not just about letting go, but depends on gaining knowledge and skills. And creativity can be taught if teachers can recognise potential and provide the right conditions. The problem is that current priorities and pressures inhibit creativity in young people and those who teach them. This is embedded in the inferior place of the humanities in the curriculum. It is reflected in the fact that creativity-based outside organisations have education and outreach programmes, but these are poorly funded. It is institutionalised in the training of new teachers. To redress these factors there needs to be a systemic approach, not just rhetoric about creative education as a subject to be integrated within the curriculum and as a general function of education. It is needed and wanted because of the skills desired by the business community, and because organisations want partnerships with schools.

The growth of concerns with creativity is set apart from two things that might produce opposition. One is the feeling that this represents the success of a lobby group for the arts. The other is that this is a victory for, and a return to, 'progressive' teaching ideas. Art as a form of expression does matter, as an environment for the expression and discussion of emotions, giving them form and meaning, not just venting them. But it also matters in science, to produce fresh conjectures and the re-evaluation of ideas. It matters in problem-solving, which is connected with creativity but is not the same; problems can be solved without creativity, and people may be creative without problem-solving. But it is a facet of intelligence, a multidimensional capacity rather than a present/absent faculty. People need to find their medium; some capabilities are domain specific and do not transfer, but others do. Being able to create in one medium, for example music, may not transfer to painting; but some of the core skills are the same. So creativity is not pure free expression; it involves applying knowledge and skills, a reciprocity of freedom to create, and the mastery and control of a medium.

Finally, the context for all this concern with creativity in education is envisaged in a cultural context rather than a purely artistic one. For the hope is that through enhanced creativity there will be better cultural education, enabling young people to engage with complex and diverse social values and ways of life. Cultural understanding becomes more important with increasing diversity, so increasing respect for different values and traditions; and the engine of cultural change is creative thought and action. So cultural development, not just the arts, is the context. Sectoral definitions of creativity associated with the arts, or elite definitions about creativity being related to rare people with unusual talents, the exceptional and great, are misleading. This is a democratic definition of creativity: there is potential for creative achievement in all fields of human activity.

Why now?

That there is potential for creativity in many fields of human activity, the democratic definition, has been reinforced in management research. Research linked to creativity in the corporate setting has sought to link creativity with central functions, like leadership (Tierney *et al.* 1999; Williams 2001; Shalley and Gilson 2004; Tierney and Farmer 2004). Krohe (1996) goes further, suggesting that as creativity is so important it ought to inform a whole new employment paradigm, with employees being like artisans in ateliers or studios. The relationship with management is then that of art patron and artist; the patron supports and inspires and in return gets dedication and the artist's best work. Others add that training is not enough; there is a need to alter the environment as well, or else it is at odds with exercising creativity (Simpson 2001; Williams 2002; Baer *et al.*, 2003). This kind of concern with creativity has been a forerunner of the full-blown concern with aesthetics. Much management interest in creativity has been fragmented (Henry 1991). The identification of varying perspectives on creativity, how to manage it, and exploring creative processes were all significant to understanding the development of creativity which was perceived to be central to the future. The academic and practical context, the theory and the reality, was one of fragmentary insights being collected and collated. But now that the interest in creativity has shifted from the margins to the centre, this collation is inadequate. There is a growing strategic concern with creativity, which is emergent and expressed in various contexts: for individuals, for groups and for organisations. The challenge is to move beyond the fragmentary insights and research base and connect creativity with HRD and strategic significance.

The reason these issues matter now is the emerging belief that creativity is foundational to HRD, and the inclusion of creativity as role and outcome of HRD is being emphasised as of growing significance. Two contrasting examples illustrate this. First is the example of the country considered by some to be the home of global cultural leadership around creativity and the open society, the USA. There, as long ago as the early 1990s, a Secretary's Commission on Achieving Necessary Skills (SCANS) identified creative thinking and the ability to generate new ideas as foundational skills for the workplace (SCANS 2004). Creativity is multifaceted and multidimensional, and not limited to technological innovation or new business models. But as Florida's (2002) subsequent analysis of the creative classes shows, even within a country like the USA there can be massive variations in cities about the extent to which they can attract and satisfy the creative classes. States and cities should be reorienting HRD as a practice and field to fuel human creativity at all levels and in all types of jobs in any organisation.

Oldham and Cummings (1996) reflect this foundational view of creativity in organisations by arguing that creativity can be generated by employees in any job and at any level of the organisation, not just in jobs that are traditionally viewed as necessitating creativity. And within the US research into HRD, creativity has been conceptualised into: a product-oriented definition; a personal nature or trait; intellectual or artistic outcomes that can be critiqued to be novel or useful; or a dynamic process involving individuals' interactions and transactions with their social, psychological and physical environment. HRD-related research into creativity is likewise fragmented and diverse, concerned with: defining models of creativity; analysing work-groups and environments; psychological factors; cognitive style; and gender. Although these research concerns do not capture the abundance of research on creativity, they highlight factors and issues that warrant visibility and discussion when relating creativity to the field and practice of HRD.

An alternative example is provided by the recent report *Remaking Singapore* (Balakrishnan 2004), where the dilemmas of encouraging creativity represent a different kind of challenge. Singapore has been known for two things: for economic success built on human resources, given no natural resources, and for a kind of 'big brother' authoritarianism. That latter repressive image, antithetical to creativity, reflected a culture concerned with micromanaging, even down to guidelines on the flushing of toilets. This has been perceived to be a problem, and proposals have been produced which include allowing for more creativity. The *Remaking Singapore* exercise was aimed at addressing challenges in the social, cultural and political spheres, and at complementing the efforts of an Economic Review Committee. Collectively, these recommendations aim to unleash the creative potential of Singaporeans, and to attract discerning talent to live and work there and fine-tune Singapore's safety nets and engender a more compassionate society. At the same time they seek to expand common spaces and strengthen social cohesion, creating more opportunities for Singaporeans to contribute to the country and strengthen their 'emotional bonds' to Singapore.

The background concern was that, amid recession and with other countries in the region luring companies away, the government wants to restrict itself to containing undesirable activities. The major proposals include allowing schools and tertiary institutions greater flexibility in admitting students, setting up a pre-tertiary independent Arts School, and modifying the ranking of schools. They also involve the consolidation and rationalisation of various assistance schemes for those affected by structural unemployment and facilitation of employment for the disabled.

Alongside these are many other changes, of often smaller import practically but of great symbolic significance. Homosexuality is now not 'unwelcome' in the civil service; people in bars can dance on tables; night-clubs can open twenty-four hours; *Cosmopolitan* magazine will be available.

However, proposals to loosen public entertainment licensing and establish 'free art zones' were rejected. These are supposedly significant but paced changes. They are seeking to change the mindset of the intelligentsia, to make them more innovative. Alongside economic, employment and public policy reform, attention was also given to:

- ceasing prior vetting of plays;
- relaxing rules on busking;
- easing registration of societies;
- expanding the sea and water sports scene;
- streamlining the management of arts events.

These proposals echo, often in weak and diluted forms, the beliefs of Florida about the conditions for attracting and satisfying the creative class; but they are also clearly connected with changing broader cultural and political traditions, opening up the society, and that brings with it substantial challenges and difficulties. Creativity is not an easy option.

So creativity, whether present to a greater extent as in places with existing strengths like the USA or to a lesser extent in more 'closed' societies like Singapore, is a whole package that many want to see increased; but catalysing it is interconnected with catalysing other, broader, changes in conditions which are more fraught and problematic. This widening and escalating of understanding what creativity entails and requires is essential.

This development, a widening and escalation, was inevitable. It was overdue because creativity is never an isolated subject in its own right; it is always a part of a bigger and broader phenomenon, developing a culture, evolving an economy, transcending inherited social problems, and so on. The emergence and establishment of an aesthetic perspective enables the fragments of creativity to be drawn together in the area of HRD. This chapter is a step on the way to that, opening up questions about matters of meaning, research and the significance of these connections. It offers some focus around three problems – the problems of the meanings of creativity, of HRD strategies and of values – on what the step away from the fragments towards the strategic would involve.

Strategic connections and inquiring into creativity

From the strategic perspective, accessing and managing creativity in organisations means overcoming barriers. For the workplace is naturally creativity-averse, normally anti-creativity. These barriers can be thought of as constraining (see Table 2.2) at four different levels (Tobin and Shrubshall 2002).

The concern is that being in an introverted, rigid, 'left-brain' and fear-dominated environment will kill any and all creativity. Such an environment will only nourish compliance, inertia, suspicion, tradition and censorship.

Table 2.2 Constraints on creativity – four levels

	Inward focus	*Backward focus*	*Sideways focus*	*Downward focus*
Dominant influence	Self	Past	Logic	Shadow
Influences Organisation's characteristics	Toe the line Self-censorship Information withheld	Values and traditions Deeply rooted structures	Bottom-line criteria No creative agenda Suspicion of creativity	Anxieties Dichotomy Opinions and actions Malaise erodes potential and causes inertia Risk avoidance and low tolerance of failure
Determines the culture	Introverted	Rigid	Left-brain dominated	Fear dominated

But by removing constraints on the self, loosening links to the past, acknowledging 'right-brain' functions and establishing blame-free cultures, creativity will flourish. For Tobin and Shrubshall this freeing of creativity requires a process of exposing these constraints, assessing their power, shifting conditions and eliminating the barriers. They suggest there are various ways to do this:

- Use new 'outside in' and 'inside out' connections; bring in new external influences and send your own people elsewhere.
- With the same people and in the same place, find new perspectives and extra dimensions.
- Provide personnel development with secure foundation and challenges.
- Ensure creative communication: channels that support the development of ideas.
- Maintain a change process of continuous improvement.
- Provide a creative culture, with beliefs, values and behaviours consistent with creativity, from the centre to the periphery.

Freeing up creativity requires, then, a strategy which is challenging to embrace – it challenges the status quo – and strategies about dealing with uncertainty and turbulence by means other than reinvention. This process, which requires a pattern of focus, withdrawal and then breakthrough, is awkward for most organisations. There are three major problems and complications encountered in expanding and escalating beyond the fragments to creativity as a strategic concern in HRD. First is the problem of process – what creativity involves – and connecting that with HRD. Second is evaluating development strategies in HRD as supportive of creativity.

Third is the problem of studying creativity within the discipline of HRD, as dominant value systems in the discipline are open to challenge. Further successful study of creativity in HRD needs to acknowledge and engage with all these problem areas. These are now considered in turn.

To take the other perspective, going down into more depth to explore what creativity is: the simplest model of what creativity means is a two-phase definition, incorporated in Amabile's (1998) much-cited definition of creativity as a duality: being creative means being both original and useful. In the context of the values-based perspective adopted here, this is clearly adopting the language of the economic values system to legitimise a discussion of creativity, as the concept of 'usefulness' is foregrounded. Setting that aside for the time being, the analysis here is that in Phase 1 creativity involves being imaginative, or using divergent thinking. In this phase old connections are broken and new connections are made, with judgement suspended. People let the mind play, probe for possibilities and seek new associations. The second phase of creativity is then about the practicality, needing convergent thinking. In this phase there is a need for judgement and evaluation, drawing on logic.

In seeking to blow away the mists obscuring creativity, it is the first phase of creativity that presents most challenges in the corporate setting. More than the provision of training courses designed to develop creativity is needed; there is a need for a learning culture 'where collaborative creativity in all contexts, relationships and experiences is a basic purpose of the culture' (Jaccaci 1989, p. 50). For Jaccaci the pursuit of creativity radically alters thinking about learning, for it sanctions idealism as the core of learning and recasts mentoring as focused on purpose and fulfilment, and training becomes HRD. The encounter with creativity transforms trainers, training and organisations, producing higher-level goals and aspirations for potential development. Stern (1992) analysed creativity in the corporate context, studying the factors that contribute to the expression of corporate creativity in Japan. The research noted several Organisational Development (OD) and HRD-initiated behaviours that contribute to creativity: study leave, participation in in-house training, team communication, and professional conferences and self-development. Robinson and Stern (1997) describe environmental considerations for the development of creativity around five features that the corporate world can manage:

- alignment: creative ideas must be directed towards organisation goals, so employees will recognise and respond positively to even a partially useful idea;
- self-initiated activity: intrinsic motivation is needed, so people need to be allowed to pick a problem they are interested in and feel able to solve;
- unofficial activity: informal meetings should be a safe haven, giving ideas a chance to develop until they are strong enough to face judgemental resistance;

- serendipity: discoveries may be made by fortunate accident in the presence of sagacity;
- diverse stimuli: new setting or situations provide fresh insight and drive people to react differently or try something new.

But when the mists obscuring creativity are blown away, they reveal not only positive things about creativity. There is more. Lyman (1989) describes some of the other aspects of creativity, and counsels for circumspection about what the encounter with creativity entails. On the one hand, to be creative people do not need to be taught anything new, only to have resurrected the child-like mind, a spirit of wonder and the natural curiosity they have shut away. Creativity entails being able to make mistakes, to fail, to shed conformity. But on the other hand, the qualities of creative people (see Box 2.1) that follow are distinctive: are these really what organisations want to contemplate encouraging and developing among their workforce?

Caudron (1994) acknowledges this side of creativity, that creative people can be 'high maintenance', requiring considerable amounts of attention and careful handling. In workforces the challenge is not making everyone equally creative: the underlying challenge is getting creative people and non-creative people to work together. There are those who say that the two worlds, the creative and the non-creative, are not that different. Kao (1996), for example, compares general management with jazz, as both are based on

---

Box 2.1 Traits of Creative People

- different and they do not mind being so
- playful; nothing is taken seriously
- do not play by the rules; be outlaws, thumb nose at conformity
- adventurous
- spontaneous; need no script for life, take direction from events
- independent; work alone or be alone, against objections, stubborn
- sensitive to art and beauty in all things, not just art
- enthusiastic, idealistic and responsive; hyperactive
- bold; charge ahead single mindedness
- acting not thinking – even mistakes lead towards the goal
- driven and passionate; to overcome obstacles in the way
- not content with the obvious, the mundane, the mediocre, the cliché; go beyond the first answer
- are alright feeling lost or experiencing ambiguity
- faithful to their vision, craft and the belief that the creative process will work
- courageous; to withstand objections and criticism

Source: Lyman

improvisation. And others would perceive the conflicts associated with handling creative types as being functional (Van Slyke 1999). Optimum conflict is needed for creativity, with an ideal intensity needed to fuel creativity rather than just disaffected behaviour. This requires having people facilitating creativity who can listen and understand various perspectives, needs and interests rather than reasoning for their own position. Ultimately the issue with defining creativity is about what is implied for practice. If organisations wish for greater creativity, do they have to take on the whole package of individuals with creative traits and cultures which accommodate and encourage these? Or can they pick and choose the bits they want, some traits and some elements of culture, but not have to deal with the rest? The answer to that depends on the extent to which the organisation and its tasks are seen to involve the creative process as it is in the artistic world.

The strategic and the discovery movements come together around a central dilemma: is creativity to be nurtured through affording its unfolding or by actively instilling it? For Gardner (1982), extreme creative behaviour is so unusual that it only occurs under special circumstances. The preschool years are a golden age of creativity for every child; each has the potential to go on, but then a corruption takes over and some become artistically stunted. Drawings drop, language sheds its poetry. The creativity associated with knowing and mastering symbol systems then succumbs to convention, to following rules and tolerating no deviation, no novelty. Adolescents become the toughest of literalists, concerned with hyper-realism. Some will stay in touch with creativity as audiences, but few resume artistic activities. Many never seek again to appreciate style, expressiveness, balance and composition, or to tolerate the experimental.

A very few – the creative personalities that succeed, need to succeed, want to excel – live with uncertainty, and risk failure and opprobrium to return time and time again to their projects until they satisfy their own exacting standards, while speaking with potency to others. But the roots of this are not mystical and irrational. Rather, the genius engages in painstaking, chaotic, persistent, active, fully engaged whole thinking. By that Gardner means the genius will:

- work to organise scattered theories/facts into a coherent synthesis;
- establish a network of enterprises, not a single one, producing a complex of searches around major nodes;
- work with dominant metaphors within a wide scope, rich, open to exploration;
- be goal-directed with a guiding purpose, animated by self-conscious projects they are determined to complete;
- develop their own skills tirelessly;
- get new peers, then abandon them;
- have a rich affective life and strong ties to the subject;
- love work and derive pleasure from it;
- have the strength needed for a solitary existence.

There are two theories about nurturing creativity to produce this kind of person. One is that this only requires an unfolding, and the other is the need for an optimal training of artistic skills. The unfolding model envisages the child as a seed, which contains all it needs to grow to virtuosity; all the teacher needs to do is to prevent damage and the effect of malevolent forces. Everyone is a potential artist, if only a tutor like a Rousseau could shield them from the pernicious. The alternative is to directly train and direct, with special cultivation and firm guidance to attain skills under a gifted teacher or artist. This is a dilemma that faces educationalists and those in the corporate sector.

Conditions, domains and core process

One option is to identify discrete conditions in which creativity is significant; another is to explore lessons from creativity in different domains; and a third is to identify core elements of a creative process. The first option is to identify the conditions in which creativity matters. Creative thinking is of value where certain conditions prevail as problems are identified and solutions are sought. These are conditions where there are uncertainties, where problems cannot be comprehensively stated, and they require subjective interpretation. They are conditions where there are many different solutions but there are no optimal solutions. Initial solutions are often holistic responses, as the creator cannot map solutions to problems exactly. These solutions represent steps to progress, not the final outcome. They are also conditions where new solutions become parts of other problems.

The difficulty is that these conditions are all conditions that exist in many workplaces, occupations and organisational situations An alternative approach is to explore how the practice of creativity has been developed in and for many discrete areas, such as graphic design, product design and building design. Lawson (1997) provides a way of framing this initially by locating creativity via design thinking as a phenomenon that can be located in the middle of a continuum (Figure 2.1). At one end is a kind of thinking which is about informed, but mechanical, calculation: logical, problem-solving thinking oriented on use value. At the other is free, imaginative thinking, associated with aesthetic value. Creativity involves elements of both these, being able to produce solutions which combine both calculation and imagination – solutions that are both functional and beautiful, that are novel and useful. In this sense creativity is a capacity which draws on an

Using informed mechanical..................................... calculation	Producing the functional and.................................. beautiful	Free .... imaginative thinking

Figure 2.1 A continuum of creativity (*Source*: Lawson)

appreciation of both objective science and subjective artfulness, requiring a combination of quantitative and qualitative judgement.

The development and enhancement of creative thinking is possible and valuable in many areas. As well as giving weight to an appropriate aesthetic appreciation it also involves understanding users and their needs, for creativity is not the free act of an independent individual. It is a social act, learned in close contact with others and practised in specific social relations. Novices need apprenticeships, for in seeking to be creative they often begin by offering solutions of great complexity but eventually recognise the need to keep things as simple as possible. They move from overly self-conscious and introspective thinking to being more unselfconscious and 'action based'. This produces better functioning and more beautiful solutions.

The final possible fulcrum is to consider the common elements of the creative process. This can be defined in various ways. One option is to define a sequence of defined activities, completed in a logical order. One logical sequence for guiding creativity has been given as:

1. **assimilation**: collect information;
2. **general study**: investigate problems and solutions;
3. **development**: refine solutions;
4. **communication**: of solutions to others.

While this has face validity and makes sense, it is a flawed model. In real rather than ideal creativity there will be transitions, revisions and unpredictable jumps, rather than a logical and sequential completion of these stages. Creators can get stuck at each stage, for example slavishly collecting more and more information rather than moving on to development. It is not unusual to reach the end of Stage 4, 'communication', only for clients to then see that they have defined the problem badly, and then it is back to Stage 1.

The creative process is better defined as involving three activities that are applicable at all these sequences or stages: activities of analysis, synthesis and appraisal. Analysis is the exploration of relations, looking for patterns, classifying objectives, generating divergent outcomes, and so the opening out of an order and structure for dealing with the problem. Synthesis is needed to move forward, to distil from among the relations and patterns and create a solution. And appraisal of solutions in relation to pre-set objectives is needed before decisions to move from abstract creation to actual making are made. This kind of definition is more helpful, as it exposes how the issue for the creator is that 'problem and solution emerge together' (Lawson 1997, p. 47). This means that the problem is never fully understood until some solution to illustrate it is provided.

This way of thinking about creativity also raises a further problem for the creator and creative thinking: the problem of escalation or regression in redefining problems. The definition of a problem may be perceived, when a creative solution is offered, to have been too narrow; problem redefinition then escalates. This means that what is to be analysed, synthesised and appraised increases. Take as an instance an organisation seeking to improve the security in their premises: they may think of a solution in terms of new kinds of locks for their doors. They may be offered a solution using new locks which are far more secure than the existing locks. Yet as they appraise the solution they may have thoughts about the additional time needed to open and close these doors given the new locks' complexity. Maybe, instead, they should be restricting the movements of some people in some areas rather than increasing security everywhere; indeed, do they need doors at all in some areas? Maybe they should redesign the existing building to allow for certain areas to be relocated, some into more secure areas, others into less secure areas with fewer doors. Or maybe the existing building is inadequate for that, and they then need to relocate to a new building. Thus an escalation into ever wider questions ensues as a result of creativity. Regression is the opposite movement. This is where a 'big' solution that is initially proposed becomes revised down to a smaller act. So the problem of security in their premises might have led the organisation above to first consider moving building; but as lesser options are also considered they may ultimately decide to become more secure just by putting in new locks.

The underlying issue is expecting the use of creative thinking to be able to produce solutions which fix specific 'symptoms' or to identify and deal with the underlying 'causes' of problems. In fact, creative thinking may open up Pandora's boxes when looking at general causes of problems; there are always multi-dimensional and interconnected elements to problems. It can then appear as if more and more analysis, synthesis and appraisal is needed, and no natural end, or point to stop design thinking, can be found. But to escape this trap is often to fall into another: the trap of over-precision, defining a discrete problem to fix. This may not actually help creative thinking; it rather precludes it. If the value of creative thinking is that it is needed where subjective judgement is important because there is no 'correct' or optimal calculable solution, then being over-precise in determining the problem initially is not helpful.

Conclusion

Creativity continues to inspire considerable inquiry and provides a focus for a multitude of varied interests. Connecting creativity with HRD is emerging as a significant issue in its own right, not a side issue. That concern takes attention up, towards strategic concerns about organisational effectiveness, and down, into the depths of human psychology and social interaction. The promotion of creativity in education as a common and central good raises many HRD issues. HRD is concerned with realising people's potential. How the gestalt of realising people's potential is perceived changes. Different elements are emphasised and highlighted.

Creativity has now become a prominent part of that concern. Perhaps not all workplaces are in need of creative revolutions, and classes other than the 'creatives' are still the producers of wealth, but creativity remains a higher-profile concern as an end of HRD, because creativity is a part of realising all kinds of people's potential.

The challenge of creativity then mirrors past challenges in HRD, when a desire to connect HRD with a key transcendent capability or competence has been proposed. A previous example would be, for example, a concern to develop generic 'problem-solving' competence, or a 'critical thinking' competence; or interpersonal soft skills and emotional intelligence. Here the construct of concern is creativity – that is, the thing to be taken apart and understood in order to then define a curriculum. In other disciplines creativity has been given considerable attention and analysis, in the worlds of the arts and of design most evidently, but it is also evident in the sciences and associated fields like engineering (Norman 2001). These previous studies provide starting points, but cannot in themselves provide the knowledge, concepts and theories needed to incorporate creativity into the discipline of HRD.

Further, as HRD is connected with creativity, research is oriented towards new questions and interests. The questions that such connections raise are about the biases and distortions of other dominant value systems on shaping and informing human development and learning dynamics. The more dominant value systems, which will be considered in the next chapter, can all be reformed by considering creativity. Finally, the connection with creativity can enlighten the professionals. There are practical and actionable conclusions from exploring the connections of HRD and creativity. These are related to the areas of the 'creativity in learning', 'learning creativity' and the socio-economic context of creative capabilities. Some of these questions and issues are already considered alongside other factors in studies associated with knowledge management and learning organisation research. The need is to situate creativity as the central focus within aesthetics, and not to lose it in the shadows of these grander constructs.

A framework (see Figure 2.2) for mapping the exploration of meanings and methods for integrating creativity with HRD applications is possible. There are themes in the area of defining what creativity is that connect directly with traditional HRD concerns about the kinds of expertise, knowledge and affective capabilities needed to map and guide the realisation of people's potential. And there are challenges faced in adapting the various methods that HRD typically affords to support and structure the realisation of people's potential in this way, as some methods and systems that are commonplace are not suitable for eliciting and reinforcing creativity. For it is entirely possible that the methods and systems of HRD may, in themselves, pre-empt the development of creativity by defining HRD needs in ways that neglect the whole person, by acting in ways that require passive compliance among learners, and by assessing people's learning in ways that seek adherence to customary and regulated standards. If these rather than the needs of the whole creating person, the adventurous experimenting person and learners seen as potential producers of original and incomparable ideas and objects provide the infrastructure of learning then HRD may oppress and defeat creativity rather than support and realise it.

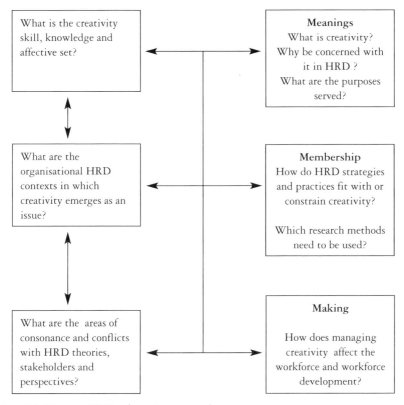

Figure 2.2 Mapping HRD and creativity research areas

3 Valuing aesthetics

> Aesthetics has become too important to be left to the aesthetes.
>
> (Postrel 2003, p. 4)

Introduction

There are several different frameworks that can be adopted to structure and enable a discussion of aesthetics and HRD. The one adopted here is based on a theory and model of how value systems underpin and shape human behaviour and understanding. This highlights the concept of the aesthetic. The aesthetic exists as a discrete value system, an equal alongside other value systems, that can be used to illuminate in part the interaction of HRD and creativity. The renewal of HRD in an age more sensitive to aesthetic imperatives is not a displacement of old values by new values. It is a re-ordering, a re-alignment and a fresh mixing of enduring, universal values. Knowing what it means to adapt to the age of aesthetic imperatives, conceptually and practically, can then be organised around an analysis of values.

There are two ways in which the term 'aesthetics' is commonly defined. In a narrow sense aesthetics has been concerned with matters of style and beauty, and the processes of delighting the senses (Beardsley 1966). This is most commonly associated with the creation and appreciation of art works and the creation of pleasing objects and environments, and, of course, our creation and appreciation of ourselves as human beings. There are some already existing connections with aesthetics in these senses. A concern with design in the development of courses or organisations is, conceptually at least, embedded in HRD. And the concept of aesthetic labour, for example, has generated some debate about how our creation and appreciation of ourselves is intimately connected with employment in certain jobs and sectors of employment. Aesthetic labour in the retail and hospitality sectors refers to the style and look of people considered presentable in an organisation seeking to project a particular image.

In a broader sense aesthetics involves understanding and exploring the complex of mind, body and sensibility (Howard 1992; Mellander 2001) which people possess and use to make sense of reality. In this sense analysing aesthetics is not confined to understanding the discrete and special experiences of appreciating art, or the dynamics of how style and look matter for specific kinds of people such as employees in certain jobs. It is a perspective on understanding human consciousness and behaviour. It contrasts with rational-logical perspectives (Cazeaux 2000). In the narrow sense, then, to explore aesthetics is to encounter the processes and challenges involved in delighting the senses, a concern primarily associated with art and design. In the broader sense, to explore aesthetics is to encounter debates and challenges about human nature, consciousness and morality, a concern primarily associated with philosophy.

Aesthetics in either of these senses may be relevant to HRD. Is delighting the senses, being like an artist, relevant to HRD? Is understanding the mind, body and sensibility complex, as a philosopher might, relevant in HRD? Some will answer positively, that it is at least relevant in some ways on some occasions. Design permeates all aspects of human endeavour (Lawson 1997; Norman 2001) and HRD is not exempt (Strati and Guillet de Montoux 2002; Shani and Docherty 2003; Bredeson 2003). Others would answer negatively, that HRD is a domain founded on scientific theory and professional practice, and aesthetics are not an essential or integral part of that (Phillips and Soltis 1998; Piskurich *et al.* 2000; Schram 2002). But to introduce aesthetics in either of these senses is a challenge to the prevailing norms and values of studying HRD.

Values analysis

The theory that value systems are central to human behaviour and understanding, and provide the basic wellspring for people's beliefs, has been influential since the dawn of consciousness. It underpins a more rigorous mode of analysis since the middle of the twentieth century, with Rokeach's (1970, 1973) systematic approach to exploring value systems. For Rokeach a value is 'an enduring belief that a specific mode of conduct or end-state of existence is personally or socially preferable to an opposite or converse mode of conduct or end-state of existence' (Rokeach 1973, p. 5). For Rokeach, values have a 'transcendental quality' that guides 'an actor's actions, attitudes and judgments' beyond immediate goals to more ultimate ends (p. 18). While values are then a source of reference they are also potentially problematic, as they are not necessarily mutually supportive. For example, it is possible to value both thriftiness and charitability as worthy behaviours, yet there are also potential contradictions in being both thrifty and charitable. As these conflicts among values are resolved, either consciously or unconsciously, a hierarchical arrangement evolves, and a value system coheres. A value system then is simply a rank ordering of values that serve to guide a person when choosing among alternative behaviours, and to help resolve conflicts between social concerns and personal desires in making those choices.

Rokeach's analytical interest was in different value systems,[1] value systems within specific cultures and across different cultures. It was also about how social conditioning and relationships underpin the creation, assimilation and evolution of value systems. This was partly evolving in the context of arguments about reorienting human sciences on understanding human experiences and human problems in ways that were considered relevant to enhance the 'humanising' rather than the 'de-humanising' of human science theory and practice. In this context, for Rokeach, value systems are also organised around two main objects. Some values, which he calls terminal, refer to desirable end states. Other values, which he calls instrumental, refer to modes of conduct. These values may be about self or other people, about ways of living, or about any other aspect of being that bears on how people should live and what ends they should pursue.

In shaping and pursuing this stream of thinking he came to be concerned with analysing what he termed the 'open' and the 'closed' mind (Rokeach 1960), and their differences as expressions of distinct value systems. The open mind was his ideal: to be able to think flexibly, sympathetically, independently and intelligently, to be free from bias and prejudice and dogma. The open mind was a precondition for democratic politics and culture, for science and research, for reason and rationality. The closed mind, by contrast, was rigid and dogmatic; indeed, Rokeach describes it as being more like a network of psychological defence mechanisms organised as a shield for a vulnerable mind rather than a mind in itself.

The closed mind was a problem; it was the psychological foundation for authoritarianism, prejudice, an intolerance of 'non-believers' and a sufferance of dysfunctional fellow believers. Closed minds were a prerequisite for societies which produced tyrannies, of both 'right' and 'left' authoritarianism. The promotion of the open mind, the opposite of the closed mind, was ultimately a project about securing the foundation for free societies. Rokeach used the values model and the ideas of the open and the closed mind to explore various related issues: how the formation of new belief systems occurred, how party-line thinking and loyalty and defection phenomena could be explained. In practice the main focus of his work became the analysis of, and the challenging of, intolerance and prejudice.

Rokeach argued that people could, and should, be categorised by the congruity of their values and beliefs, feeling that this was in fact more important than, for example, race or ethnic categories. He proposed a structure for values and belief systems which involved levels of 'central', intermediate and peripheral beliefs. Central beliefs were to be defined as 'beliefs you believe everyone else has'. Intermediate beliefs were those related to evaluating different authorities, determining those to be given credence and those to be rejected. Peripheral beliefs were those that were derived from the core and the intermediate, the 'superficial content of everyday believing', being actively sifted and sorted according to compatibility with these core and intermediate areas. The organisation of belief was psychological, not logical; this meant that contradictions could exist without undermining the functioning of the belief system. Managing disbelief was also important, considering the ways in which one belief system could be embraced and a series of other belief systems rejected.

Modelling values

The issue encountered here is different, but the method of analysis can be similar. Rather than analysing closed or open mindedness, and tolerance or authoritarianism as an outcome, it is the diversity of ways of understanding HRD, and the terminal and instrumental values of HRD participants. That is, do the values associated with concern about these matter in determining what the end aims of HRD are, and do they matter in shaping how HRD is actually enacted? The blunt answer to that, on the surface, is a clear 'no'; they do not matter, as values associated with other ideas about terminal and instrumental values prevail. HRD is for economic good, or for social good, or for political good, and to be understood via scientific research. HRD does not exist to express or exhibit imagination, creativity and beauty. HRD is not a form of art. A more sophisticated analysis, though, reveals a much more intriguing answer is possible.

Underlying Rokeach's theory that values affect behaviour and under-standing was a framework of a hierarchy: some values were superior to others. But it is possible to consider that various kinds of value system are possible, and equal, that they are different expressions to an underlying impulse, articulating in various forms an underlying ethical position. People's sense-making and ideas about right goals – terminal values – and right behaviour – instrumental values – run along varied but predictable lines. People are active agents, sense-makers, depending on these values to anchor their sense-making; each person, affected by the group, social and cultural environment they inhabit and help create, seeks to achieve certain goals in life which are consistent with their sense of right goals and right behaviours: their ethics.[2] These are not a hierarchy of values with some supe-rior and others inferior, some culminating in an open mind and others in a closed mind; rather, they form wholes, identifiable and recognisable wholes, or gestalts, which have in theory an equality of function and meaning.

Various models are available to map a range of equally valid sets of gestalts. The one adopted here is based on the original framework proposed by Spranger (1928). Spranger identified a totality[3] of values in which there are six different sub-systems. For him the interest was in how these could be seen to underpin and affect the organisation of the individual personality (Teo 2000). Here the interest is in how these might influence an instru-mental and terminal understanding of HRD. These gestalts were defined as the veritistic, economic, social, political, spiritual and aesthetic. Immediately the significance and relevance of this classification is seen, for the aesthetic stands as an equal alongside other gestalts which are conventionally taken to be influential in determining the instrumental and terminal nature of HRD. Each of these factors, and their associated value systems,[4] can be outlined briefly.

The veritistic

The priority instrumental and terminal value of those acting within a theoretic value system is veracity, the pursuit and discovery of truth. The ordering and systematisation of knowledge, the contesting of claims to determine truth, the process of inquiry and research are all desirable. These values are most obviously expressed and embedded in the pursuit of the goal of the 'cognitive', seeking to observe accurately and to reason: ultimately, to theorise. The veritistic value system considers HRD and aesthetics from the point of view of scientific truth, reason and logic.

The economic

The primary instrumental and terminal value of those acting within an economic value system is utility, being useful. It is expressed in valuing most the good of satisfying material needs. The interest in utility is most obviously expressed and embedded in the organisation of businesses and the accumulation of tangible wealth. Being thoroughly 'practical', and judging all else through that lens, is also a hallmark. The economic value system considers HRD and aesthetics from the point of view of practical use, as potential to be applied rather than wasteful.

The social

The primary instrumental and terminal value of those acting within a social value system is the care of others, and successful interaction with other people to achieve that. The values are expressed and embedded in all forms of altruistic and humanistic behaviour, through loving. The social value system considers HRD and aesthetics from the point of view that sees being kind, sympathetic, unselfish and humanitarian as the ultimate good.

The political

The primary instrumental and terminal value of those acting within a political value system is being in leadership, and around power. The political type need not be a politician, but will express a striving for power and authority. This may be expressed and embedded in relishing competition and struggle, which is embraced as a large part of their life. 'Winning' through to have power will be seen as the most fundamental of motivations for all. In the case of HRD and aesthetics, this value system considers power to be the apex of personal and organisational renown.

The spiritual

The primary instrumental and terminal value of those who act within a religious value system is to act in ways consistent with a moral and metaphysical system of belief, a unity. They seek to comprehend the universe as a whole, and to relate themselves to a totality. The value system may influence HRD by considering it either as a facet of encouraging a retreat into mysticism or in experiences of active participation in the world through missionary-type work of a social or environmental kind.

The aesthetic

The primary instrumental and terminal values of the aesthetic value system is the creative attainment of good form and harmony. Sensibility, not rationality, provides the lens, and judgements about style and grace, charm and symmetry prevail. Those so influenced need not themselves be creative artists; they are aesthetic if they find their chief interest in the artistic elements of life. The aesthetic values system considers HRD as a domain of the sublime and the beautiful.

The HRD context

In the context of HRD the use and integrity of the last two forms of value has been questioned. First, there has been the separation and exclusion of the religious value system and participants. This is perhaps easiest to make sense of. In the broadest sweep of history there was both the decline of traditional religious beliefs among some populations, and the containment of faith-based doctrines as being of private concern, separate from government and the processes of institutional human development in specialist settings such as schools and the workplace. The outcome was that religious rooted values have neither singly and alone, nor in conjunction with any other value system, been explicitly used to help understand and explain the dilemmas and challenges of HRD, of realising people's potential. In general, developing expertise, skills, knowledge and aptitudes related to work and organisation, the curriculum for anything associated with that, has had no religious component nor any religious participants actively involved *as* religious participants.

Of course, for some people religious values have indeed continued to function as a fundamental influence, motivating a concern with human development, providing a source of moral instruction, and offering a substitute for rationally attained knowledge. But that is generally all done behind the scenes and privately, for it is not part of mainstream HRD.[5] And, of course, the underlying characteristics of the religious value system, a concern with morality and metaphysics, has been manifest in forms other than traditional faiths. It would not be possible to review major influences on HRD in recent times without citing, for instance, the growth of equal opportunity moralities and metaphysics, and the same in the establishment of codes of ethics in 'professions' and the supervision of licensed practitioners.

The second separation and exclusion, that of the aesthetic value system, is less easy to explain. Why have the aesthetic values and participants, matters of cultural/artistic sensibility, been neglected, or indeed repressed, in HRD in a way similar to that experienced by those with religious values? There are two lines of inquiry suggested. One line of inquiry is that aesthetic values and participants have in fact not been neglected or repressed; they have been incorporated, but using coded language and concepts, existing in masked forms. So matters of cultural/artistic sensibility have been influential in shaping how we make sense of human development, but they have been disguised. Everything from the look and feel of the classroom to the 'image' of what a fully developed human being should look and feel like embodies an unconscious inclusion of cultural/artistic sensibility at the heart of HRD. And artists have been involved, but mainly invisibly, affecting the look and feel, providing ad hoc tips and techniques on performance before audiences, producing videos and programmes which use drama forms and methods to structure communication.

The other line of inquiry is that aesthetic values and participants have indeed been excluded and repressed. This was because they raised too many awkward questions, both intellectually and practically, about the structure and functions of realising people's potential. Essentially for them, engaging with learning and development is not for the purposes of work and employment, or social progress, or to win votes and power; it is for itself, and for the fulfilment of the creative spirit. Just as religion had to be contained 'elsewhere' as it could contradict the leading and ruling understanding of what human development could and should be, so with the aesthetic value system and participants. They had to be contained in their own world, set apart from the world of HRD, and be seen as doing something different. That was art and culture, set apart from developing people's potential, skills and performance capacity.

The extent to which the prevailing economic, social, theoretic and political forces and agents have ever been in danger of being questioned, interrogated and undermined by agents of either faith-based or cultural/artistic sensibility is questionable. The key agents of cultural/artistic sensibility used to be closely intertwined with the powerful, their patrons, who were either religious or political. The growth of some independence from that in the market place also shackled them equally to economic demands. Some have been associated with social movements, seeking to raise consciousness and accompany change, but many have not been. But now we should not be happy to settle for what they were given: the ghettos of arts subjects in the curriculum, and a few art schools, instead of a role integrated at the heart of human development.

The four dominant value systems and HRD

First is the economically grounded value system. For some of those concerned with utility, developing people's potential matters only because it is a means to an end: to have individual or organisational economic success, or improve individual or organisational performance and productivity. For others HRD is an end in itself; it is necessary and right to be concerned with realising people's potential in and for itself. Anything that impedes human growth and development is to be seen as malign, and treated accordingly. This, of course, introduces an interesting tension, as the requirements of certain economic 'ends', and the institutions of learning and practices that support them, can be seen as then impeding rather than supporting the realisation of people's potential. If, for example, the ultimate end is to service the needs of economic growth, then vocational education, producing the required skills, should be the central logic and value of HRD. We would then expect that people would become estranged from HRD, from realising their potential, where they can see no economic benefit in it for them. Thus schools alienate and fail 'non-academic' pupils. They should be given a second chance, later, to get back into productive roles or higher productive roles.

This is the reality of the totality of HRD seen from the participants within an economic value system. But for others this is in fact the main malign influence on realising people's potential: that their use as a resource, a skilled resource, is alienating. It is part of the problem, undermining a system of more general, universal, culturally oriented potential development. If all that *really* matters is producing the competent workforce, then the participants in the system will see that and respond accordingly, including becoming bored, estranged from knowledge and study and dropping out. Reinforcing the economic totality logic is not the solution to this; it will make it worse in the long run.

Second, there is the social value system. This raises debates about the desirability of either undertaking social engineering or revitalising institutions to attain better HRD. The kind of concerns and areas of action brought into HRD in adopting this value system can be briefly illustrated by exploring how a sensitive social issue displaces initial economic concerns. For example, it may be proven that the greatest economic returns come from the earliest investments, the circumstances in which children are cared for and learn up to the age of 5. This then is a social problem; 'negligent' care entails estrangement from effective development. A conclusion is posed: condoning state intervention in the lives of under-5s with problematic family lives is sensible – not because the children face any immediate threat or harm which would warrant removing them for their safety and welfare, but because they are not developing well. Such a view of HRD as a means to an end, of better productivity and children growing through development to personal success, is to be achieved at the cost of intervening in the fabric of the most social situation, relations among a family unit. That this may quite possibly ruin the development of several people's potential and lives all in one go means little as long as those in power think it socially expedient.

Third, there is the political value system. Power is organised through processes for attaining it, contesting it and managing co-existence among different interests. Realising people's potential is integral to that. In making sense of HRD, either a hegemonic or an emancipatory standpoint may be adopted. Hegemony suggests an exercising of dominance through manufacturing consensus, around 'common sense', rather than through a more explicit and direct exercise of positional or expert power. A political value system may influence HRD so that policy and practice fits with the 'common sense' constructed by those in positions of power and authority. This is most evident around the development of government policy in HRD, but it is not confined to that. In the economic value system, hegemony currently resides with the triumph of capitalisms, and the productivity and profitability concerns that entails. In the social value system it resides with the modernisation of the family and associated institutions of education and care. In the HRD theoretic field, hegemony is most evidently attained by the various positivistic schools of psychology, concerned with individuals, and of social psychology, concerned with interpersonal and group processes. In the political context hegemony means a balance of power between HRD as a responsibility of private businesses and the state. These hegemonies inform the otherwise fragmented world of HRD.

But there is also an emancipatory perspective in HRD. This may be expressed as HRD challenges to aspects of capitalism, manifest around calls for corporate social responsibility or more fundamental challenges to the goal of greater wealth creation. In social terms the emancipation perspective may be expressed in the language of work–life balance issues, or more radical conceptions of changing what work means and what working lives entail. In theoretic terms it may be that perspectives other than positivistic psychology can inform our understanding of HRD, and theories of ethical and moral behaviour represent one alternative approach. In terms of political philosophies and analyses of power there are those standpoints which see the need to resolve conflicts by altering the terms of the whole HRD process, in the interests of those oppressed or exploited under current arrangements and structures rather than those privileged and rewarded by them.

Fourth, there is the veritistic, or theoretic, value system, and those who would seek to provide a 'top-down' account or a 'bottom-up' account of the realities of HRD based on human sciences. Top-down accounts are possible and needed from 'on high', above the subject, mapping the whole underneath them. These accounts are useful for various purposes: understanding supply and demand, identifying social priorities, providing 'meta' theoretical frameworks and informing top-level policy-making. But top-down accounts are remote from human realities. Bottom-up accounts are also possible, grounded in experiences among people and an understanding of up close interaction. These are, again, useful for many purposes: for appreciating how economic actors feel and think, for empathising with the intricacies of actual people in social situations, for 'micro' level data about people and for gauging the impact of policy in practice. It is the equivalent of appreciating the quantum and chaos elements of HRD. But it is hard to make sense of greater issues from amidst the chaos of particular human situations.

So the veritistic-based view of HRD may also be concerned with different kinds of capitalism and their impact on HRD, different kinds of social analysis and their impact on HRD, different systems of governance and their impact on HRD, different kinds of natural science truth about people, and different kinds of morality with metaphysics impacting on HRD. There are also the economic, social and political kinds of bottom-up veritistic accounts: qualitative, close and personal, hermeneutic understanding of individuals realising their potential in work, in their communities, as sense-making agents, as political agents and as moral agents. There are dialectics as these interact and compete. The aesthetic value system has to enter and engage with this dialectic. Having some familiarity with both the whole picture and many multiple, local and intimate accounts is the constant intellectual challenge. By analogy, if the natural world encompasses both an infinitely vast universe and particles so small that they cannot be detected, then so it is with understanding the realisation of people's potential. The aesthetic value system does not transcend this dialectic.

System-building or spontaneous activism is an associated part of this dialectic. For HRD is action and knowledge that encompasses parents parenting, teachers teaching, employers funding training departments, and individuals everywhere seeking to manage their learning and development across myriad activities. Should there be greater system-building, to control and integrate all these various actions and knowledge, to join them up in some way to ensure that there is better connection and articulation under an HRD theoretic Leviathan? Or should there be an acceptance of a spontaneous activism, with involvement and innovation of an autonomous kind promoted, funded and valued? With the former arises the desire for a single unified theory; with the latter a plurality of various and many theories informing what people do.

But the development of apparently good things, such as evidence bases and research-grounded understanding of HRD, may be complicit in making the situation worse rather than better. For there is a danger that in seeking to hear, see and speak about the realities of people and their purposes in realising their potential, the measurement process masks the realities. Where is the theoretical account and understanding of what developing potential means to the living, insecure, ambitious, desiring, beings we humans are? And in the rush to propose and adopt policy and practice for more effective and efficient HRD, there is a risk that this underlying flaw, this drowning out of the human account, becomes worse. The alienation via theory from our subject, and ourselves, is just masked in the accomplishments of producing journal articles and reports for policy-makers which satisfy the 'top-down' intellectual appetites of those audiences, whether they be of an economic or a social justice kind.

Aesthetic interplays with prevailing paradigms

The aesthetic value system may be seen to interact and interplay with these dominant value systems, rather than being an independent source of valuing and understanding HRD. With the economic value system, it is where and when the valuing of utility either fits or conflicts with the aesthetic. The costs and benefits of imagination, the supply and demand of creativity and the free market or state control of the production of beauty can all become important factors in the rise or decline of wealth, the boom and the bust of the beautiful. The forms of innovation, the making of all things, and the production of beauty: all may be for the general good, or for the consumption of luxury and conferring status. Surpassing others in wealth may be then a driver of the aesthetic imperative, or a destroyer of it. In interplay with the economic and utilitarian values the aesthetic has variegated the processes of business, and associated image-related manipulation through advertising. Many of those committed to aesthetics can see this as a debasement and an affront to the values most important to them.

Aesthetics interplays with social issues around pursuing caring and compassion, and loving as the ideal form of all human relationships. In its purest form the social values system attains selflessness, though the more general form would be to be humane, humanistic. Aesthetics again can be seen both to fit with or to conflict with this. The artist, the creator, may be actively humanistic and seek to introduce more beauty as a driver of producing caring and compassion; or they may be themselves entirely individualistic and self-sufficient, even misanthropic in finding through use of the imagination and creativity an escape from the social world.

Interplays between the aesthetic and politics are evident, but in contrasting ways historically and in contemporary times. Historically, the use of imagination, creativity and beauty was integral to organised religion and monarchies, courts and the elites who ruled. In more modern times aesthetic movements have continued, in a free market system, but tended to produce the opposite alliance, with an avant-garde radicalism associated with challenging powers that be rather than endorsing and hallowing them.

Vertical integration

Important themes and issues are raised which can be vertically integrated across the various value systems: matters of style and appearance, ideas of the beautiful, unity of mind, body and sensibility, and the debates of analytical movements concerned with the aesthetic. These can be interpreted in relation to the concepts and debates of HRD, and this can be applied to thinking about HRD. For individuals, organisations and communities, the aesthetic connections with HRD that have been 'invisible' are increasingly being seen. The model presented in Table 1.1 above was designed to open up HRD and potential issues in the relationship of aesthetics to HRD. I would expect there to be some ambiguity still. I do not believe that can be resolved, but rather it may motivate useful thinking about and practice in HRD.

The legitimacy, or otherwise, of exploring these connections depends on seeing HRD as involving an aesthetic imperative as well as a scientific enterprise. But suggesting that understanding aesthetic value is central to HRD, in the senses cited above, rather than either materialistic questions associated with 'economic models' of human capital or phenomenological questions about constructing better learning organisations, raises further questions. Better understanding aesthetic value can be a means to desired ends, more people involved in better HRD. And it is an end whose pursuit in itself can make overcoming trials and troubles, the vicissitudes, easier rather than harder. Certainly, once the associations between human development and aesthetic value are glimpsed, it is difficult to ignore the implications these have for all education, training and development, including that in the work and organisation context. Practice in and perceptions of HRD are limited only by one thing: our imagination.

One origin and expression of this is the argument about design: that design, careful and deliberate considered styling, is now everywhere, and everywhere is designed. Aesthetic valuing now permeates many more kinds of choice, not just clothes and accessories. Customers for all kinds of products and services are style-focused and aware, and seeking through their style choices to express their identity. And so professionals in many walks of life now must adapt to the age of aesthetics. The era's iconic company, according to Postrel, is Starbucks, whose success reflects less increasing demand for coffee and more the participation in a kind of sensory experience and image, echoing images from popular culture. Ford as the icon of industrialisation and mass production and McDonald's as the icon of globalisation and convenience are consigned to history. And as they are, so HRD must adapt to the demands and curves of this new era.

Though Postrel and others do go beyond the superficial aspects of this aesthetic valuing, and seek to connect it with core matters of diversity and individual identity, they still work with a limited and narrow view of aesthetics, and therefore of the origins and direction of an era which, whether it is more or less aesthetic than others, is definitely more concerned with the idea of aesthetics. A deeper and broader view is needed, one that sees the re-ignition of a concept that has been associated with the philosophy of art as having at its heart a constellation of constructs. These now feature at the hub of socio-economic policy and practice: the constructs of imagination creativity, and beauty. Why these concepts should matter so much now, embedded in the idea of aesthetic value, and how they present a challenge for HRD goes beyond minor adaptations to an era where Starbucks stars; it goes to the identity of HRD, its meaning and purpose, its priorities and promises.

And this is why aesthetics has become too important to be left to the aesthetes, and why it needs to be applied to HRD. Now the aesthetic imperative, the compulsion to think clearly about look and feel in and beyond image, has taken root outside the enclaves of those with luxurious lifestyles and the specialist domains of art and culture. It is becoming a concern for all kinds of consumers in all sorts of situations. It requires the refashioning and adaptation of the economic, the social and the political. It even extends into the hallowed domains of the academic and the spiritual, places whose look and feel are entrenched in long histories. We think of the costs of not looking and feeling right, the increased pressures to be beautiful, the perceived power of the impression and spin – all commonplace contemporary phenomena. But the oldest of HRD domains trade on a certain kind of aesthetic. The universities strain to escape from that, and to re-invent themselves using e-learning. But the struggle they face in altering themselves is not just their image but their very architecture and substance, the enclosure of subjects in disciplines with tribes zealously guarding their territories. It is their identity and image, their look and feel.

Conclusions: pretty smart?

So the look and feel of HRD, the style of HRD, the aesthetics of HRD matter when succeeding or failing to engage people. Applying the logic of an aesthetics analysis, look and feel, style, can and should be better connected with HRD if the theory and practice of HRD is to keep pace with broader personal and cultural developments. The experience of learning and development, for individuals and organisations, has to match and better the other experiences people are willing to invest in, from individuals playing computer games to fantasising about relocating to a new country, and organisations seeking 'creative accounting' solutions rather than people-based innovation. If not, the risk is that those who fail to adapt to the age of the aesthetic become moribund and die off. Now that may mean that some producers and providers of HRD die off, leaving those that do adapt to flourish. But it may also threaten HRD as a whole. If HRD as a whole were to wither and become moribund, that has, of course, substantial repercussions for the hopes and aspirations of many. That risk is real.

Understanding and interpreting HRD is influenced by values: instrumental values and terminal values. One model of value systems defines the types of value systems possible. In understanding HRD, four of these have been dominant paradigms and two have been marginal. Creativity raises again the prospects of and an interest in the neglected aesthetic value system, which was one of the marginal ones. As a value system in itself, and in interplay with other value systems, with consonance or value conflicts possible between it and the five others, it is being resurrected.

The re-emergence of dominant aesthetic values reflects a greater interest in creativity in circumstances where the primary HRD dialogue is fixed around strategy, performance and major government policy reform. There seems to be little room for the 'philosophical' or 'artistic' language of aesthetics to be adopted here. Yet elsewhere, as Postrel rightly notes, from the grand scale of the physical environment we inhabit, the buildings and homes, the furniture and products we use, to the detail of the food we require for nourishment, everything is now much more consciously and explicitly informed by aesthetics. The concern with the aesthetic challenge is real, and part of progress elsewhere. Why not HRD?

Objections to an aesthetic perspective and the lines of inquiry associated with it here can be identified. These tend to centre first on objecting to the 'superficiality' of concerns with look and feel, with style. They are concerned about the negative or ideological aspects of dealing in aesthetics. There are objections to the idea that effective HRD means anything other than harnessing the 'success' of psychological models of learning and behaviour. It does not require an understanding of the nebulous unities of mind, body and sensibility at question in aesthetics. For some the objection is that engaging with the problems of 'continental philosophy' in which the contemporary study of aesthetics is seen to be entangled (Eagleton 1990). This is a diversion from the real tasks faced in HRD.

Yet the issues raised by considering the nature of an aesthetic imperative can be seen to matter for practice in and perceptions of HRD. In a minor sense they suggest a need for creativity, innovation and imagination to be taken more to heart in the world of HRD; there ought to at last be some discussion of them in major HRD texts. The case for a major role would require seeing the aesthetic imperative as part of confronting, in the broadest context concerns, the failing infrastructure of instrumental, functional and rational HRD. That is to say that the edifice of the physical, cultural and pedagogic facilities, relations and institutions that embody HRD are failing acutely and chronically; they are failing those at the bottom and at the top, the champions and the losers. The whole edifice of the infrastructure, the buildings, professions, technologies, systems and processes of education, training and development are part of the problem (Laurillard 2002). Design methodologies and approaches to education, training and development, or managing and organising, can be perceived to be inadequate in the learning societies, knowledge economies and global culture we are supposed to be seeking to construct.

There is a requirement for transformational change and rather limited reform, and the infrastructure we have inherited needs to be questioned. An aesthetic perspective offers one way of doing that. Is the existing infrastructure up to the job, is it in the right physical and cultural places and is it a socio-technical system allowing us to do the right things? There is a superficial sense in which the aesthetic imperative might be relevant, where it is about the 'packaging', the superficial appearance and style, or lack of it, of

HRD systems and practices. The branding or presentation of HRD may benefit from an aesthetic sense; and instructors, coaches or other HRD agents can benefit from an improved presentation style. HRD packaging can and should be made more exciting rather than plain, to make it more attractive to clients and to learners. But this is a limited case, as aesthetics does not improve HRD or drive its development; it is really what is 'inside' the packaging that matters.

4 The illusion of potential
Imaginative truth

> The value of a game lies in its ability to create an illusion – that is, to provide a separate reality in which you can experiment and take risks without great penalties for failure
>
> (Gallwey 1986, p. 228)

Introduction: the imagination and HRD

In one of the few texts that treat imagination directly, Egan (1992) considers in detail the imagination of students in the 8–15 (or puberty) age group. She identifies several elements that affect the typical imagination of this group:

- extremes and limits;
- romance, wonder and awe;
- association with the heroic;
- revolt;
- concern with matters of detail.

Extremes and limits rather than the local and familiar engage this age group; they will be engaged by the bizarre rather than the prosaic. The distant and different, the exotic and the amazing need to be used to frame learning which is ultimately about the everyday aspects of any subject. The dialectic is to relate these to the familiar as the end point, not the starting point. For this age group, uncertain about and questioning of norms, extremes suggest limits and a context for norms.

Romance, wonder and awe rather than 'critical analysis' are the natural mindset.

Braving dangers, encountering wonders, having adventures, pursuing noble causes are the modes of exploration favoured. The archetypal plot of the quest which heightens the significance and enlarges the meanings of people, encounters and the world around us requires objects of wonder, the extraordinary, the rare or strange.

Seeing the everyday as wonderful, feeling adrift in mysteries but with the prospects of coping through remarkable power, despite bewilderment, is the hook of religion, poetry, the supernatural, and horror films for this age group.

Associating with the heroic is integral to this age group, who feel growing power but are essentially powerless. The world, to the romantic imagination, is peopled with heroes overcoming constraints with confidence, ingenuity, energy and persistence; which is, they feel, what could be their personal experience. They empathise with that, they admire that, they wonder about it. Participating in heroism does not mean fighting monsters; it may centre on compassion, gentleness, revolt, patience, courage, virtuosity, beauty. As associations with heroic qualities play such a role in their imagination, then through heroism they can be engaged.

Revolt is experienced by parents, teachers, authority figures and others in many ways at many points. This age group both resists the adult world and seeks to find a place in it. Questions of power and independence provide a constant undercurrent of tension. This is not a smooth transition for anyone, and often a sense of injustice lingers in this age group. Some may express ideals, or try on new roles, increasing idealism. This is the emotional reality, and knowledge is to be embedded in it, not copied lifelessly from a textbook. And matters of detail also matter to the age group. They like to explore in exhaustive detail, and to discover everything about something within its boundaries. Their collections and collection skills and mentality offer much to work with.

In sum, Egan seeks the humanising of knowledge in order to better manage the learning experience of this age group. The call is for the human interest angle, for emotions, actions, hopes, fears, to be taken into account, whatever the subject. Knowledge exists only in minds, and connections between minds are best made and channelled through knowing and sharing hopes and fears, intentions and imagination. It is a plea to resuscitate learning from suspended imagination, to think about it in human terms.

This is the beginning of an alternative to the standard model of 'Set Objectives, Develop Content, Choose Methods, Structure Evaluation' used to design learning: to be organised into the alternative is to adopt a narrative structure, with initial access through strange content, a narrative line which enables the hopes, romance and awe, ideals and revolts to be considered. This clearly cuts across much conventional thinking and the common view that HRD involves systematically establishing the knowledge, skills and attitudes for the lives that people should, and will, lead. The alternative view is to see HRD as freeing people from being bound by conventional ideas and beliefs, to be autonomous; awakened to thinking about the possible. For Plato it took a fifty-year curriculum to free a learner from convention, enabling them to apply their reason independently. For Rousseau it was necessary to avoid education of the young being infected by second-hand ideas. For Dewey it meant training in becoming scientific and inquiring, rather than imprisoned in conventional ideas. Traces of these perspectives prevail in HRD, alongside the mainstream and conventional. The tension between order with regimentation and balancing freedom with autonomy is central to all HRD culture and its discontents.

One acknowledged aspect that the mainstream and conventional view has mainly excluded, for example, is emotion. Learning implies knowing a lot, but that implies nothing about being able to think. This is HRD that treats the mind as a recording device yet the mind is a complex of meaning structures. Learning that gives great pleasure, examples of it show imaginative engagement. This is not about producing whoops of joy all day long but about engaging with the learner. While being developed does mean coming to know a lot, it is not just that. Engaging with the imagination entails using a range of levers; social virtues conveyed through stories; fictional stories and thinking things may be otherwise; information; and events and emotions. A good facilitator of learning needs a good stock of stories, not just a limited selection of some right ones. They need to go beyond objective knowledge, to get through the tools they use, including language, to the very heart of their materials, their subject. They should be able to manage visualisation, originality, creativity, to form images and to use guided imagery. The key is to engage the narrative mind.

What is imagination?

Imagination is a faculty, a distinctly human faculty: that of forming new ideas, images or concepts about objects not present to the senses. It is a faculty which is both lauded and pilloried, sought after and hunted down. This reflects ambivalent feelings about the psychology and the politics of imagination. At a psychological level, imagination can function in individual human understanding in two different directions, one much desired and the other the root of many a problem. The positive extension is to use imagination to be resourceful in resolving challenges encountered in reality. The negative extension is to use imagination to resolve the challenges of reality by withdrawing from them, the danger of the imaginary substituting for the real. The self-same thing, the power of imagination, may generate either a genius or a dangerous fool.

At the political level the characteristics of those broadly on the left and in the right of politics could be drawn in terms of judgements about imagination. Those of the left conventionally accuse the right of having little or no imagination; they are stuck defending what exists, not what might come to be. They are ensnared in the way things are, the system, resisting change in the name of order. For those of the right the left suffer the contrasting flaws: their faith in progress through change is grounded only in the imagination, having no basis in reality. Being more passionate about change only means becoming more detached from the natural order of reality. Those of the left make the basic mistake of believing that imagination precedes and catalyses substantial change; they are dreamers. This is always utopian, the triumph of hope over experience; every major attempt at attaining well-imagined change results in tyranny. Those of the left retort that the right have to say that, in order to buttress and mask as an 'eternal, natural order' the particular features of their temporal system. And, in practice, the right do have an imagination, which when given any reign leads to fantasies of absolute and total secure order being acted out and becoming dystopian nightmares of societies ordered around race or nation with awful consequences. In considering the imagination, both these positive and negative extensions, and left-wing and right-wing perspectives, are relevant.

The legacy of all this is of integrating the imagination with the workings of consciousness, rather than it being a distinct and separate part of the mind. There is not a special faculty of imagination: it is rather a feature of the way in which the mind functions to make meaning. It is wrong to conflate imagination and visualisation, for imagining and forming an image are not the same thing. Einstein famously imagined himself riding on a beam of light, and got to the theory of relativity. That act of making an image, though, is not the heart of imagination. Imagining is the capacity to think of things being other than they are, to hold new, different and multiple ideas about possibilities beyond what we are immersed in.

This is the key to freedom to think of unusual and effective possibilities. For phenomenologists it is by means of imagination that we make ourselves; we are able to see various possible directions of action and various possible selves engaging in them. In this there is both great freedom and also great risk. For to imagine is to conceive of that which might possibly be so, including the novel, original, generative. This includes developing what amount to, in other terms, fantasies and world views detached from 'reality'. A belief in alien abductions, as well as producing theories of relativity, is the outcome. Being 'unsubdued' by habit, being unshackled by custom, being able to transcend the given world placed before us, means that the faculty of imaginativeness can lead either way: to ingenuity or disaster (see Figure 4.1).

Imagining

The positive connotations of imagining, the rational, sensible and constructive side of imagining is prone to being hijacked. Williamson (2003), for

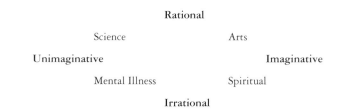

Figure 4.1 Mapping the imagination and rationality

example, represents a contemporary USA-based spiritual activist example. This might be expected to represent a good example of the imaginative and the irrational, but is proposed as other, as wrapped in some elements of the artistic and the scientific. Williamson has assembled essays from thinkers on imagining changes in health, food, community, the environment, family, feminism, children, the soul, religion, political parties, activism and identity. The purpose is to inspire people to take positive action to impact the future, addressing 'Inner America' and catalysing readers to elevate their personal lives, and 'little by little' impact greater change. They seek to contend with the doomsayer theories and gloomy forecasts. The book is also associated with the Peace Alliance Foundation (formerly the Global Renaissance Alliance; GLRA 2004), an organisation which extends that spiritual activism, based on 'peace circles'. They pursue a 'little by little' strategy in organisational terms allied to a belief in the power of meditation and striving for personal balance and serenity.

This contemporary use of the idea of the power of the imagination continues a long tradition, stretching back to ancient views, of defining what the imagination is alongside our broadest conception of human nature. The ancient belief was that imagination was bound up with rebelliousness; the belief was that some gods or humans had usurped the power of others to control and determine humankind's lot. They had been tempted to obtain knowledge or control beyond what was rightfully theirs, and the power to imagine what it was not given to them to know. One myth and symbol of this is the gifting of fire, with the god Prometheus incurring the wrath of Zeus for giving fire to mere mortals. The other is the Christian myth of the fall, with humanity coming to possess knowledge of good and evil. There is, then, in any use and exercise of the imagination, an element of two significant actions: a rebellion against higher powers, and a transformation of the merely human into the divine.

The imagination provides another cross-cutting take on the aesthetic imperative. The concern with being imaginative as a desirable and necessary characteristic in those supporting learning and learning itself is striking. To be imaginative can be interpreted literally as meaning being able to hold images in the mind. What is special about such imagining is that these images provide an intersection of memory, perception, emotion and metaphor. To be concerned with engaging the imagination is then to be concerned with engaging all of these. But, alternatively, to be imaginative may mean to have a capacity to think in a particular way: a capacity to think of what may be possible, rather than crystallising actuality via memory, perception, emotion and metaphor around an image. To be concerned with engaging the imagination is to be concerned with the phenomenology and nurturing of this capacity, asking 'What if?'

In either sense, imagination may be given the status of wellspring of all creative activity and human success. But it is in this latter sense, with going beyond what is given, that the imagination is most revered (White 2003), underpinning the capacity to think for ourselves. People with imagination are the wellspring of progress, of change, of enduring ingenuity. For White there is a good reason to isolate the imagination particularly: it is to define and defend this capacity. For the major problem our cultures face now is the erosion of imagination and an attendant triumph of the mediocre, flooding and saturating what should be the world of the imagination with the banal, not the beautiful. The net effect is to remove engagement with asking 'What if?' questions and instead to substitute for that an engagement with the 'dumbed down', the vulgar, the gross, the ridiculous. The itch of the imagination is not even scratched. Consequently, people are left yearning for something else, something more; the disenchanted look around for the sublime rather than the ridiculous. When they do not find it on TV, or at the cinema, they can seek for it in the performing arts. For these are reputed to be still a refuge for the true spirit of the imagination, where people concerned to have both their intellectual and their emotional natures engaged can find satisfaction. The performing arts are not implicated along with mass communication in complicity with distorting desire; they are against the process of continuing misdirection and domination of people's desires, as they afford instead dialogue and reflection. So there is a great value in, and need for, the re-ignition of the idea of the imagination and its worth, to start a blaze whose flames could consume all that is mediocre and banal, inauthentic and false. The creative and the compassionate would rise again.

Links to HRD

Egan (1992) argues that, socio-political issues aside, learning works best with good teachers; and good teachers are imaginative. This means that they adopt unusual and effective methods to teach, and are able to give pleasure. Myth, memory and emotion are all intertwined in the systems of 'information management' and communication which stable groups, as cultures, have. Knowledge coded in stories, rather than in lists, theories or laws, persists. The power of such stories is their connection with affective engagement, as through vivid and strange images they enable strong memory recall. The contemporary 'invention' of techniques such as 'mind mapping' are versions of this, the oldest of methods to tame the wildness of forgetting. It is from myth itself that we inherit Mnemosyne, the goddess of memory, mother to all of the other Muses: those of poetry, literature, music, dance. They all had their cults, then and now, but could not exist without the underlying common source. It is also pertinent to remember that Plato and Aristotle established the first academies as cults for the Muses. Today, modern academies, universities, would not consider themselves either cults or much in the thrall of Muses, and only the name lingers on with 'Museums' being places of education and research. Yet the idea that the imagination has been excised from modern academies, universities, is wrong.

Contrary to the elevation of imagination as a seat of human power, Plato preferred to elevate the cultivation of reason; this was the way to gain secure knowledge of the truth, and secure knowledge of the truth was the ultimate goal. Imagination and, downstream, the arts had a lesser role; they were only about mimicking and entertaining rather than accessing truth. Not even the highest of art could match the meanest of maths as a source of insight to reality. Mankind could not approach truth through painting or poetry. The Platonic ideal, then, was to cultivate reason and accumulate and clarify bodies of knowledge; that was the high road. For Aristotle, art was more than mere copying. It afforded, through particular articulations, glimpses of the general and universal. Nonetheless, art was not a big deal, and reason was ever superior to the imagination.

The imagination was then consigned to a secondary and supporting role in the lifeworlds of humankind. With the Enlightenment, the function and status of the imagination was reconceived and rehabilitated. Philosophers such as Hume reconfigured the relations between sense, image and reason. Hume's starting point was that our perception of the world is fleeting, partial and founded on constantly changing impressions, yet the mind appears to have a stable, clear, and constant image of it. Such stability was generated from the flux because the imagination achieved it. Rather than it being an inferior, marginal, problematic capacity, it was imagination rather than the faculty of reasoning that provided the foundation of sense-making and the whole mind. Reason was the slave of the passions.

Following this, Kant (Lyotard 1994) went further; he argued that people do not experience a problem with processing a 'flux' of impressions from the world for a different reason. This was because the imagination structures what it is possible to perceive, what we can perceive. The mind does not, through senses processing information managed by reasoning, 'copy' the world accurately; each person is constituted of capacities that both enable and limit how the world is to be perceived. If people perceive structure and order, sensing the external world as already structured and therefore sensible, that is so because these qualities are attributes of the mind, and its specific, limited ways of seeing and knowing. These are not attributes of the world. What the world is actually 'really like' can never be fully known, as the instrument used to apprehend it – ourselves – is so specific and limited.

Playing with fire

So the imagination is reinstated with an active and central role; it provides the lamp with which people may seek to lighten the darkness beyond what they know. This is why it matters, not because it is a part of the mind as a mirror reflecting the world 'as it is already illuminated'. There is then a world within, the world of our imagination, affecting our sense-making and what exists externally, beyond our immediate awareness. One logic might then proceed to consider how, the better the imagination, the more darkness that might be lit, affording greater views around us, beyond the immediate both physically, temporally and socially. We can see into the past and ahead into the future, beyond our own lives and cultures, across cultures, only in as far as we have the imagination for that. The meaner the imagination, the more darkness that would prevail, enclosing people in the immediacy of their own lives, circumstances, times and conditions: claustrophobic, confined and therefore miserable conditions. Imagination provides, this asserts, the structure for enabling conditions in which the individual and the whole culture could be best nurtured and act.

This case for the imagination is both prefigured and expressed with the subsequent rise of the Romantic movement. This was founded upon and identified with the belief that imagination, and downstream creativity, could be the source of reconceiving order. The producers of new light would be the conjurors of images and words, who would find ways to unleash tides of emotion that could carry everyone beyond the dams and barriers to change, and on to a better world. Such imagination was most evident in artists; artists were producers, not reproducers, agents of change, not mere copyists. Associated with this view there arose a belief in the purity and power of childhood, which as a golden age for imagination was to be revered and whose corruption or loss was to be lamented.

The belief that adulthood involved steady progress upon breaking with childish things was decried as a fiction of development, and questioned. Retaining in some way, or recapturing, the wonder-filled experience of childhood was the ideal, and imagination was the vehicle for that.[1] The culmination of this was that artists were the ones who could attain an under-standing of truth and reality greater than philosophers, a view best expressed by two of the great Romantics. First was Keats, and his incanting that 'truth is beauty, beauty truth'. Second was Shelley, who described poets to be the unacknowledged legislators of the world. This was a high tide for the cult of the imagination, and its underpinning of creativity and the arts. The subse-quent course of events, and of social, economic and technological progress, embodied in the early effects of industrialisation, rendering the quality of life greater for some and grimmer for many, overshadowed the hopes of the Romantics and altered the whole landscape in which the imagination had to operate. And the failure of either reform or revolutions to bring about the desired emancipation and change foreseen, and indeed the defeat and trans-formation of that into terror, undermined the heart of the Romantic enterprise. All passion was not spent, but the only hope that remained was a hope that artists and their imaginations were still potential powers that could provide an impetus and foundation for a new beginning. Yet instead of artists displacing philosophers as the agents of truth-seeking, it was to be scientists who played that role. Their experimental methods, objectifying perspective and production of theories provided the infrastructure of change, not the imaginations of artists and their creations. These sciences would be what the Romantic and the imaginative would now have to contend with, or make peace with.

Playing with fire again

This connects with the modern concern: the extent to which gameplay and computer-based learning is a positive or negative foundation for supporting learning (King 2002). Games have always been a part of human culture. Now videogames represent a major worldwide phenomenon, shaping culture, where more money is spent than on movies. The context is that this is a serious business. Some are concerned that this is an arena defined by young men for boys; trends and ways to become more relevant are needed. One study (Grossman and DeGaetano 1999) claimed to show that videogames trained people to kill. Police forces do use Firearms Training Simulators (FATS), where the constant practice of repetitive firing allows them to act in real life. They are trained to overcome the innate distaste for taking human life. This is a version of operative conditioning. On the other hand, simulations enabled the first astronauts to learn to fly to the moon without ever leaving earth.

Most videogames are non-violent, or harmless fantasy. But few studies have been done, compared to TV. People identify potential problems with role-playing: taking new identities, the weirdness of identity. They are anti-theatre, censoring it. But games most often give authority figures the power of violence; only a few give that power to criminals. There is also a concern about isolation: a narrow world, socially unprepared. But one major phenomenon, Pokémon, required interpersonal communication, and laborious collecting. People are ever fearful of youth; but rock and roll produced baby boomer materialists, not anarchists.

In terms of art, games are a mix of the narrative and the spatial structured for spontaneous play. They offer totally constructed environments. Early games were just simple contested spaces. Now they have the whole globe as a form of game board, with degrees of realism beyond imagining. The world is sighted through gunsights and consists of clear levels. These worlds are designed for affordances: spaces or objects with hidden potential for action. They may be minimalist or elaborate, from 'Super Mario', childlike, bright realms to realistic noir worlds. Hard rails are set, but there are also multi-directional, multi-linear options. Players need to be led, without making them feel led, by giving them embedded information. Realism works, but raises expectations too high, rather than having clear goals and possibilities. Immersiveness is not photo-realism but a sense of being there, with some things exaggerated to make it exciting. That may come from any conventions: expressionism, Romanticism, surrealism.

The central character is the star, from the deformed cartoon characters to those replicating humans consistent with key cinematic conventions and physiques. There are simple controls for complex movements. Competition is the key; there are winners and losers. Experiences may be highly networked, with a self-organised playing population customising and extending games. They create and modify them: a decentralised approach which learns, adapts and selects best practices. Narrative itself is another metaphor within which players quest. The quest typically involves the following elements:

- having a goal;
- encountering obstacles;
- accessing resources;
- getting rewards;
- facing penalties;
- obtaining information.

Thousands of games are produced along these lines, following this recipe; only a few are successful. Those that are become a central part of the pop culture ecosystem. As they get more realistic, and potentially more immersive, the lines between the real and the imaginary may blur. What if we could not tell the difference between a computer-generated image and a live one? The movie series *The Matrix* explored this area from a dystopian perspective. The potential for these synthetic virtual words to afford an experience of beauty beyond anything available in everyday reality could become a powerful pull on all kinds of consumers, not just typical computer game players. The high promise of these technologies providing such fresh paradises is countered by those who would be anxious that they were in fact new wildernesses, the most isolated environments possible in the modern world; places where people can be lost, alone, in fantasy worlds in which through mastery of a game they become heros; but only to and for themselves. As the real world becomes more fantastic, so the fantastic world becomes more real

In seeking to connect gaming with learning there is confusion. This will be explored in detail in a later chapter. At this juncture the point is to note that this confusion is inherent where a scientific approach to learning is adopted and the nature of the imagination is excluded from making sense of learning and HRD (Winch 1998).

'Much current thinking about learning … is confused and barren and should be discarded without regret … the possibility of giving a scientific or even a systematic account of human learning is also mistaken' (Winch 1998, p. 2). Which concludes that this means we can, at best, understand the connections of gaming and learning only in a piecemeal way. It has done that in favour of grand theories of learning. But context is important, and these other factors are critical, so all grand theory is undermined. We cannot describe and understand what is before us, or only in a piecemeal way. There is a need to clarify matters of epistemology: how knowledge is acquired. Learning theories rest on faulty epistemologies. They have a common epistemological root, that knowledge is acquired by individuals with a conscious awareness; human beings are mental beings primarily and corporeal only secondarily. That is why the practical, social and affective can be neglected. There are different versions of this:

- modern empiricism: people are automata, learning in one sense part of the natural world, behaviourist;
- modern Cartesianism: people have separate and distinct cognitive, neural structures and processes;
- developmentalism: learning accompanies stages of growth, from Rousseau, via Piaget;
- liberationism: learning accompanies being free from authority, utopian and anti-authority, after Rousseau.

Yet all these fail to appreciate the normative nature of human life, and the impact of child-rearing. That is to say that learning is always managed in a value-laden context, not a value-free context where the 'right' scientific answer can be defined and applied. For Winch, much development is training: a normative activity designed to get people to conform to rules. Development through learning rules, by making mistakes and being corrected, is the central normative activity facing children seeking to becoming competent members of their community. It is interconnected with the essentially social nature of life, and the basic task of producing the next generation. In the past that kind of development meant learning the myths, making the artefacts and knowing the beliefs of the tribe. The modern individual faces the same task, but the developmental context is institutionally complex and specialised. There are many separate compartments and spheres, of which most people remain ignorant most of the time. Even child-rearing is a specialised activity, not a common group function. And as specialist and autonomous institutions are established and persist, they develop their own discrete values.

The illusion of games

The way that development can be structured within older forms of games, physically demanding sports, can be explored. Here there is also a role for the imagination. Games have designated beginnings and ends, with physical boundaries, with goals and obstacles to be overcome, governed by a set of rules. But they are simulations, pretend realities. Games, of course, require to be learned, and they thus aid growth and change; but to participate in them relies first upon the imaginations of the players – that is, the illusion that the game matters. Children's games are part of learning as well as enjoyment. Adult participation in games is also common. Games are considered important because they are simulated realities; competition as channelled aggression, for example, is allowed and mistakes can be made without dire consequences. Through improving their performance in games people engage in efforts conducive to more general learning and growth, but this is not the aim and what happens is not of great importance. The enabling and ultimate illusion is that the game is important, that results are important and justify elation at winning, despair at losing. The function of this commitment to games and their outcomes can be hijacked by governments for the purposes of distraction; a claim levelled in ancient history about the Roman Empire and its use of games, and in contemporary societies about the function of rivalries in sports supporters within and between nations.

Consider any game that is played, or sporting activities that people enjoy and would like to be better at. If a person decided that their current level of performance was frustrating, they could set about trying to improve their performance using the following options:

- Read books about it for tips.
- Practise or play more.
- Get a top instructor, specialist coach.
- Consult a Zen guru.

These options offer a ranking of options in order of their likely choice. Understanding why, and why the final option may be the best, is to introduce the imagination again to development. The shelves of bookstores are full of books with tips on every game and sport. Reading these does not often produce the desired results, as understanding the principles does not translate to improved practice. Indeed, more practice without insight can be quite harmful. Many people think that the best solution is to obtain a top instructor and specialist coach. Books are a cheap substitute for that. But this might actually perpetuate frustrating levels of performance. Learners take it for granted – and it is the norm – to have an instructor instruct you, a coach coaching on the discrete skills; and learners may feel cheated if they do not get that. But the process of instruction and coaching may be based on a fundamental flaw: that you have been persuaded to mistrust yourself and your natural learning process. Most education and training is based on passively acquiring 'do-instructions'. Learners are told to 'do' this and 'do' that. This is couched in terms of the needs of mastering either conceptual or practical aspects, based on the authority and power of the instructor as a possessor of the secrets and mysteries of the activity and the learner as a blank slate.

However, learners have their own natural, innate, learning process; they can learn anything without instruction, from experience. This model actually requires that the natural mode of learning be neutralised, and the most effective way of doing that is to introduce the learner to self-doubt, suggesting that they cannot learn or improve without 'do-instructions'. There is then a vast business of trying to analyse actions into concepts, then into 'do-instructions', and institutions devoted to then giving the learner their immersion in these as the way to learn. It is partly successful with children, increasingly problematic with young people, and with adults there are often major problems:

> **'I do not understand'**: communication gaps between teacher and learner; the teacher knows what they are talking about, the learner does not. At best the learner has to master the vocabulary first, but learning the vocabulary becomes all that happens: there is no change in performance, just reinforced self-doubt.
>
> **'I cannot do that'**: the learner understands intellectually but is not able to act; the instructor may be asking you to do things that are currently beyond you, so the performance does not improve. Not being able to meet expectations, to follow the instructions at that stage, produces reinforced self-doubt.
>
> **'It makes no difference'**: the instructions may be wrong or misguided; they are generic and do not deal with your underlying performance problems, simply reinforce self-doubt.
>
> **'There is too much to think about'**: there are too many instructions at one time; there is too much to attempt to consciously manage, so the 'lesson' has no impact, and the experience of overload reinforces self-doubt.

This kind of 'do-instruction' model, premised upon and reinforcing self-doubt about a natural ability to learn, is ingrained in the education and training of children and adults. The struggle to remove it from adult learning, and use alternatives, is ongoing. Adults struggle through learning episodes, seeking to work around the chronic problems engendered by the prevalence of self-doubt, with the systemic effect of reinforcing it. Worse, the 'do-instructor' of learning episodes takes up residence and becomes ingrained internally; learners replicate a 'do-instructor' presence in their own consciousness, the voice that sows the seeds of doubt, that interferes with performance and with trying to learn to improve performance even if they are not in a formal learning situation.

Gallwey has a model of the mind as being split and divided against itself; this duality is similar to models that set the conscious against the unconscious, the left-brain against the right-brain – indeed, the mind against the body. There is a natural way to learn: through experience and trusting yourself to find a way to effective performance, all on your own. A system has been established which is based on 'do-instructions', and that becomes prevalent and is institutionalised. That was due to the perceived superiority of, and victory of, conceptual knowledge, of the academic. Any system based solely on this is imbalanced. It produces, among other problems, dependence on 'do-instructors'. Instead, people need to manage their own inner game, remove self-doubt, concentrate, be aware.

It is in this context that the 'Zen guru' option comes into its own. For such a person can help the participant develop the awareness, concentration and self-control required to let their natural learning process prevail. They can learn to trust themselves and develop via experience to deal with their own performance needs, and improve performance. What the coach should do is help them develop insights about the inner game and leave the rest, the mechanics, to them. For they are capable, they can learn anything naturally, and can improve performance through experiential learning. Removing the interference of the tense, doubting, egotistical, results-fixated, narcissistic self is what works. Decrease self-doubt, develop relaxed concentration and awareness, trust in themselves, and they can improve performance. Everyone can. And learning – that is, growth and change – will occur not just in performance of the activity but more broadly as well.

Such a view is widespread and popular. Yet there are benefits and successes of 'do-instruction' systems, both for helping to impart conceptual elements that affect performance and for other kinds of learning. The various ways that the mind can be modelled as subject to a split may include the trustworthy inner competent and the interfering 'do-instructor', but it is the practicalities of combining cognitive, capability and affective processes together that is the underlying challenge. Ultimately, while Gallway is against learning founded on the communication of tips he himself is actually providing tips.

Just removing self-doubt and improving concentration and awareness cannot substitute for capability. And leaping from connections with improving performance to connections with existential and spiritual matters, matters of illusion and reality, is questionable. If people really need to buy into alternative philosophies to perform well then that is what they should be supported in; but that leads back to questioning the whole point of playing any game. The critique of Western education and learning systems favouring Eastern-based philosophies is an academic one; going by results, it seems the Western system produces more winners, without the inputs of Zen gurus. The Western mix is one which approaches sport and games combining the romantic, the pragmatic and the militaristic. When competing, that seems to produce a sports psychology capable of sustaining winners, though their qualities as human beings may fall short of what a philosopher, Eastern or Western, would condone.

5 Caring about beauty

Beauty, though not a source of knowledge, is, nonetheless, the source of knowing.
(Kirwin 1999, p. 63)

All cultures are beauty cultures ... every civilisation reveres it, pursues it at enormous costs, and endures the tragic and comic consequences of this pursuit.
(Etcoff 1999, p. 245)

Introduction

A study of UK business growth and decline reveals that professions catering for beauty, body image and alternative therapy have increased dramatically while traditional high-street shopkeeping businesses have seen sharp declines. Aromatherapy businesses have increased by 5,200 per cent in ten years, alongside cosmetic surgery, weight control, make-up services, psychotherapy, hypnotherapy and counselling (Yell 2004). The pursuit of stress-free perfection seems to be producing a new employment landscape, and it is one where the subject of beauty is unavoidable.

Accompanying the emergence of greater interest in aesthetic values and debates, the discourse of beauty has become more significant. The exploration of this concept proceeds by defining and critiquing four major theories of beauty: the metaphysical, the rationalist, the structure of feeling theory, and the biological theory. The structure of feeling theory is considered most fitting for connecting with understanding and interpreting HRD. This is examined first by looking at the importance of the structure of feeling of beauty to a group's world views. Second, a direct textual treatment of this idea, derived from architecture, is explored. The structure of feeling of beauty is, finally, to be situated and analysed as a form of social construction as well as an element of biology. Social construction is integral to connecting beauty with HRD, producing insights but also provoking contests and resistance.

The idea of beauty

Following the identification of a general aesthetic value system and a role for imagination, the natural culmination of analysis is to encounter the concept of beauty. The aesthetic and the imaginative converge on the concept, either because it is believed the job market clearly rewards beauty or because the myths of beauty are considered to be a source of fundamental and ongoing distortions. The influence is subtle and complex. Why are attractive people seen as more skilled, capable and warm? Why is leadership associated with certain features, a type of face and being tall? Why are there links between weight and pay differentials for 23- to 31-year-olds, with the hourly wage of fat women 20 per cent lower, on average, than the pay of women of average weight (Averett and Korenman 1996), and husbands of skinny women earning on average 45 per cent more than those of fat women? Why are workers' earnings affected by their overall looks, rather than just their weight? Very attractive men and women enjoy hourly earnings about 5 per cent higher than those with average looks, even after adjusting for factors such as education. Plain women earn 5 per cent less than average lookers, plain men 10 per cent less (Hamermesh and Biddle 1994).

There is something of the childish about all this. Beauty myths, after all, are for the child; beauty is embedded in the pleasure of anticipations, promises and belief in them, a world new and free of scepticism. Becoming adults means not letting beauty myths eclipse all else; people are wiser about naive passions aroused by beauty, and with greater knowledge comes more scepticism and a world with less beauty in it. To take beauty seriously is to approach the front lines and the trenches around which various battles rage. There are battles between the mass media, seeking to control conceptions of beauty and hook consumers into consumption, and the avant-garde, seeking to oppose the mass media and flout any and all aesthetic canons. There are battles between those promoting an interpretation of beauty in the world that is integral to a world view and others seeking to dissent from that and to provoke alternative beauty, or beauty-free, interpretations and world views. There are battles between those who believe the main maxims that beauty is in the eye of the beholder, that you should never judge a book by its cover, and that beauty is only skin deep, and those who claim that the evidence shows that these are myths, that beauty does matter, and that beautiful people do have advantages (Langlois *et al.* 2000). There are battles between scientists who seek to reduce beauty to some essential attributes and those who contest any such reduction (Ramachandran and Hirstein 2000). The problem for each side in these battles is that they are all fighting a losing battle. This is because we live at a time that has been characterised as one with an endless tolerance for diversity in what is deemed beautiful, merging and amalgamating all past icons, where a polytheistic creed prevails (Eco 2004). What may be deemed beautiful, or be undermined and flouted, is now so diverse that there is no single ideal of beauty to either use or target. Beauty can be understood and interpreted in this context.

Most importantly, the perception of beauty is not confined to or governed by the reception of art. Indeed, in modern art the idea of beauty is rigorously excluded; interpreting artefacts with no a priori limiting conditions by an institutional artworld displaces that. Art becomes its own subject matter. Being a work of art is a relative concept, with no absolute criteria. Art is a normative concept, a space whose limits are always changing, not just filled anew. So beauty and aesthetics are not to be conflated, but have a kinship. Artworks can be classed as beautiful objects, but many beautiful objects are not artworks. Art may seek to make some kinds of beauty eternal, but ultimately that is impossible. Beauty is a term for a structure of feeling and form of perception which is itself a necessary and sufficient enough condition; there is no need to warrant it in relation to archetypes and ideals.

Defining and theorising beauty

Starting at the most basic level, the quality of beauty can be attributed to a sunset, a flower, an object, a moment, a face, an experience, a person, a work of art. What these various and diverse phenomena share when the adjective 'beautiful' is earned is membership of the 'good' versions of the category; and the association is that the attractive is healthy, the disgusting associated with disease. But beauty is also deceptive. It may be artificially manipulated, to make the bad seem good. It may be shallow and superficial. It may be transient, a brief phase in a process. What exactly the psychological dimension is, how experiencing the beautiful as a structure of feeling works, has been the subject of theorising.

The psychological dimension is considered by exploring what makes for beauty; what, for example, makes a face beautiful? The entire cosmetics industry is based on answering that. Yet one answer is that a face approaching the average is considered beautiful; a beautiful face is the mean, that is, of all faces. The social dimension, why and how equations between being and value exist mediated by that structure of feeling, is explored by considering the functions of art and the Bohemian response to status anxiety. A direct connection to importing beauty into thinking in HRD, via the importation of the metaphor of architecture, is considered. The culmination of this is to have to interpret beauty and its functions in HRD as a socially constructed category. This means that, along with being a subject of real psychological gravity and high impact and social function, it is also a subject associated with the problems and contests of legitimation surrounding the idea of beauty and the beautiful.

To explore beauty is not to become embroiled in criticisms or affirmations of aesthetic labour. It is not the purpose of HRD to produce a generation of Venus and Adonis clones to staff the style bars and boutique hotels, or other centres, of the 'faking-it' economy. It is instead desirable and necessary to understand how different theories of beauty imply different things for HRD. Theories of beauty, and ideas of the beautiful and the ugly, while not knowledge in themselves, are nonetheless sources of any knowing. That is, they precede rational and logical evaluations, they inform our desiring and others' desiring, and therefore any inter-subjective agreements about the world, what is in it, and whether that is good or bad. This permeates all we can know, including knowing about what could and should be done in the name of HRD.

This takes a preliminary definition of the beautiful: the beautiful is that which pleases immediately, producing an instant and necessary delight. This is how Kirwin (1999) defines it, arguing that this experience represents a structure of feeling which is innate to the human condition. For Kirwin, beauty is a phenomenon where there is no gap between perception and judgement for rational understanding to bridge; it just is, or is not. If so many diverse things, and different things, and even contradictory things, can be beautiful to different people, what is there to hold on to? Kirwin answers that the common term 'beauty' is a shorthand for a structure of feeling, even if the objects and subjects of it are so diverse. The question then is to explore and refine our understanding of that structure of feeling. Kirwin identifies three different theories of beauty which aim to provide answers for this.

The metaphysical theory

The first theory is the metaphysical theory of beauty. This is that the structure of feeling exists as a reflection of the presence of the ultimate. In the idealist version of what beauty represents this will be the presence of God. The experience of beauty in ancient and medieval thinking was indeed connected with knowing the divine. To experience beauty was to have some form of contact with the great creator: the great creator who was the 'beauty beyond beauty'. The creator could be glimpsed in the beauty of nature, of other people, in artefacts, or in the 'beauty' of morality. Whatever the trigger, the metaphysics of beauty were the same: that God could be seen and known through these signs and traces. If a person wanted to track down God, they looked for, and found, these signs and traces.

This was a theory that was bound up with, and therefore formed part of, a bigger and broader argument: that the existence of God could be derived from the presence of 'design', the teleological argument. Thus beauty was not an isolated idea, set apart from the rest of existence and to be debated in isolation; it was central to a whole way of life and thinking that centred around faith and belief. Beauty, then, had to be only and completely associated with virtue and life, and not just superficially but in its essence. If the beautiful was a sign of God, then all things of beauty were sacred, to be revered, and to remain pure, in order to fit with the virtues of the 'creator'. And the corollary was equally firm and set: the opposite of beauty, defined as ugliness, had to be accounted for within creation. It was either the work of the creator, associated with punishment, sin and death, or the work of evil, acting against the creator and the virtuous. Through this equation, then, anything perceived to be, or defined as, ugly would be associated with punishment, sin and death. Beauty as a structure of feeling was then a token of something else, not a simple presence of necessary delight. It was not a consummation of something corporeal but an intimation of something metaphysical. And it elicited, for all that, a polarity whose other side, the ugly, could then be harnessed to guide and target fear and loathing.

The rationalist theory

The next big theory, which challenged this faith-based view, came with the Enlightenment. This was the rationalist theory of beauty, where the experience of beauty centred around the operations of the individual's mind: it was not in the world but was rather based in the eye of the beholder. This theory offered a different kind of idealism, that beauty was a subjective category made up by humans, not an objective attribute of the divine. Differences about what inspired, attracted or elicited this structure of feeling would exist among individuals and groups, reflecting matters of taste. There was to be no universal agreement on the things, people or experiences that evidently and rationally betokened the existence of God, or any other first cause of beauty; there was just the subjectivity of the beholder, and that within the inter-subjectivity of the culture. This transformed the idea of beauty to a structure of feeling founded on the essential subjectivity of the rational individual, and a knowing of beauty which was based on the rational individual.

This conclusion was then a dead end. For while everyone has the same capacity for the structure of feeling, its operation was impenetrable to reason and science. For it was not possible to define scientifically the common or absolute properties necessary and sufficient for objects to be beautiful to a rational being, though some had a go at the time (Burke 1998). Consequently, for the rationalist and science, whereof they could not speak thereof they must be silent. So the analysis of beauty, and the sublime, faded from any science, living on only in the humanities and the arts.

The inner structure theory

Yet Kirwin argues that it should be possible, and valuable, to study the structure of feeling itself in the rational individual, for 'What is extraordinary is not that sometimes even apparently antithetical qualities are considered beautiful ... but that the connotations of the word "beautiful" remain stable' (Kirwin 1999, p.4).

The structure of the feeling should not remain impenetrable to science and rationality. What was an irritant at the time of the Enlightenment, restricted to one rational speculation on taste, was all 'in the eye of the beholder'. Yet even the basic formulation is itself limiting, as to make vision the sense that is the primary channel for apprehending beauty is curious. To assume that seeing and that form, proportion and measure are the most significant, is evidently both partial and limiting. It may be that harmony or a rhythm – musicality, for instance – might better afford an analysis of the core experience of beauty. But in this theory, the eye of the beholder theory, it cannot. Beauty, following this confinement in the eighteenth century, could be discussed only relative to good and bad taste. And that was a kind of antinomy, which is to say that whether an object, person, or experience was really beautiful or not was a question that had to be asked, but could not be answered, by rational individuals following the structures of science.

Kirwin offers a third theory. The structure of feeling of beauty is neither a manifestation of God nor of individual and arbitrary 'subjectivity'. Instead, it expresses and represents a basic existential feature of being human: people have vain desires and are caught up in a web of impossible desires which they seek to both make sense of and contain. The essential desire, as Kirwin sees it, implanted in people is a desire for happiness. Human desiring, the hope of happiness, is in origin an internal process: that is, it begins in the organism. But it seeks to be attached to things perceptible, to objects, events, people. The structure of feeling embodying desiring seeks to become arrested, it seeks a vanishing point, somewhere to stop and rest. The choices of vanishing point, of arrest, are experienced in consciousness as an awareness of beauty.

So, for Kirwin, that which arrests our desiring we call beautiful. But no matter how many people, places or experiences we can identify as such and then try to take apart and analyse, we will not reveal what beauty is. For their common properties cannot account for beauty itself. That is inside us, in our desiring; it is not external, in the world. The dilemma is then that in the act of seeking to go beyond the moment of being arrested, to explore what it is that has arrested us, the whole experience changes. In seeking to measure we are both looking in the wrong place and at the same time changing the vanishing point. While desiring we may encounter beauty; but in seeking to analyse what we find beautiful we are no longer desiring. The structure of feeling we seek to consider has been switched off, and is therefore no longer accessible. Then when it is switched on we are incapable of reflecting upon it, as the structure of feeling, the feeling of a yearning without an object that suddenly finds an object, allows no such detached and external observation. There is then an eternal mystery about beauty, and it excites an endless yearning.

That is part of the strangeness of beauty: that it is so desired but cannot be known. But it is not the strangest conclusion about beauty for Kirwin. The strangest thing for him is that there is ever-present a foreknowledge of the impossibility of ever being satisfied by attaining the vanishing points, finding that which elicits the structure of feeling of beauty. Human desiring may be momentarily arrested in the presence of beauty, but it is never satiated. People could be dejected by that, and give up on beauty. Yet people are not dejected by it; they do not find it depressing and futile. They still find and take a pleasure in seeking the beautiful, but it becomes a pleasure mixing both delight and regret, desire and resignation.

The biological theory

Etcoff (1999) provides an illustration of an alternative theory of beauty, in the context of perceptions of human beauty. The sense of pleasure is always visceral, indicating perception of something that is pleasing and tempting; and people live with their beauty scanners permanently on; that is why the manipulative industries of advertising seek to catch people's attention with beauty. There is no formula for beauty to be found, but there is method in the madness of spending as much as people do on cosmetics, clothing and plastic surgery. This is because the science of beauty confirms that there are biological advantages, and that evolution includes the 'survival of the prettiest'. The prettiest people are those with the right faces and bodies. There is a core of a few basic geometric proportions and exaggerated features, which may be incarnated in various types of face and body, that serve the purpose of providing an advantage in attracting mates for reproduction. Thus 'beauty is a universal part of the human experience ... it provokes pleasure, rivets attention, and impels actions that help ensure survival' (Etcoff 1999, p. 25). She directly challenges the idea that beauty is only in the eye of the beholder, that is that it represents an arbitrary cultural ideal, which varies across cultures and, indeed, within them, as fashions unfold. There is both a permanent and eternal element and a variable element. The evidence for this theory is associated with several kinds of study. Studies of babies show that beauty is not learned; babies can and do discriminate between faces on beauty lines, and have preferences for the beautiful. It affects perceptions and attitudes in everyday life; good-looking people have advantages. As looking good has survival value, people are prepared to invest in it, and hence in clothing, cosmetics, adornments and plastic surgery. It functions as a feature of courtship, signalling physical splendour, nubility, fecundity and health.

Etcoff clearly appreciates that people are ambivalent about beauty. It is both a source of strength and also an enslavement. Historically this was so for women in particular, but it is now more generally true for men as well. Is seeking cosmetic surgery a sign of a healthy or an unhealthy interest in appearance enhancement? Is the fact that more money is spent on the beauty industries over and above so many other educational and social causes tragic or comic? Is it significant that the cultures becoming more conscious and concerned about beauty are also the one with major problems in obesity and eating disorders? Etcoff acknowledges that valuing beauty so highly presents difficulties for cultures, and for women in particular; the past may have seen the attainment of beauty as a cover for low self-esteem, a sense of shame and worthlessness. Now the challenge is to bring the idea back into the realm of pleasure rather than denying that it matters. For denying that it really matters actually means leaving it to the powerful forces and industries seeking to capitalise on it, rather than helping people become more conscious and reflective about it.

This containment of analysis to the human and the reproductive is limiting, though. The way that art forms, for example, capture certain conditions of beauty, instances of it, in relatively stable forms, is not the beginning and end of beauty as a subject. These demonstrate rather that shared tastes and values of a community evolve and change. Art exists to evoke a constellation of feelings, not one kind of sensation of the transcendental truth of beauty and its goodness; but even the aim of art is not centred on beauty. That is the premise of aestheticism, of art for art's sake: that beauty is a matter of choice, to be approved of or disapproved. For many, art exists, rather, to move people, not to refine prettiness. The survival of the prettiest is only a part, not the whole.

Application to HRD

The structure of feeling, beauty, and why it should matter when we think about realising individuals', organisations' and societies' potential is then not something to be glossed over. It is necessary to explore the breadth and depth of the interconnections of beauty and HRD, to enter into a plurality of meanings and issues, with contest and conflict about the meanings and facts, knowledge and action, rhetoric and reality. Any of these theories could be connected to HRD, and worked through. In the metaphysical theory of beauty, the connection is with the divine and the sacred, the idea of God as the creator, or other concepts of the absolute being behind beauty. The connection with HRD would be to perceive HRD, in realising people's potential, as in some respects divine and sacred; it would lead to an integrative analysis towards the spiritual rather than the creative. These are issues that are worth exploring and will be explored in Chapter 8, 'Beyond artfulness'. With the rational theory of beauty, where the problem of beauty was quarantined in the limbo of taste, the arbitrary influences of a culture, the connections with HRD would be to situate analysis of strengths and weaknesses in HRD within such cultures. To what extent, and in what ways, might HRD be subject to fashion, to arbitrary cultural tastes? The overall impact of this theory, though, was to remove beauty from being scientifically explored at all, and thus to remove it from the world of HRD where that was scientific. It was a dead end. The mantle of science is now reclaimed by those like Etcoff, who adopt an evolutionary psychology perspective and explore the biological contexts of beauty. This connects with HRD to the extent that HRD may be complicit in the fashioning of the self to meet ideals accompanying plastic surgery and fashion to help people engage in successful courtship. This provides more questions than answers, though, as it fails to transcend the old and futile search for the key elements of proportion, and is confined to beauty as an interpersonal experience alone. That leaves the structure of feeling theory, existential experience of yearning, the vanishing point theory of beauty, as of possible relevance to connecting with and understanding HRD.

The vanishing point theory proposes beauty as a motivating force, combining a mixture of the vain and the insatiable. People both embrace the vanity of desire and realise the impossibility of fulfilment; gratification is not just to be deferred, it will never be. Rather than being overcome by despair and angst with the consciousness of this, people persist; they construct value around experiencing beauty as a central part and parcel of being human. Some of that informs the practice of the arts, some of that informs our rationalisations about what is good and healthy. But beauty exists not in the world at all, it exists in us.

That ploy in beauty terms may be backed up by materialist explanations, such as there being mathematical forms of symmetry in the world. Or it may be made more than transient and vain through idealistic explanations, as represented by ideas about beauty being 'God shining through all'. The point is that beauty appears as something people react to, yet it is all the result of an action on our part, the action of having vain desires, of projecting our yearning arrested on an object. Searching behind that for order in the universe, a God behind appearances, signs of grace and goodness, is searching in the wrong place. Beauty is still to be respected, in the vanishing point theory, as it involves an identity of being and value, a preservation of desiring in the face of rationality. It is, in Kirwin's phrase, a holding fast to that which exists only in its slipping away.

How may these conceptualisations of beauty as being a projection of our own yearnings rather than a feature of an external reality be applied to HRD? HRD also is an attempt to project our desires, but then we delude ourselves that this is not just a ploy to avoid recognising it for what it is; a transient fixation of vain desires. Searching for order in HRD, a theory behind appearances, a policy beyond reproach, a practice above our vain desiring, is also searching in the wrong place. Also, HRD exists not in the world, but in us. As we project and 'see' beauty in the world we also suppress awareness of our projecting. We can then pretend that it is the world itself that has in it beauty, and pretend that this is not merely a momentary, and transient, fixation of our vain desires.

So with HRD beauty is still to be respected, for similar reasons. The opposite of beauty in this theory is not ugliness, which is actually another form of being and value identity, but vulgarity. And the vulgar is that which either erodes desire despite rationality, or allows rationality to override desire. It is letting go of that whose slipping away is to be avoided, or holding fast to that whose slipping away is to be preferred. And the beautiful, like HRD, is ideal for engaging with the unreasonableness and capriciousness of people, and their unions of being and value and their embodiment of beauty.

Beauty and the social context

The social rather than the theoretical contexts in which an interest with beauty may arise are many. One recent and illuminating social analysis (De Botton

2004) considers the problem of status anxiety, and explores how interests in beauty can be linked with resolving that anxiety, or at least containing that anxiety. Status is one's value and importance in the eyes of the world. Possessing status is good and matters considerably, to the extent that people hunger for it. Status anxiety is a pernicious worry that we do not conform to the ideals of success that prevail, or that we may be stripped of what sources of status we currently have. Self-conception depends on others, on signs of respect to feel not just esteemed but also tolerable. In contemporary society, status hangs on achievements, and the fear that failings in achievements may occur and lead to humiliation, shame and bitterness. Status now hangs on performance, not an unchanging identity. There is, therefore, uncertainty: the pursuit or possession of status may be thwarted or depend on things outside our control – fickle talent, luck, employers, profitability, the global economy.

So others' attitudes shape our own self-images: being a failure, unimportant and dim or intelligent, important and successful. These are highly conditional on achievements, leaving people vulnerable to and craving the petting of others. This is a powerful enough phenomena to account for the feeling that despite material progress, overcoming poverty and famine, there persists a sense of relative deprivation; that what we have is not enough. People continue to envy those they consider like themselves, their reference group. And most people's sense of a reference group now is wide and diverse; as they compare themselves to more people, they experience more anxiety. Status systems structured around achievement, not a place in a hereditary hierarchy, create new problems; more envy follows equality. The exceptions of some rags-to-riches stories do not change the basic rules; and there exists an underclass, feeling betrayed. The new servants are, when young, cheerful, but either leave that life behind and become embroiled with other status battles, or darken and become bitter. Self-esteem is a variable considered to determine in some way a person's fortunes. High self-esteem is associated with success and thriving, low self-esteem is associated with dysfunctional behaviours and outcomes. In a world where it is commonly believed that wholesale personal transformation is possible, and the rapid attainment of vast wealth and great happiness is attainable, those who succeed must have high self-esteem and those who do not have low self-esteem.

The old stories about poverty and status were favourable to the poor. For the poor were not responsible for their condition and were indeed to be considered the most useful in society. Being of low status had no moral connotations, the prime example culturally being the most exalted, Jesus being of the poorest. The rich were sinful and corrupt and owed their wealth to robbery of the poor; all had been rigged, by the cunning and mean against the blindfolded and abused. Now there are different stories about poverty, being poor, stories about failure. The foremost is that it is the rich who are the useful, not the poor; the pursuit of wealth drives all else and is therefore most useful. Amassing and spending brings benefits to all. The greedier the better; the rich are heroes. Second, one's status does have moral connotations. In egalitarian systems the best reach the top: meritocracy accepts them if warranted, replacing half-wits and nepotism with the meritorious. So those who do succeed are better. The view of money changes, and so does the view of religion, and the work ethic. Finally, the poor are sinful and corrupt and owe their poverty to their stupidity. From being unfortunates they become failures and are seen as either targets of direct contempt or in need of a big dose of self-help. Compassion goes: let them flounder if they cannot help themselves.

Several systems for mediating and reinterpreting ideas about status to contest this system of status allocation have emerged over time.[1] Among these are systems of status allocation proposed by those interested in aesthetics, embodied in art and the Bohemian response. The production of art is often attacked as being entirely negative; it is an activity peddled by unrealistic and unpractical people, promoted by and for pedants, only an excuse to lure people from the workshops to recite songs. In its defence the case for art is that great art is rather the most useful activity; it interprets and gives solutions for the deficiencies of existence, helping to remove error and diminish human misery, and making the world better. Art is the criticism of life, explaining our condition to ourselves. In art the realities of status may be challenged. In novels and pictures what is important can be changed and modified. In the form of tragedy, status-driven thinking can be challenged. There is sympathy for those in catastrophes, the dishonoured, without forfeiting the right to be heard/respected. These are ordinary types of person making a spectacular mistake due to temporary slips which lead to a reversal of fortune, losing everything. The lesson is to acquire modesty about our capacity to avoid disaster and to sympathise with those who meet it. All follies are traceable back to features of common human nature, so we may be appalled by what people do yet also remain compassionate. Through imbibing the lessons of tragic art, we become less foolish.

The ultimate variation on this is the Bohemian way of defining and allocating status. In various eras and in various forms the Bohemian response to status has been pitted against meritocracy, success and reputation. Instead, Bohemians value sensitivity over worldly achievement, and creating and/or appreciating art. They will dress oddly, live cheaply, read a lot, be melancholic, be concerned with emotions, and pursue unconventional sex lives – anything to avoid being respectable. For at heart they dislike intensely the bourgeois, materialist prudes, immersed in trivia, cynical on the one hand and slaves to sentiment on the other.

They will be martyrs who sacrifice all to write, paint or make music. They will be free spirits, happy doing nothing, indolent, daydreaming, having bittersweet thoughts after glimpsing a beautiful face. For to do anything else just corrupts the soul. They do realise that this state, if attained, together with their peace of mind, is all too easily shattered, so they limit who they spend time with, restricting this to communities of kindred spirits. They will be clustered in certain districts, restricting contacts simply to close friends.

They redefine the meaning of failure. Commercial success is damned. Those who succeed are rarely wisest or best, but pander to their audience's flawed values.

They like being misunderstood outsiders; despite rejection they are superior. In cycles they reappear, incarnating the belief that to be a great artist meant offending the bourgeois, being immoral monstrosities, irritating the respectable. And thus the endless incarnations of Bohemian values appear in movements time and again: in Dada, Surrealism, Futurism, hippies, punks, grunge, gangsta rap. Unfortunately for the Bohemians, most people are not inclined to be too irritated any more by such movements and antics. They await the forces of commercialism reshaping the phenomenon, reeling it back in and taming it for the purposes of money-making. The inevitable shift is from hoping that Bohemianism might be a basis for radical change to simply valuing originality and emphasising the non-material. Aiming to surprise or shock the bourgeois with music, art, theatre or any form of art is no basis for radical change. The legacy is that the Bohemian does still stand upon the value of beauty to challenge mainstream status ideals:

- that people fail to understand the limited role that wealth pays in a good life;
- that people are too hasty to condemn worldly 'failure' and venerate outward success;
- that there is excessive faith in sham notions of propriety and respectability;
- that accruing professional qualifications equates with having talent;
- that neglecting the value of art, sensitivity, playfulness and creativity, and being over-concerned with order, rules, bureaucracy and time-keeping is harmful and boring.

Ultimately the Bohemian provides legitimacy for alternative ways of life, and subcultures where other values prevail. It is in some respects an emotional substitute for Christianity, suggesting a case for the spiritual rather than the material. The infrastructure, the garrets and cafés, the clubs and festivals, the low-rent districts and alternative businesses provide a refuge and fellowship. Sidestepping the mainstream can still lead to being distinguished and successful, but really it is the wayward and absurd that is worthy, serious and laudable.

Neither the valuing of beauty and art nor the Bohemian response seek to do away with status; what they offer are new ways of determining esteem and distributing status, based on other values. They are still differentiating between success and failure, good and bad, shameful and honourable. One conclusion is that we need to understand the producers and consumers of HRD in terms of the extent to which they are Bohemian, or need to be. The need for status may never be removed, but the worst is to suffer the oppro-brium of audiences whose values we really respect. Ultimately, being able to stand back from the hegemony of a meritocracy fixated with commercial success and monetary standards should be helpful to all those who are unable or unwilling to subscribe to all dominant notions, but who know they are not losers and nobodies. For the commercially successful and honoured and privileged are not winners and 'somebodies' without qualification; they are beautiful, until the losers say differently.

A concrete example: architecture and Venustas

Beyond the theoretical and the social contexts there are examples of people directly introducing the concept of beauty into discussion of HRD. One is found in Bredeson (2003), who uses the metaphor of architecture for discussing the redesign of the professional development of teachers. The architectural metaphor provides a triangle of concerns (see Figure 5.1). The metaphor leads to a discussion of 'the creation of learning spaces using appropriate materials and structure that are useful, and when artfully done, even beautiful' (p. 153). The aspect of function encompasses listening and responding to needs, interests and priorities of HRD clients. Who are the clients of HRD? The aspect of structure involves analysing the structural and material components that need to be brought together for concrete experiences of HRD to be enabled. The language for discussing both of these aspects of the metaphor are in many ways acceptable and exist in other discourses. It is the element of beauty which provides an aspect of the

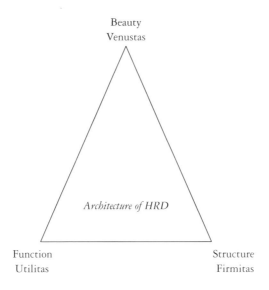

Figure 5.1 The architectural model

metaphor which is newer and challenging; the emphasis on the aesthetic elements, artistic arrangement and use of materials as being equally important. The overall intention is then 'to create artful designs for learning (venustas) with structural integrity (firmitas) that appropriately meet the needs of ... (those) they serve (utilitas)' (Bredeson 2003, p. 8).

From this model Bredeson deduces six design themes for a new architecture of professional development in the context of schools and teachers:

- professional development is about learning;
- professional development is work; it is very important, not marginal;
- professional expertise is a journey, not a credential;
- opportunities for learning and improved practice are unbounded;
- performance, professional development and mission are intimately related;
- professional development is about people, not programmes.

The metaphor of architecture introduces not just the language of foundations and space development, but the issue of Venustas, of beauty. Architecture stands at the intersection of societal need, available technology and artistic theory. We hope there are architects like Lloyd Wright, who can revolutionise architecture with a vision and ideals reflected in where people live. He identifies a need to break the mould of traditional staff development structures. Using the architectural metaphor there is a need to build first beneath the surface: footings and foundations, making them wide, deep and durable. This is to enable the aesthetic: the artistic arrangement that seems evident in architectural wonders. What are the aesthetic elements, and if beauty is such an essential component why has so little attention been given to it? In practice he identifies several contexts for the creative design of learning opportunities for considering the architectural mix of structure, function and beauty:

- development as work; legitimise development as work, not something other than work, at the margins;
- development in work; opportunities embedded in daily work to gain and reflect; individual–collaborative, formal–informal
- development at work; on-site learning opportunities;
- development outside of work; conventions, visits, often individual; need to share these;
- development beyond work; learning and growth experiences for the heart, mind and soul.

Bredeson also appreciates and discusses the challenges of this way of trying to rethink the design of development. The challenges he identifies are:

- There are commitments to powerful traditions and norms which work against redesign taking account of Venustas.

- Many people are sceptical: will redesign incorporating Venustas really be different, and better?
- The conditions of the site, in his case schools, are often not conducive; sites need clearing out first, the debris removed.
- There is no one set of design specifications for Venustas, just common characteristics.
- The new foundations must be both enduring and changeable, and this is a paradox.
- To move ideas from the 'design studio' to the workplace requires rethinking, restructuring and culture change.

What Bredeson actually proposes is an amalgam of current thinking on learning and development, for example that there are informal aspects as well as formal, that 'communities of practice' matter, that the environment for learning matters. This is wrapped in the language of architecture, but the most challenging part of the design triumvirate, the beauty part, is the most underdeveloped. The questions he raises about the aesthetic aspect of redesign, and the intent to design better development experiences using the criteria of beauty, remain unanswered.

The social construction of beauty ideals

The problem of beauty continues to exist, in theory, in social contexts and in HRD practice because it is a part of the social construction of reality. The social construction of reality (Berger and Luckman 1979) involves several kinds of legitimation (see Table 5.1). Each of these kinds of legitimation brings problems with it.

A pre-theoretical legitimation of beauty is one that can exist without any strong 'truth' and 'knowledge' claims. There just is 'natural' beauty. The starting point of incipient legitimation is differences and choices; electing to take some things as justifiably beautiful and others as not. For that view to persist over time, from one generation to the next, cultural transmission becomes necessary. That means that rudimentary theory, and then explicit theory, arise to explain and justify why beauty exists and how, in the name of a 'natural' order, it is expressed. The ultimate outcome of this process is to incorporate ideas about beauty into a complete symbolic universe, providing

Table 5.1 Kinds of legitimation and challenges

Kinds of legitimation	Challenges
Incipient legitimation	Pre-theoretical justifications
Rudimentary theory	Elaborating schemes (adages, maxims)
Explicit theories	Differentiating 'bodies of knowledge'
Symbolic universes	Integrating knowledge into a totality

a 'sheltering canopy' over a whole institutional order. Certain ideals are legitimised and others are stigmatised, including ideas about beauty.

But with the establishment of such a symbolic universe, and all its advantages, a new threat is posed. In such a closely interconnected weave of significance, any questioning of a part can have a significance beyond its immediate functions. The functions of ideas of beauty may be to warrant certain types being seen as preferable, But the questioning of that, and its violation, can be dramatic in its implications for the whole. This accounts for the depth of feelings experienced over threatened symbols, reflecting the way that they are intricately threaded through the whole 'sheltering universe'. The fragmentation of the whole universe would bring chaos. Keeping chaos at bay becomes the underlying rationale for defending ideals and symbols. Participating in rituals and solemn reaffirmations at critical points becomes important.

First is the form of rudimentary theory and the problem of simplification. The underlying issue is that an increasing complexity accompanies the success of any specific social construction of reality. One way of managing this complexity is simplification: to reduce legitimation to a low common denominator which is easy to communicate and defend. An example would be the 'compression' of the teachings of the Christian religion from being based on reading all of the Bible down to knowing the ten commandments, or the seven deadly sins. The need for such simplifications is attributed to 'human beings are frequently sluggish and forgetful ... frequently stupid ... meanings tend to become simplified in the process of transmission, so that the given collection of institutional "formulae" can be readily learned and memorised' (Berger and Luckman 1979, p. 87). So alongside the evolution of ever more complex symbolic universes there also occurs a process of simplification, where recipes and formulae are derived to inform and guide people. This need for simplification contains within it some of the seeds of a threat to the complex symbolic universe. For as simplification occurs, generated meanings can become more accessible to and subject to a variety of interpretations.

A second problem of social construction interpretations of beauty is the evolution of 'sub-universes'. This reflects how

> the increasing autonomy of sub-universes makes for special problems of legitimation ... outsiders have to be *kept out* ... at the same time having them [the outsiders] acknowledge the legitimacy of this ... insiders have to be *kept in* ... [this requires] procedures by which the temptation to escape from the sub-universe can be checked.
>
> (ibid., p. 105)

The threat of emerging sub-universes, subgroups or subcultures presents a persistent challenge. It may be indeed that the symbolic universe evolved in part to exclude certain subgroups; those groups have a stake in setting up a sub-universe for themselves. If one type is considered beautiful, and we are not in that type, then why belong to that universe? We will establish our own subculture, in which different standards prevail. Or it may be that social changes create subgroups that are outside the established order. Social changes may include or involve changes in what is deemed beautiful, producing new disenfranchised groups. Even without social change there are always temptations for some of those within the system to detach themselves, out of the frustrations experienced through being within the dominant universe They may then seek to align with subgroups to challenge the dominant symbolic universe. The history of religion, politics and indeed art forms are replete with groups who have split from the main symbolic universe to establish alternatives. Ideals of beauty are therefore susceptible to firm defence on the one hand and contest among subcultures on the other.

Either the challenges of simplification or the maintenance of a dominant symbolic universe present issues in managing the basic processes of social construction. These are processes of cultural transmission, of handling deviants and heresy, and managing contacts and confrontations with the different symbolic universes of 'others'. Any symbolic universe has to be dynamic, has to expand in time and in space. Otherwise the institutional order can be questioned and challenged by others that are themselves expanding alternatives; new generations, other cultures. The long-term trend of legitimated ideals to be undermined, despite reassertions of order, is attributable to changes in many fields. The rise and fall of civilisations and empires may be due to many economic, social, theoretic, spiritual and political causes, but the underlying dynamic is that of a symbolic universe expanding and then having such great boundaries that it cannot be defended and sustained. And once the cracks appear they spread dramatically across the web of interconnections.

Fourth, there will be problems with the media associated with legitimation. These can be categorised in order of their genesis. The oldest medium for legitimation is the mythology stories about gods in human form creating the world and its morality. Then arise the theological legitimations, with a more metaphysical view of morality based on mediation with gods, and through key figures and the texts they produce. Third is philosophical legitimation: the use of speculative but organised thought to pursue wisdom about the world in a scholarly way. Sometimes this was based on theological debates, sometimes on investigating nature. Finally there is the growth of scientific legitimation, based on observation and testing theories, with the role of educated elites using rationality as their method of legitimation.

Each of these kinds of media continues to offer legitimising functions, creating layers of legitimisation as civilisations progress. Myth is overlain with theology, then with philosophy, then with science. The implication is that there is a continuing role for each of these kinds of media. The specialisation of knowledge and science at the more advanced levels makes common and comprehensive knowledge impossible for any one person or group, but never eradicates myth. Indeed, in these areas expertise may become detached from the pragmatic necessities within which their forerunners were more intimately involved. In legitimation terms a conflict may arise between experts and practitioners (lay people), and between experts and the general population. Berger and Luckman (1979, p. 137) conclude that in the course of social construction and legitimation, 'there is always a social-structural base for competition between rival definitions of reality and the outcome of the rivalry will be affected, if not always determined outright, by the development of this base'.

In their own time and context they envisaged and endorsed there being a core of cooperation and tolerance among a number of sub-universes: a recipe for relativism. This pluralism discouraged the search for a single truth, but also encouraged scepticism and innovation in accommodating conflicting views and beliefs.

Conclusion

The theoretical context reveals beauty to be a significant concept that may be connected with HRD. It may be connected via theories, as with the theories considered here. Kirwin sought to pin down a new theory of beauty, beyond the metaphysics of religion and the rational individual, the containing vanishing desires theory. De Botton described how such concerns with beauty and art exist in a social context, where the containment of social as well as psychological pressures matters. And Bredeson provided an example of how one attempt to contain the concept of beauty, as ideas are translated from one discipline, architecture, to HRD, plays out. Or it may be connected more generally, as the social construction analysis suggests.

The opportunities and problems faced in HRD in seeking to connect these expressions of the idea of beauty to HRD are evident. The processes of legitimation surrounding beauty become a problem for individuals, groups and entire cultures. These problems are imported into HRD. Expressions of beauty are manifest in a context of simplifications, a reduction of norms to recipes, the growth of sub-universes, and the problems that arise for specific institutions whose tasks centre around beauty. Should HRD pay as much attention to exploring the concept of beauty as to learning or ethics? Would HRD be better theorised and practised if it were viewed through Bohemian eyes, and constructed more openly around the communities and practices that entails rather than those of science? For is it not the case that eradicating that which is considered ugly, vulgar and disgusting, and the pursuit of and expansion of beauty, is an unalloyed good? Becoming more conscious and reflective about the effects of beauty, what it means and why it matters, is to reanimate HRD, the attainment of people's potential, not to denude it or misdirect it. For the world in which HRD has to maintain its footprint, and expand, is one where beauty means something and matters.

Part II

Concepts

6 Artful HRD

Pleasure for pleasure

The message ... is not to promote a new magical instrument, a new 'quick fix' for business ... It is an attempt to define the contours of 'artful creation', a new paradigm that draws on our full human potential (body, mind, heart and spirit). Artful is here defined as a quality of expanded consciousness that evolves through profound personal experiences, and is often facilitated by artistic processes.

(Darso 2004, p. 18)

An opening scene

As some oil workers gathered at an airport for their helicopter journey to offshore oil rigs, they suddenly encountered a woman dressed only in red stiletto shoes and wrapped in a white sheet. She told them how she had just spent the night with a stranger she met in a drunken stupor. Her husband was confined to a wheelchair two years earlier after an avoidable accident; despair had driven her to the final humiliation of a loyal wife. The offshore environment is a hostile and dangerous one, and this was a part of a safety campaign, developed around an actress providing a performance. It grabs the attention, using shock tactics. The company concerned had thought about using a real victim to present the message, but decided against it. Those who have experienced the performance describe it as both excellent and awful. The presentation has been recorded on DVD, for future use (Page 2004).

This kind of artful HRD initiative is an outcome of thinking and making as an art more than a science. The concerns with process that this raise can be explored: the extent to which a model of artfulness contrasts with a model of expertness can underlie HRD. Behind the practical issue of process is a theoretical difference of paradigm, with the 'measurers' contending with the 'pleasurers' for the control of structured and formal HRD. The focus on either discipline or freedom associated with these represents a division of belief about the fundamentals of HRD. In conclusion, the ways that arts may support artfulness, the freedom paradigm, and the pleasurers' view of process, is considered by looking at the theoretical framework of Darso and the practical applications of Earl.

Introduction

HRD requires inventive minds at work to animate learning (Boud and Miller 1996), and the example above illustrates that; the method used, the timing, the situation are all striking and unusual. Yet this is not about applying theory from psychology directly to development. It evolves from observations and reflections about human learning and growing, and seeking to influence that. This need for artfulness is both a long-established axiom and a constant challenge. Knowles (1984) entitled the opening chapter of his seminal text on adult learning 'The Art and Science of Helping Adults Learn'. What he meant by 'art' was that the process rather than the content, setting the right climate and involving learners at every stage of the learning in planning and design, was important and could not be definitively stipulated and copied.

This concern with process is integral to a view that learners are problem-solvers and decision-makers, and all kinds of activities, methods, procedures and resources have a role in development. Developers need to be process-orientated. They need to be enquiry-centred, 'doing' things with learners, and to be experience-oriented. HRD should provide a totality for a well-spent youth, a transition to adulthood socially and vocationally, and help throughout life to meet the demands of growth and change. It should harmonise individual needs with those of society. And it should always be remembered that learning environments are not just places for preparing for life: they are life itself for learners, trainers and teachers and those concerned with the learners. HRD should combine and balance the three key kinds of processes that people will encounter in life. These are processes of enquiry: exploring, experiencing, explaining. They are processes of making: inventing, designing doing. And they are processes of dialogue: with objects, creatures, persons, self. And HRD must be concerned most with what the person can be now, not what they might do later; it is about the personal, not the vocational.

In achieving this, HRD can be done artfully as well as scientifically. The directly artistic use of artfulness in HRD is reviewed by Pollok (2000). Actors joined by artists, musicians, storytellers and other professional performers, including comedians, are working in organisations to support HRD. Drama-based training is used for role-plays to bring issues to life. Staff are taught music to learn about creativity, and by musicians to learn listening skills. In doing this organisations are sloughing off the macho culture embodied in old-style versions of artful development, found in, for example, the use of outdoors training. Allen (2003) does review how new generations of outdoor courses, going beyond the old SAS survival-style macho events, are being devised. They target more accurately on exercises that are more carefully designed as true metaphors for the workplace, explicit parallels. They involve shorter courses of one or two days rather than four or five days. They aim to help break down barriers between management and workforce, and promote team work. They may be used for leadership and senior management development. Or they may be specifically targeted at needs regarding change. They may also help fulfil Corporate Social Responsibility goals, for example through renovating inner-city facilities. Yet it is more than the activities. Old-style development was about controlling, with some people knowing everything and protecting that. This is no longer possible. Further, the use of the whole brain rather than just the rational-logical capacity means that experiential learning is a better choice. That is why the arts are used, to be in touch with emotions: more creative is cool. There is an equation of the 'soft' with the anti-macho, so that these process options are an alternative to masculine preferences. So the arts promote higher skills of neglected brain areas and the nurturing of soft skills.

Earl's model

Earl (1987) provides one of the few extended and in-depth engagements with these kinds of ideas specifically targeted at HRD. These are ideas of thinking about course design for training rather than teaching as an art and craft. For Earl, design is 'the plan, structure and strategy of instruction used, conceived so as to produce learning experiences that lead to pre-specified learning goals' (1987, p. 13). For learning experiences to be effective, valued, liked and efficient it is necessary to give time and attention in the design process to being creative, not only to rational analysis. Earl argues that the art of design depends upon combining intuition, creativity and logical thinking. He then provides a number of ideas and models to assist with creative design thinking, and analyses issues in translating designs from the drawing board into practice. Attention devoted to this increases the likelihood that learning will be effective, valued, liked and efficient. In describing design thinking, he suggests three points of reference which are particularly significant for aesthetics. First is a set of design principles.

- Is this an active, not a passive, experience, involving the learners?
- Will you get meaningful responses from learners? Are learners doing things that are relevant, possible for them to do, and necessary to reach the goal – an increment in learning or strengthening of learning?
- Who exercises control? Is it complete trainer control, or shared, or complete learner control?
- Respect, but outwit, constraints; there is limited time and resources, but find ways around these to give something of value.
- Provide feedback; give information on progress, positive results.
- Make good use of media; look at your plan, and ask whether you could get the same result if you dropped something. If so then it is not critical, even if it looks good.
- Double check that what you do will meet the learners' needs; make the course good for them, not for you.

The creative thinking needed to deal with these is not a smooth process from start to finish. As with any artistry, it will have its ups and downs. Work may be halted from boredom, fatigue, from not knowing how to proceed and being stuck. Nonetheless, work always continues, as ideas incubate on unconscious and non-conscious levels. From this work, or from testing out ideas, there is a growing awareness that illuminates or lights up new directions, other approaches, a different path to the solution. The designer balances three aspects (see below) while the overall process can be mapped as in Figure 6.1:

- intuition: sensing when you are on the right track, and trusting that;
- creativity: a richness of ideas and originality;
- logic: testing, selecting and rejecting ideas relative to the end goal.

Designers may copy or revise from existing designs, or diagrams and notes about designs. They will think about which stimuli (information, materials, criteria for decision-making) are needed to obtain desired responses (what learners are to do, to write, decide upon). Various forms will be found in different training events, along with the different devices available for providing feedback, asking questions and preparing people for the next event in the chain. The design point is that for each stimulus–response (S–R) event a training situation needs to be created. A session is a series of these events, and this provides the building blocks for larger units and

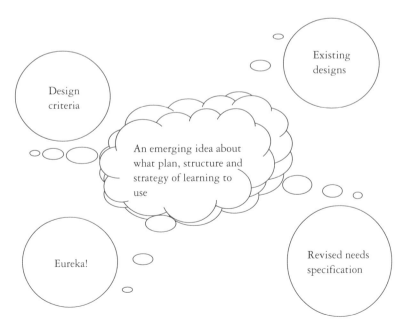

Figure 6.1 Map of the design process

courses. Revised needs specifications may arise as session ideas emerge, and a sense of what is possible and desirable alters while the event is taking shape. The methods and media available, the success criteria, the actual content may all vary as the end goal is reconsidered and refined.

Ultimately, in design there will be the 'eureka' moment. For adhering to all the above advice is not enough to produce a coherent session; everything only really 'clicks' into place when all the pieces of a puzzle that have been gathered become more than a jumble of bits. Then the designer is no longer uncertain how to proceed, how to organise it all, how to put it together. The insights or devices that trigger such moments tend to have two properties: they provide a picture of what the training-learning situation is going to be, and can serve as an anchor point and stimulator for trainees' learning. They become the leitmotif, the theme that can be constantly returned to. Such devices may be:

- a simple quote;
- a picture or an image;
- a pedagogic device, e.g. using maps;
- a person or case;
- a saying.

These generate for the designer an insight into the training–learning situation. It provides for the learner an anchor point throughout the whole process. Earl describes the phenomenon of what happens when all these come together as the design beginning to talk to you: writing materials, making diagrams, selecting concepts, preparing training aids, all becomes clear and smooth. The sequencing of material will follow a pattern, and an appropriate one has to be selected: the route map of order in which to meet the content:

- chain: a fixed set of events – a forward chain or a backward chain;
- necklace: a cycle;
- spiral: simple to complex;
- network: interrelated parts but not in any order, arbitrary;
- hybrid.

Any event should ideally be tested and revised before being installed. The designer is testing for the unexpected: for wrong responses, difficult attitudes, common mistakes. These tend to fall into the following categories:

- Missing imperatives: learners like being told what to do, they demand attention and action.
- Missing overviews: learners like to know where they are going, to have a navigational aid. Provide a clear and common frame of reference.
- Missing melody: there is no melody to the session.
- Impractical design: it is beautiful but not functional.

- The non-integration problem: the bits don't fit together. The sequencing of the stimulus and response pathway is faulty.
- Neglecting in the design: one or some of the five SPICE functions which humans seek to satisfy and fulfil: spiritual, physical, intellectual, career, emotional (by spiritual is meant a sense of purpose and meaning).

The main test is the implementation of a good design. Learning is effective when the learning goal is met; it is valued when the learner has found the learning experience worthwhile; it is liked when the learning experience has been enjoyed; it is efficient when the time and energy spent has been optimum. For Earl the conclusion is that those responsible for learning need to nurture and use their intuitive and creative capacities as they engage with course design. In practice this means developing a database of diagram and good designs, looking for the 'eureka' anchors, and working with the design principles. His particular approach is informed by a behaviourist understanding of learning, expressed in the S–R model of events and experiences. Stimuli are pictures, words, statements, film, content; responses are demonstrating understanding, doing, analysing. But this does include 'encounters' and therefore self-construction as elements of learning. The point is to create an environment of stimuli to which the learner can respond, is willing to respond, likes to respond, and as a result of this learns. Avoid adopting wrong stimuli or eliciting inappropriate responses.

Theoretical frameworks

Being artful, and the process of being artful, is of greater significance than that, though Coleman (2004) makes the case that artists should be training trainers, or teaching teachers, to help learners. This is because the artist is in a position to address challenges that extend throughout any and every curriculum. Persistent failure in training and teaching is in part due to practitioners working with a specific model of what constitutes 'intellectual seriousness'. She characterises the model that currently permeates teaching as being one of 'experts' teaching their isolated subjects. Students are passive recipients and the teacher's task is to inject into students what the teacher already knows. The artist offers a different model, which allows for other possibilities: that learners could be seriously interested in more than one thing at the same time, and that developing knowledge and understanding is not confined to being in the presence of an expert who 'knows' it all as a non-expert who knows nothing.

The pedagogy of the 'artist' contrasts with the pedagogy of the expert. It is a pedagogy of making. Such a pedagogy has evolved for learning the arts, but need not be limited to that. It may be applied wherever the work of a group or class cannot be completely governed by the trainer's or teacher's actions and decisions, where the student must assume responsibility for what is happening. Activity and accountability are shared by both the

teacher and the student. When learners make something, it is their choices at work. The learner is being more active in the learning process and can then be held more accountable.

While this pedagogy may offer an alternative model for learning, it is ironic that the reality has been one with a marginalisation and an under-resourcing of teaching in arts subjects. There is an interest in correcting that, and at the same time realigning arts education with a world demanding a 'creative workforce'. Creativity, as discussed previously, is conceived as the engine for innovation and new ideas. Yet artistic creativity's functions regarding emotions and feelings should not be overlooked. Artistic creativity is inspired by and for producing affect as much as it involves effective cognition. This too has a place within HRD, recognising the importance of emotions, affective resonance and emotional 'intelligence' in development. A holistic view of artistic creativity should be applied. For instance, artists rely and depend on a studio, or a studio environment. Whether other kinds of learning that seem to rely mainly on information processing, reading and talking can be transferred to studio environments is open to question.

Proposing a broader theoretical framework, Darso and Dawids (2002) and Darso (2004) suggest that there can be a creative alliance of arts and business, an inspiration for renewal of business and management from a source other than science. This is possible as innovation is an asset, and creatives are taken to be good at that. The ways business may learn from arts are given in Table 6.1.

Conceptualising and prototyping, previously called metaphor, is to help communication through different kinds of language, shifting focus and thinking. This is going beyond diverse and multiple interpretations of organisation and management: teamwork is 'jamming', organisation is 'improvising', leadership is 'conducting'. It is about, for example, exploring the language of poetry to make shifts in thinking, and so produce new images and thoughts. Social and product innovation is also fairly conventional; any policy or product is the outcome of design-influenced processes, the creation of actual policy or physical objects, services. Innovation can be improved by, for example, having artists-in-residence working alongside policy or product development teams. Both of these are well established and defined. More ambiguous, but on the increase, are two other aspects. First is learning from arts capabilities and competencies as they are parallel to

Table 6.1 Matrix of what business can learn from the arts

Well-defined aspects	Artful capacities and competencies	Social innovation Product innovation
Ambiguous aspects	Conceptualising Prototyping	Collabs Practice spheres
	Art as role model	Art in action

Source: Darso and Dawids 2002; Darso 2004

organisational learning needs, particular crafts and skills like actors communicating well and more general core capabilities like being creative. Second is the development of 'collabs' and practice spheres. This extends the idea of using arts events such as shows, exhibitions and performances. It is about going past entertainment to produce spaces and occasions where, through art on walls, forum theatre, creating dialogue and so on, people can experiment and discover. Altogether, for Darso, these options represent forms of what arts can give to business generally: that is, trust and dialogue, bringing people together and facilitating the new and change.

Paradigms: the measured and the pleasured

Coleman's idea that the learning process should be participative, experiential and collaborative sounds great and makes sense. There are other aspects of the artful, beyond the process, that could be applied to HRD as well. There are the ways that people have of interacting, viewing and interpreting the arts. The products of the arts can provide a source of references, much like a text, for academic-oriented dialogues and pursuits. However, in an educational and training environment that is increasingly preoccupied with standards and measurement, it is difficult to convince those who are not predisposed to see the value of artistic approaches in education (Eisner 2002). This paradigm of measurement is antithetical to artful HRD, whose paradigm is pleasure.

Institutes of higher education do not encourage a 'making' or collaborative pedagogy, centred on pleasure. In classrooms, corporate and educational, the measure of pleasure is rarely found. There is no research that points to pleasure-oriented indicators and pedagogy as improving HRD outcomes. Rather, standardisation is the system, and tests are the key measure, promoting HRD that works to pass the test, whatever that may be. Such a measurement culture is intended to satisfy perceived public interest or senior management mindsets about tracking performance and making people in the system accountable. This is a vicious cycle for the pleasure paradigm, as until concrete results can be demonstrated very few will care to experiment.

These concerns echo long-standing debates about conceiving of HRD as something that could be modelled on the preparation of artists. Any aspect of the curriculum can be seen as, in some sense, an act of making. The features that underpin performance in ballet and poetry can be applied equally to management or accounting. Making could be material or it could be about ideas; in either case it involves qualities of an artistic character. And by an artistic character is meant qualities such as coherence, harmony, expressivity, skill, imagination. Artistry in development makes it possible for learners to function artfully in any realm in which they work.

The artful perspective is a nagging concern for some at the forefront of current concerns and for others an irritating distraction from technological change and economic valuing. Concerns with, for example, school

improvement can be seen as largely mechanistic and rationalised approaches to both curriculum and training processes. People hope to identify 'what works' independent of the context in which what worked was found. Artistry as a regulative ideal for HRD shifts the paradigm to reforming the HRD environment as being modelled after the studio, not the assembly line. The focus on 'standards' is then less about covering required material, and more about the quest for real quality. Learner projects should build from the ideas of former learners, and through imitation and improvisation advance upon that. That would more usually be seen as 'cheating'. But that is an essential part of an ethic of excellence (Berger 2003). Berger is a master carpenter as well as a teacher, and is guided by a craftsman's passion for quality, describing what's possible when teachers, students and parents commit to nothing less than the best.

A paradigm shift to the artful could change the way HRD is practised, but could it also engage with another critical factor that impedes HRD? This is overcoming the problem of broader social factors which impeded HRD (Nicholls and Nicholls 1975). For much of a learner's learning occurs outside the formal environments of schools, classes and so on, whether they are studio environments or not. It happens in the course of their more general social being. In school, learning is disciplined, organised and sequenced, with checks on progress and provisions for remediation, fulfilling definite, known purposes in a purpose-built environment. Learning outside that environment is not organised; aims can only be inferred from opportunities taken and all is guided by the chaos of the systems of punishment and reward that are in operation. Development happens, if at all, by chance, not design.

This is a learning environment with little regard for the needs of the learners. It is necessary to be sensitive to this, though, and to the varying needs of the social being, as that impacts upon the person's learning and development. Developers may otherwise be prisoners of their own social background and expectations. They can seek to collect information about their learners, to research the learners, not just for the sake of it but in order to better have an effect, to make an impact. Inside the environments they control they can strive to create relaxed social relationships and the right environment. But the factors from outside their control, in society or the workplace, mean that learners all arrive different: more or less problematic, with more or less distrust and antipathy towards any person with designs for helping them develop.

To get some unity, or agreement and overlap, between these two different realms, the structured and formal and the general life world, is difficult. There is the natural chaos of learning outside the formal environment, with the vagaries of parental influences, peer groups and mass media influence all playing a part. But more than that, there is inconsistency in the structured and formal learning environment; between espoused aims and actual practices. Davies, for example, explores the assumptions behind the centrepiece of most learning, the setting of objectives (Davies 1975). Assumptions underlying the setting of objectives may be simply stated as defining and letting people know the end point of the journey. But development is not just getting from A to B; there must be reasons for making the journey. The first approach to setting objectives was that they ought to embody and guide the development of mental discipline: improving the habits of thinking, improving memory. This underpinned the classical and systematic approach that prevailed throughout the first two-thirds of the twentieth century. Learners were passive, accepting of direction; they were too immature to initiate meaningful activities. Teachers and trainers were benevolent autocrats who realised their objectives by motivating, controlling and modifying learners' behaviour through talk and chalk. Learning environments were task-centred and teacher-dominated. Discipline was the key watchword.

An alternative approach in opposition to this evolved and came to prominence later in the twentieth century. This has been termed the Romantic approach. The core belief here was that each learner brought varying attitudes, values and goals with them. There were incomplete parallels between personal and social goals; what the learner wanted and what the organisation wanted. Because of this there were often goal conflicts, and ensuing problems with discipline expressed as contests over power relations and their management. A more human-relations oriented view of the context suggested that approaches other than discipline could be used. The alternative was to give more freedom. Appeals for more 'freedom' for learners and teachers, and experiments around that, evolved. For some this meant, at its logical extent, having a personalised and dedicated curriculum for each learner. For others it became axiomatic that all developers could really do was try to develop adequate, fully functioning people. And some suggested that experiences in art provided the only way to self-discovery. Movements in education expressed these most clearly, though the impact was felt throughout the world of HRD. Leading individuals, such as Montessori and Steiner, became figureheads of this general trend. The underlying and ultimate rationale and objective of HRD was to be human growth conceived as self-actualisation. This struck a chord with all those who saw disciplined learning as stifling, boring, oppressing, holding out the promise that it could be exciting, enjoyable, satisfying.

Misunderstanding these concerns about discipline and freedom can mean that even the best-set objectives are not attained. Rather than having objectives imposed on them, developers should work on understanding the learners' concerns and be more than technicians for behaviour modification. An amalgam of these two major approaches is the legacy, the ambiguities of the classical-Romantic approach, of discipline and freedom.

Conclusion

Imaginative HRD is an outcome of thinking and making as an art more than a science. The concerns with the artful process raised by this can and should be explored. The ways that arts may support artfulness are considered

by looking at the theoretical framework of Darso and the practical applications of Earl. This is not just about using some additional techniques: it is
about migrating from a model of expertness to a model of artfulness, and a
freedom paradigm, and the pleasurers' view of process. Alongside the practical
issue of a more imaginative and creative process is a difference of paradigm,
with 'measurers' contending with 'pleasurers' in influencing structured and
formal HRD. The focus on either discipline or freedom associated with these
paradigms represents a deeper split about the fundamentals of HRD, what is
believed and valued.

The downside of emphasising the artfulness of managing the process can
be seen in Mole's critique (1996) of the management training industry. This is
an industry in which many people seek lucrative returns, but in which scientific
credentials are rarely offered or sought. People present themselves as masters
of an art and experts on the process. Yet what they actually offer is far from
artful; it is usually 'genre training', pre-packaged courses of short duration and
unfocused. They are homogeneous on content and delivery, and typically:

1   intend to modify individual behaviour, in skills that can be readily
    transferred and acquired;
2   change the person's behavioural base, not their knowledge base;
3   are completed in a short time scale – a few days, possibly residential;
4   use language and a style that sounds impressive but is more emotional
    than rational;
5   offer solutions that seem comprehensive and absolute but are not.

These artful and process-oriented practitioners of HRD disregard the
systemic properties of organisations, and situations, and instead trade on a
popular fallacy: that performance issues are grounded in problems with individuals, not situations. This approach gets bought in from key stakeholders:
professionals, stand-up trainers, sponsors and trainees. This is because the
approach fits with their comfort zone, the economics of buying in help from
'process' experts. What they get is usually off-the-shelf courses which have
been derived from a culture of imitation, the practice of mimetic isomor-
phism, leading to the same mix of models and techniques being used widely
in different contexts – for example, the use of diagnostics for team roles or
learning styles, and so on. The buyers of training as contractors for services
use schemas of acceptable solutions to judge what they are offered. They
often seek brevity, deal in variety and accept high levels of discontinuity.
They settle for quick answers, easy reads. They will actively avoid much
reflection on needs, and go for sustained and in-depth engagement – that
which is needed for changing the knowledge basis. And for the typical
trainee the process issue is whether they will be sufficiently entertained, not
whether they will learn. The ultimate result of attention to process is
mediocre and inappropriate training. That may be artful in the sense that it
is entertaining as it is experienced, but it is not effective.

7 Arts-based HRD

Introduction

Arts-based HRD (AHRD) is learning and development that is designed and delivered by artists and delivered using arts practices. The most prominent proponents have been theatre groups and musicians, but AHRD also includes the visual and linguistic arts. There are, though, few explanations of how AHRD works or why it should be used. Some options would be:

- The task case: the arts involve tasks like organisational tasks; they can be matched and a basis for experiential learning; management is like conducting.
- The process case: working on arts tasks enables the group process/soft skills to be surfaced and analysed; rehearsing a performance shows how communication, trust, etc., matters in teams.
- The affective connection case: HRD requires the affective dimension to be accessed and elicited; artists can access and elicit emotional responses; music has charms, inspires, moves and satisfies.
- The creativity case: the creative capability is sought and prized among the workforce; involvement in the arts encourages the creative capability.

AHRD is actively promoted by important organisations in the arts world: in the case of the UK, by the organisation Arts & Business (A&B), whose role is considered here. A case study of one initiative, developed by the Ensemble Orchestra, is analysed in detail.

Developments of arts in business

Contextual developments around managers learning from how artists work (Austin and Devin 2003), or beliefs that 'creativity' underpins innovation and growth, and artists are the archetypal creators (Kingdon 2002), are popular. They provide a context within which AHRD can be located and legitimised, and also critiqued (White 2003). It seems that there is contextual rather than theoretical legitimacy for AHRD. That in itself is interesting and worth exploring. That contextual legitimacy includes the emergence of an aesthetics of organisation and an affinity with the ideas of creativity and imagination, both realms of the artist, in organisation analysis and management. Faced with uncertainty and change, the tools of the arts are brought into management, alongside the tools of science. But can a scientific approach to research and analysis sit comfortably with an artistic approach to imagination and creation? Evidence is presented about the concrete, material and specific issues raised by the use of AHRD. These can be more clearly grasped and explored if a better theoretical picture is to be developed, instead of being entangled in a debate about contextual trends and attitudes towards them.

It is the case that AHRD is actively promoted by various agents, including, in the UK, organisations like Arts & Business (A&B). A&B are very active in promoting what they brand as 'creative training and development'. They do so as they believe there are benefits to business (Wilkinson and Foster 2003). They argue that the arts engage people's hearts and minds with unique immediacy. Using those engaging and transferable skills from the worlds of theatre, music and the visual arts, the workforce can be stimulated to think in new ways. Businesses have employed artist-trainers to unlock the creativity of their staff, help build effective teams, enhance leadership and personal impact skills, boost confidence, improve external and internal communication, develop future scenarios and instigate and maintain change programmes. Benefits to the arts are partnerships between business and the arts. Motivating, memorable training for business provides a valuable revenue source for the arts and gives artists the chance to use their skills in a new and challenging environment. A&B seeks to run courses to help arts organisations develop the skills necessary to run training courses for business effectively and in a professional manner. They also act as brokers, for qualified trainers and facilitators with experience of arts-based techniques. They can deliver bespoke training packages such as forum theatre, participatory workshops, conference interventions and more traditional role-play in order to influence behaviour in a company, accelerate change, improve communications, release creativity.

The financial context for the marketing of AHRD is shown in Table 7.1. There is a decline in general business sponsorship, and a consequent concern to reconceptual of the partnership between arts and business.

A&B

There is an organisation in the UK called Arts & Business (A&B). Their mission is to bring arts into business and business into the arts. A&B seeks to help business people support the arts and the arts inspire business people, because good business and great art together create a richer society. Their vision is to help strengthen communities by developing creative and effective partnerships between business and the arts. They believe that through

Table 7.1 Grossed up estimates of total business investment in the arts (£ millions)

Category	2001/02	2000/01	1999/2000
General business sponsorship	54.3 (down 6%)	57.6	59.6
Corporate membership	14.9 (up 32%)	11.3	10.9
Corporate donations	6.5 (up 55%)	4.2	12.5
Sponsorship of capital projects	14.5 (up 61%)	9.0	45.7
Sponsorship-in-kind	14.1 (down 22%)	18.1	11.3
Awards and prizes	6.2 (down 17%)	7.5	7.0
Millennium projects	0.5 (down 92%)	6.6	3.4
Total investment	111.0 (down 3%)	114.4	150.4

Source: Arts & Business survey data 2001/2002, 2000/2001, 1999/2000

the encouragement of partnerships between business and the arts, our communities can be enriched, our individual values enhanced and our society renewed. As an advocate for relationships between individuals and organisations in business and the arts, they also deliver a range of services to both sectors.

Funding from central government helps A&B to foster innovative and long-term partnerships between business and the arts through a grant scheme, 'New Partners'. With support from both the private and public sectors, they also run a series of professional development programmes which promote the exchange and development of skills between the business and arts communities. Funding from their supporters enables A&B to be a national and international advocacy and lobbying body, encouraging leaders from every sector to further the cause. They still want to embed the arts more deeply into individual businesses, with the ultimate goal to increase business investment in the arts. Encouraging sponsorship alone is no longer the most effective method of doing this. Partnerships with the arts need to be deeply rooted as an integral part of business culture.

A&B have a long history of seeking to place artists in residency with companies: poets, creative writers, visual artists. Many practitioners will be familiar with the other end of the continuum: learning about the use of voice, the creative presentation of ideas using storyboard techniques, role-plays and narrative. The newer area is the one in the middle, where practising or former artists seek to offer products and services in corporate training and development. This used to be called 'arts-based training', but it has now been renamed 'creative-based training and development' (CTD), as the 'arts' term was thought to be off-putting. When an employee of A&B sought to work with artists concerned with AHRD to help them identify their needs, they unanimously expressed a need to better understand the business environment, in order to be able to promote their services effectively. That A&B member therefore organised a day where members of the business community would provide development for them on that. Not a single artist came. The event was rescheduled. No one came again.

Trainers using........Artists supporting training..........Artists in
performance   and development   residence
techniques

Figure 7.1 A&B continuum of artists in business

CTD is meant to help businesses to work with artists on innovative and creative training programmes. The arts engage the heart and mind with unique immediacy. Using those engaging and transferable skills from the worlds of theatre, music and the visual arts, the workforce can be stimulated to think in new ways. Businesses have employed artist-trainers to unlock the creativity of their staff, help build effective teams, enhance leadership and personal impact skills, boost confidence, improve external and internal communication, develop future scenarios and instigate and maintain change programmes. Motivating, memorable training for business provides a valuable revenue source for the arts and gives artists the chance to use their skills in a new and challenging environment. There has been a clear trend for them to engage with AHRD. The A&B perception of the opportunities in HRD is that a continuum exists (see Figure 7.1), going beyond just offering training sessions.

The Ensemble Orchestra case experience

An illustrative case can be given and analysed, that of the Ensemble Orchestra (EO). The EO was a long-established name, with a fairly stable group of musicians involved in the Ensemble. They usually number around fourteen musicians, with violins, violas and cellos. The EO work without a conductor, in rehearsal and performance. Rather, they are led by the principal violinist. They have been performing in venues throughout the UK and Europe. They have also been involved in education projects in schools and communities. They were funded by revenues from these activities, and through the sponsorship of a large UK corporation. That sponsorship deal has recently been ended, and no new deal has been struck. It was in this context that the EO began thinking about offering products and services for the corporate training market. The EO worked with consultants to develop a core product, a one-day event for team-building and development. The thinking behind this is that this is a world-class team, which forms and learns many times a year, without a conductor. Effective communication in rehearsals is the basis of the world-class team. The team is able to attain world-class standards with less rehearsal time than others, so they must be really effective as a team. The day event they offer is based on the following elements:

- They perform a piece for the trainees to demonstrate their abilities.
- They then rehearse a new piece in front of the audience.
- The trainees then discuss the rehearsal in small groups.
- They discuss their observations with the whole Ensemble.

- They then form groups to make their own music.
- Things are modified and changed during the composing.
- The groups perform their pieces.
- Learning about teams is discussed.

The EO offering clearly represents a creative and imaginative approach to learning. It is an entertaining means to a serious end. Hearing, seeing and playing music, being in the presence of world-class musicians, is indeed a great pleasure, for music lovers especially. Using this as a means of learning and developing workplace skills related to teams, communication and speed is fun and play, but with a purpose. Seeing this in action it was evident that challenges existed. These are not peculiar to the EO experience, but relate more generally to AHRD. How the following challenges were manifest in the EO case is considered next:

- Meeting needs: how is the EO experience to be differentiated from other approaches to learning for the needs considered relevant (for example, in team development)?
- Design: how does the shift in corporate context from providing training to managing learning influence the design of AHRD?
- Partnerships: what problems are presented for partnerships between AHRD organisations and corporate clients?

Challenge 1: Meeting needs

Three things were stated, with direct connections to what the Ensemble can offer to organisations seeing to meet business needs. The Ensemble is explicitly identifying these as areas of need where organisations may wish to adopt creative and imaginative approaches to learning; further, a set of constituent 'skills' were emphasised as underpinning their achievement of world-class standards quickly (see Box 7.1).

Where there are gaps or problems with any, some or all of these needs and skills in an organisation, the EO would claim, they may offer a creative and imaginative way of dealing with these. The expectation seemed to be to address a wide range of 'real teams', groups of people in workplaces. Conceptions of the appropriate audience might be:

- reasonably performing teams aiming to shift up and become world class;
- leaders of teams in organisations which aspire to be world class;
- senior management leadership wanting to develop awareness of world-class team issues;
- teams which are required to work creatively and innovatively.

Leadership needs also present an interesting challenge for groups like the EO. The EO can do without conductors; there is no need for flamboyant

---

Box 7.1 Connections of EO with Business Needs and Constituent EO Skills

Teams: This is a world-class team, which forms and learns many times a year, without a conductor
Communication: Effective communication in rehearsals is the basis of the world-class team
Speed: The team is able to attain world-class standards with less rehearsal time than others

Skills
Motivation
Decision-making
Role clarity
Goal setting
Working under pressure
Communication

---

interpretation, a soloist can set the lead and tempo. However, since the Romantic era there has been a need for conductors, to handle the potential for rubato, stretching and constricting the beat, and interpretation. The conductor is an arbiter of taste, a referee, an accelerator, a brake, the guide to the apex of the score. Conductors must be confident to get up in front of eighty musicians and tell them how to play: there is discipline through respect. Performance and the magic of that, from the mundane to the sublime, depends on a fruitful rapport between orchestra and conductor; they will turn up the voltage. The real work of the conductor, the leader, is in preparing the score and rehearsals; and that occurs away from the rehearsals themselves. Their technique and gift to deliver the goods, their ear and sense for different kinds of music, may not be evident in rehearsals. And players in orchestras are good sight-readers and can put on a show with minimum rehearsals in any event. Music-making catches fire and exhilarates because of what the leader does before or away from the rehearsal, as much as during it.

Challenge 2: Design

On one level the EO experience, and others like it, clearly represents a creative and imaginative approach to learning. It is an entertaining means to a serious end. There can be rapt attention and evident pleasure among the participants at such sessions, and good levels of informal interaction between learners and musicians. It is a version of the same kind of design found in the adoption of 'outdoors activity' based training, and other arts-based training, such as working with creators of improvisational comedy or drama.

This also fits with a number of trends: in organisations for team-based, high-performance concerns; in work for knowledge workers, professionals, creatives, the changing gender composition of the workforce; and in learning design, for more creative and imaginative methods.

A consequence of these and other changes is a shift from 'providing training' to 'managing learning'. Experiences other than classroom-based training are appropriate for organisations in which staff are expected to be learning continuously, often within a structure of personal plans and core competencies. This creates a climate favourable to innovations such as arts-based learning in general and the Ensemble in particular.

The structure of the EO day event had the following main facilitated elements, for which a framework to guide analysis of the creative and imaginative design of learning can be offered (see Table 7.2).

Table 7.2 Analysis of the design of the EO event

Morning
- All present observe rehearsal of EO.
- Small groups discuss the rehearsal of the EO.
- The whole group discusses those discussions with the EO.

Afternoon
- Form groups for a group task; 'ready-steady-compose'.
- Modify and change things for the composing teams.
- Closure; reflect on learning.

Learning design issues			*The EO framework*
Elements of learning	Importance for learner	Taster event parallels	Learning issues T, C, S
Narrative	I get information	Introduction	We know world-class matters to us; how can we better explore that and learn?
Interactive	I explore	Observe ensemble	This is an unusual team which can be observed; what does this surface?
Communicative	I discuss	In a small group	We can compare our experiences and issues about our teams, and change.
Adaptive	Then I try out	Make music	We get to try out the changes; we work as a team with new insights.
Productive	I can now do	Performance	Because we have changed we can perform better; we have really learned something.

Notes:
T = Team; C = Communication; S = Speed

A number of features of the EO event design can be highlighted. One is that there appears to be full use of all elements of learning, which is a very good thing. No element is being left out. On the other hand there is a split between the early elements based on working with the Ensemble and the later elements based on the music-making exercise. The later adaptive and productive elements are focused on music-making, not on 'real team' operation. In the later stages the lead is necessarily being taken by musicians, otherwise the task could not be completed. Either some way is needed of making the adaptive and productive elements music-based but under the control of the 'team' who are putting into practice what they have learned, or a different kind of task is needed. Or the transfer and application to better teamwork, communication and speed has to be reinforced after the event. In that respect the changes introduced throughout the 'ready–steady–compose' element have to be much more clearly linked to the aims and objectives of the event, and feedback given on what happens when such changes are introduced.

Challenge 3: Partnerships

One difficulty encountered by initiatives like the EO providing such arts-based events is getting the form of partnership right – the form of partnership suitable for engaging with organisations to help learning rather than providing the usual arts-based aesthetic experience for the audience. Work organisations are used to the typical form of 'a day's training' and addressing core competencies, and assessing costs and benefits of learning events. The creative and performing arts organisations are used to educational formats where their learners are concerned with music and musicianship, and there are broader benefits which mean their work is subsidised. The Ensemble is a pioneer in exporting its experience to the corporate world, and any organisation which opted to engage them and import that experience would also be a pioneer. This presents a new interface between two kinds of partners who do not usually interact. On the one hand are partners whose purpose and values are economic: work organisations. On the other hand are partners whose purpose and values are aesthetic: creative and performing arts organisations.

For these two partners to interface with each other in this new and emerging way, some adaptation in each is needed. The issue of language was mentioned several times. That is relevant, but it is also a surface issue. There are deeper issues. Work organisations, and gatekeepers for learning and development activities within them, need to appreciate the potential of arts-based training. This may mean seeking forms other than 'a day's training' to engage with the partner. Creative and performing arts groups, and their gatekeepers, need to articulate what they do in ways that persuade work organisations to engage with them when music and musicianship is the medium, not the message.

And each partner needs also to sustain their values and identity. Work organisations produce or provide services in circumstances where efficiency and effectiveness are critical. Creative and performing arts groups perform in circumstances where aesthetics are critical. Trying to 'fit' those with the values of arts with those with the values of work organisations can be done. But it is not a perfect match. Indeed, the differences may be a fruitful source of learning as well. There may be friction as well as harmony in exporting the aesthetic to the economic.

In concluding on the EO event, the impact of these artists performing as a foundation of AHRD was very pleasurable and satisfying for the learners. And by the norms of the discipline of HRD this event was challenging (see Table 7.3). In analysing the event retrospectively, even a sympathetic advocate of the aesthetic perspective could not avoid slipping into critiquing the event as failing to fit these norms. And, following that, seeking to offer analytical solutions to help the EO take an approach to being better trainers that would fit with the dominant conceptions of HRD as they are most usually found. But this is to miss the whole point. Even as someone who approached this experience in sympathy with their goals, I found myself thinking about their performance in utilitarian, functional and rational terms. The point is, though, that organisations like the EO do not, and cannot, fit with that norm. What they are is what they are as artists, and the integrity of that is indivisible.

Do such initiatives in AHRD deserve the warm embrace of endorsement or the cold gaze of theory developers? Case studies, of course, raise more questions than answers; judgements on the extent to which AHRD will be embraced as respectable or rejected as fanciful and mistaken cannot be confidently based on a few cases. Certainly there are the usual range of business development issues being encountered by groups like the EO. They need to clarify their vision, the marketing and the economics of providing creative and imaginative AHRD. The proposed product demonstrated the potential, but also surfaced a set of issues about the design and delivery of an effective learning event. EO, and others like them, need to give some more thought to the basics of needs analysis and demonstrating the learning and business benefits. They need to consider modifying the design and delivery of the event to include blended learning. And they need to think innovatively

Table 7.3 Norms of HRD and EO norms

Norms of HRD	EO norms
Rigour and order	The 'chaos' of a rehearsal session
Uniformity	Musicians not trainers facilitating
Austerity	Using the joy and language of music
Discipline	Participating in experiment and fun
Seriousness	Playing and enjoying
Rational	Pleasurable

about the form of partnership possible between an arts-based learning provider and the kinds of organisations who might engage with you.

The challenge of evaluating AHRD is one recognised and faced by the whole interface between arts and business (Wilkinson and Foster 2003). There is a need to better interrelate the worlds of art and business to the mutual advantage of each other, whatever position is taken on state funding and support for the arts. The area of CTD is the most exposed part of this interface, and one where thinking and analysis might be usefully conducted to provide some ways of thinking about and dealing with this issue, not only in AHRD but more generally (Phipps and Trezona 2001).

Attempts to evaluate the impact of the arts in business still also have to contend with the problem of theorising aesthetics in HRD. One ambiguous feature of theory development in HRD is its capacity to both legitimise and question change, in the form of new or emerging methods and techniques. On the one hand, theory development is about embracing such change, and finding a respectable place for the new and emerging. On the other hand, theory development exposes new concepts and change to a critical gaze, and may mean it is rejected rather than assimilated.

The questions are asked because both government and businesses seek to face up to social issues that cannot be dealt with solely through capital investment and economic regeneration. They are both concerned about engaging communities in their local area, encouraging an active citizenship and social regeneration driven by popular engagement. Cultural policy can play a role in this, through linking citizens with one another, bridging diverse communities and providing positive common focal points for community life. The arts may also provide spaces for accessible discussion and deliberation of issues not easily explored elsewhere. The proposition is that they help build social capital. Social capital consists of the features of social life, networks, norms and trust, that enable participants to act together more effectively to pursue shared objectives with norms and trust. The idealist view of artfulness is that the process of group artistic production relies on identifying common goals, group co-operation and effective communication of complex ideas. Competition is replaced with collaboration, and self-interest is counterbalanced by group needs. The belief is that AHRD is good at doing this. The question is the extent to which more AHRD can produce better or greater results.

Arts and change

Arts and processes of organisational change are also a subject of analysis (Cowling 2004) in considering how the arts can best contribute to wider social aims. Widening access and participation in the arts has been a government concern since the policy proposals in 2001 to achieve these aims, including the Creative Partnerships scheme mentioned previously. In addition, business sponsorship provides a significant source of funding for the arts in the UK. In a difficult economic climate, businesses may also focus their activities on the Corporate Social Responsibility (CSR) agenda. As arts bodies have become increasingly adept at responding to these changes, they have also become better at trying to speak the right language and measure outputs. They are increasingly more concerned with evidence for the outcomes that reflect social policy goals, such as improved education, mental health, offender rehabilitation and community cohesion.

Whether these goals are consistent with the espoused goal of government and business arts funding to promote excellence, innovation and creativity in art for art's sake is an open question. Seeking a robust assessment of arts investment beyond aesthetics and an evaluation of the arts impact on the wider goals of public policy may mean killing off the very soul of the arts. One argument for making the connection firmly is that engaging with the arts can help with organisational change. This is because the arts and the creative process can play a role in empowering employees to effect bottom-up change and foster dynamic organisational development. Incorrect assumptions about people can be challenged and overcome by engaging with the arts. These include the assumptions that people cannot act without a specific purpose in mind; that people should seek to behave in a consistent manner, standardise behaviour, and that people should strive to act in a rational way. Yet insisting on these makes it difficult to experiment and improvise. The need to present actions as guided by purpose, consistency and a rational plan is absent from artful creation. The Catalyst project at Unilever is now cited as an example where this was the case (Darso 2004). At Lever Fabergé, up to 70 per cent of the staff engaged in varying activities associated with the arts. Catalyst initiatives included things like 'Live and Direct', in which participants develop a play, and a creative writing programme to help staff to develop vital skills in a non-threatening and enjoyable way. It was deemed to have contributed to the creation of a more challenging, creative and stimulating culture.

The proposition is that artists can offer a unique, independent view of the world. This is useful to business, not only in gaining insights about consumers, but also in helping to create a creative and innovative culture. This works partly through their ability to raise self-esteem and improve feelings towards work, life and self. They provide the opportunity to reconnect with the world and engage emotional responses. They also allow a break from the routine of just doing to examine how people feel about things. People are able to participate in imagined worlds with different identities. A neutral space is created in which it is possible to challenge ideas and assumptions and tackle difficult issues. The arts are also useful because they are a participatory form of behaviour and because they are dynamic.

It is to be acknowledged that the arts are not appropriate in all cases and do have some shortcomings. Artists are not universally more flexible than other people. Artists tend to have strong visions of themselves as artists and don't like change. Some artistic institutions can be reluctant to engage with business people and those they see as insufficiently artistic. The fundamental weakness, though, appears to be that many organisations commission AHRD as a last resort, in a moment of crisis. Integrating the arts into business is more difficult when times are good, as businesses are much more reluctant to be challenged. There is an argument for forging long-term relationships which move away from this crisis-based approach to a more open-ended approach. For AHRD to be of impact it needs to be central to the organisation's perception of its strategic direction. Yet Human Resources (HR) gatekeepers can be resistant to this. As a profession HR has spent time and effort trying be taken seriously and may be reluctant to jeopardise this with initiatives that are perceived as weird in some quarters. Mainstreaming the arts into an organisation is the issue, and progress can only be expected to be made to the extent that leaders support this.

Finally, and as ever, there is concern that there is not sufficient 'hard evidence' of the benefits. The corporate sector sees AHRD as arts sponsorship with bells on, rather than an integral part of HRD. This is compounded where organisations who use AHRD techniques are often reluctant to put money into long-term evaluations of results. This is often flagged up as very necessary at the beginning of the process but slips down the agenda once there is 'buy in' to a project. Yet trying to identify direct links between AHRD and business outcomes to justify AHRD goes against the grain of bringing artists in.

Conclusion

Considering learning from the arts leads into AHRD. AHRD is promoted actively by bodies like A&B, as well as by individual groups of artists. It is an important and significant interface for both sectors. The problem is of evaluating AHRD, learning and development which is designed and delivered by artists and delivered using arts practices.

The EO case provides an illustration of the 'task case', where the arts involve tasks like organisational tasks; they can be matched and constitute a basis for experiential learning. It also embodies the 'process case', where working on arts tasks enables the group process/soft skills to surface and be analysed – rehearsing a performance shows how communication, trust, etc., matter in teams. It implicitly rather then explicitly incorporates the 'affective connection case', where HRD requires the affective dimension to be accessed and elicited; artists can access and elicit emotional responses – music has charms, inspires, moves and satisfies. It is not illustrative of the 'creativity case', where the creative capability is sought and prized among the workforce; involvement in the arts encourages the creative capability.

This reflects the contextual rather than the theoretical legitimacy for AHRD, a theme that the organisation A&B has to engage with as it seeks to build partnerships with government and businesses and mainstream AHRD. That contextual legitimacy includes an affinity with the ideas of creativity and imagination, realms of the artist, in organisation analysis and management. Faced with uncertainty and change, the tools of the arts are brought into management, alongside the tools of science. Present evidence about the concrete, material and specific issues raised by learning from the arts, from the use of AHRD, may be more clearly grasped and explored if a clearer theoretical picture is developed, instead of being entangled in a debate about contextual trends such as social capital and Corporate Social Responsibility, and attitudes towards that.

For if there are possible benefits from the interaction of arts and business there are also potential drawbacks. The use of the arts, and their potential to produce shock and estrangement rather than create great art, introduces concerns about the functions of AHRD and the roles that artists are playing in organisations. Where the primary purpose of realising people's potential is an esoteric one, producing whole and harmonious people able to perform better, there is one kind of role for one kind of art. Taking a contrasting view, as some organisational stakeholders and some artists might, there is an exoteric purpose for importing AHRD in to organisations, to proceed through shock and dissonance to constantly break people away from their comfort zones. This is the alternative role for another kind of art; it is one that managers may seek to harness, but will also be wary of. Each may have its functions, but equally each may have its dysfunctions, depending on what the AHRD reveals about the organisation to those who experience it.

8 Beyond artfulness

Expressing human vitality

The more power of creating beyond itself a being has the more vitality it has. The world of technical creation is the most conspicuous expression of man's vitality

(Tillich 2000, p. 81)

Introduction

Beyond being members of the creative class, and learning from the arts and the arts of learning, there is a bigger and deeper question that aesthetics poses for HRD. This is that belonging to the creative class brings with it an expectation of contributing to the fullest possible expression of human vitality. At a moral level it is an affirmation that is the question 'What have you made of yourself?', which is at the heart of HRD. Yet it seems too many people are forced to defy such moral demands, and instead face negative judgements or moral rigour. Belonging to the creative class is about engaging with this purpose beyond artfulness, the purpose of securing human utility.

If HRD is to belong to the creative class it has to explore beyond learning from the arts and the arts of learning, and ask what aesthetics this aspect imports into HRD. To phrase the issue in a way that is more neutral, does aestheticising HRD and belonging to the creative class reinforce the concern with HRD as about aspiring to improve human beings rather than being about accumulating and applying scientific, objective and disembodied theoretical knowledge? The conclusion that HRD must aspire to improve people, is inevitable but rarely stated. It is inevitable that connections with manifest positive social justice outcomes are sought through HRD, and that we must believe that by practicing HRD harder and better we can transcend past mistakes. We must use the language of 'faith' to understand and interpret HRD. The aesthetic then leads to concerns that are more usually discussed in terms soteriology, the rescue or salvation of man.

The interest here is to directly address rather than understate this issue, and consider the extent to which the aesthetic and the soteriological traditions may either converge and interact or conflict. In some respects they seem to be very similar: sharing a concern with improving humanity rather than the process of accumulating knowledge. But in other respects they are divergent. Pro-aesthetic versions tend to cohere around variations on Bohemian, anti-capitalist activism. Pro-spiritual variations tend to cohere around variations of idealist metaphysics (see Box 8.1). These aspects of HRD are problematic areas to explore. In structuring that, there are four domains that need to be in some way considered (see Figure 8.1). As the domain of anti-aesthetic and anti-spiritual is considered elsewhere in the book, the concern here is with the other three domains.

Box 8.1 Interfaith employee groups: Ford

The conventional wisdom has been that religion and spirituality should not be raised in the context of the workplace. This is appropriate as organisations are secular environments, and the potential conflicts raised by proselytizing make it a sensitive issue. Yet it is being argued by some that those who feel they can bring their spiritual values to work are happier, more productive, stay longer than those who feel their spiritual values are excluded.

For example, at Ford in the USA several separate religious groups petitioned the company, each seeking designation as an employee resource group. This official status gives groups similar status to other 'diversity groups, and corporate funding and an intranet site. The company denied the requests, saying that it did not want to appear as if it were favouring one religious group, but said it would consider a proposal for an interfaith employee resource group, one with representatives from a variety of religions. The Ford Interfaith Network assembled a board composed of representatives from eight religions – Buddhism, Catholicism, Evangelical Christianity, Hinduism, Islam, Judaism, Mormonism and Orthodox Christianity.

This trend towards addressing religious identity in the workplace context has the potential to produce new sources of conflict. Again in the USA two lawsuits illustrate why employers might be reluctant to enable religious speech in the workplace. In the first, a former Hewlett-Packard employee sued the company after he was fired for insubordination because he repeatedly posted Biblical verses condemning homosexuality on his cubicle's overhead bin. The 9th U.S. Circuit Court of Appeals said the former employee was not a victim of religious discrimination and was fired legally for violating the company's anti-harassment policy. In the second case, the 9th U.S. Circuit Court of Appeals ruled that Cox Communications had the right to fire an evangelical Christian for violating its anti-harassment policy after she criticized a lesbian subordinates sexual orientation during the employees performance review.

Source: Henneman 2004

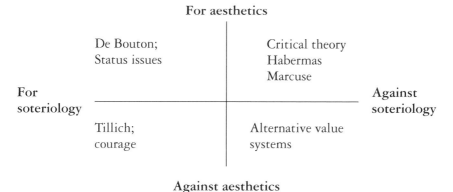

Figure 8.1 Aesthetic and soteriological interactions

Aesthetics and soteriology interactions

HRD has always constructed its shrines and rituals around the places and points of transition in life. Wherever people encounter change they will usually find themselves interacting with an HRD institution and professionals: in the classrooms, the learning centres, the schools and colleges. So where the transitions are, or where they are desired, there is HRD. The individual lifespan, the corporate body and its complexities, and the place of learning among a society's population all interact around these key points, these transitions. Problems may exist. Even where a system is well established the locations and professions around which HRD has been constructed may become less vital. More critical yet is the misplaced hope that a reverse causality can work: that simply by constructing such environments, or professionals, the lifespan transitions, change and progress, will be catalysed.

These HRD environments and the professionals have a vision and mission of causing the transitions, or enabling them. This is so for the individual and their lifespan, the discrete company and its changing needs, a society and its dynamics among the constituent populations. But all these levels and kinds of focus for HRD are not only for transitions; they are themselves all coming into being and passing away.

It is natural for a sense-making, meaning-dependent being to identify something that is not transitory, that is expressed in the individual but is outside change, beyond history. One such thing is the human spirit. Spirit may mean either the material, definitive characteristics of ordinary people, or by extension the metaphysical and ideal: the soul. For the ordinary human being to have spirit is to be energetic, enthusiastic and determined. To be dispirited is to be lacking courage, vigour and hope.

Where such spirit exists HRD is possible, as a concern with transition only flourishes in an environment where there is energy, enthusiasm and determination among those concerned. Or conversely HRD is needed to construct an environment of courage, vigour and hope, of interest so that transitions are made possible. HRD is, in the former instance, intrinsically spirited and, in the latter instance, seen as a method of enabling and evolving spirit. Because of this it is an attractive occupation, indeed a spiritual home, for those who value the cultivation of human vitality and transitions, or the more metaphysical variation, the heart and soul.

HRD is, in consequence, practised and managed by a coalition of those who have such an interest in the human spirit. This is not to attribute to practitioners of HRD a mystical role, or to endorse, a metaphysical or mystical view of people whose business is HRD. Far from it: there are tensions around the differences within different metaphysical traditions, and between them and the non-metaphysical, scientific and humanist traditions. The implication of this is that HRD evolves in part as a coalition of people who may see themselves the keepers of the shrines of the spirit, and the encounter with aesthetics in HRD is both eased and obstructed by that. It is eased because there are parallel, long-standing, deep and substantial engagements with aesthetics in the traditions of the spiritual. Indeed, religions may be defined in part by their aesthetics, the ways they bound architecture, art, music, narrative and beauty to their causes. There are clearly lessons to be learned for HRD from looking back at how past powerful religions used the aesthetic in the service of their goals. However, for the soteriologically inclined, the aesthetic is also to be resisted. The reasons for being suspicious of and contrary to the aesthetic are simple. They are that the arts compete for people's commitments when they ought to be steadfastly committed to their spirituality and religion. And, of course, the perception that the sensual and the libidinal, in which the aesthetic is intricately implicated, present a threat to moral order, where morality is defined as that which, in the name of the good, neutralises the power of the aesthetic, the denial of desire and the mastery of pleasure.

Soteriology and status

De Botton (2004) places status dynamics at the heart of his social analysis and interprets cultural and subcultural systemic response to status issues and anxiety. Status systems exist to distribute value to people according to their standing within some commonly agreed criteria. People with high status, however defined, obtain regard and the benefits that brings; people with low status, however defined, suffer disregard and the costs that entails. De Botton considers religion, specifically Christianity, as being shaped by its opposition to and accommodation of common views of status. Its strengths as a basis for opposing the norms of status allocation originate in brute mortality; mortal illness or upset reveals to people the falsity of any status system, and the futility of honouring it. Mortality illustrates clearly that status is linked to the position the person has, not to their self. The ego is mightily offended by this. Encounters with, or thoughts of, death thus lead people to revise the priorities they held based on attaining and maintaining status, favouring more spiritual priorities.

Even as the wealthiest had their portraits painted they would at the same time include symbols of memento mori, for example skulls and hourglasses, signs of mortality. The message was to set your house in order, for you must die. This should usher people towards what matters most: to become emboldened to find fault with experience, and attend more seriously to the virtues of love, goodness, sincerity, humility and kindness. Eventual demise was the great leveller; and judged against eternity, how little of what agitates us really matters? We are tortured by our ideals and high-minded sense of what we should do. Instead, we should consider our own petty status and enjoy a tranquillising glimpse of our own insignificance.

That is an anaesthetic response of the soteriological challenge to normal status relations. An alternative, an aesthetic response is also possible. For to the Christian all are within God's love. So where some might overlook, dismiss or persecute those who are deemed lesser, lower, inadequate, they will see beneath the surface to a person's humanity, their shared vulnerabilities, fears and desire for love. The view is, ultimately, of the ordinary as good rather than the high status as best. Ordinary people are not to be chastised or debased as losers and failures, as nobodies. They are as much a part of community, via the churches, as the most exalted. Earthly status and spiritual status co-existed, with earthly status varying in ways that were outside an individual's control but spiritual status being within their control. Two cities co-existed: the earthly city and the city of God. And the Christian church endowed that earthly presence with its use of paintings, literature, music and architecture. It used art to illustrate virtues, from warfare to respecting the poor. And 'through its command of aesthetic resources, of buildings, paintings and Masses, Christianity created a bulwark against the authority of earthly values and kept its spiritual concerns at the forefront of the mind and eye' (De Botton 2004, p. 268).

In the high period of success and significance the Christian church took issue with but did not abolish the earthly city and its values. It did instil in the cultures it affected a consciousness that it is more important to ask of people 'Are they good?' instead of 'Are they high status?' or, for the latter, most often, 'Are they wealthy?' It is ironic that some of the strongest opponents of religion and the churches, the enlightened advocates of reason and social progress who helped create a more secular world, now find that their other opponents, the wealthy, seek to reverse this consciousness And, more ironic yet, the alternative view, contesting the 'good' of material wealth and its influence, is rooted most among those making priority of the spirit, if not in churches then in various kinds of circumstances and intellectual spaces.

Beyond the dedication of the artist and the social milieux needed to produce the circumstances in which great art is possible, Goguen (1999) suggests that what distinguishes great art from merely good art is related to its role in facilitating meditation upon the sacred. His point of departure for arguing this is classical Buddhism, which considers the pursuit of bliss, permanence and self-existence to be undermined by the three marks of existence: suffering, impermanence and non-ego. Suffering refers not only to real and actual pain, but also to a general sense of the dissatisfactions, that hopes and expectations are often frustrated, goals are not achieved or are escalated, thus increasing the likelihood of later frustration. Impermanence refers to the transitory nature of all experience, achievements and relationships. Non-ego refers to an awareness of the fiction of the substantial self and its capacity to know. To examine human experience requires a state of meditation and a kind of phenomenological reclassification of understanding via the meditation experience.

Affording this meditative form and function was the purpose of great works of art, not just in the Buddhist context but also in the Western tradition. There has been, however, a progressive diminution of the sacred in society, and in Western art from medieval times into the twentieth century. Most contemporary artistic production is in the service of commercialism and consumerism. This would mean that people would perceive that this is not great art, and maybe not even good art; and people would seek their meditative forms elsewhere. The older tradition of which great art is a part includes believing that we do not perceive an 'objective world' that is 'out there', but rather we construct our own world, based on our values and expectations. That 'world' can then be transformed through the practice of meditation, without the usual overlays of projection and attachment. In this way, all experience can become a heightened aesthetic experience.

The aim of producing and appreciating great art, then, is not to produce mystical experiences as such, but to afford such experiences as integral to the healthy human condition. Practices in activity such as meditation in form and function, whether through religious rituals or art appreciation, enable that. They may be done in conjunction, with an interaction of both art and religious ritual (Spivey 2004). Or they may be done separately, the one without the other: indeed, consciously without the other as exemplified in pursuit of religious experience in sensorily deprived environments, or art appreciation in dedicated galleries and concern halls. Yet each will still retain undercurrents, resonance, shadows and shared elements of the other.

For the spiritual: against aesthetics

For others the aesthetic is a contaminant of the spiritual rather than a means of revitalising it. And the temptation to find affinities between the aesthetic and the spiritual may be part of the problem, not the solution. Kierkegaard expressed this historically, though the essence of the belief persists: the aesthetic is at best a detour, at worst a trap for arrested development, on the way to the ethical (Tillich 2000). This was bound up for Kierkegaard with his general view that individuals' responsibility for their own salvation had become obscured by the habitualisation of the spiritual life. Instead of working on being ethical they were part-time believers; and they would rather most of the time be in thrall to the aesthetic, to pleasure, to living for the moment, grasping enjoyment, the beautiful, the satisfying, and believing that the pleasant was the good. The consequence was that people were slaves to their desires and moods, and would seek anything to avoid the experience of boredom that came when the pleasures ceased, and behind that even greater discomfort from angst. But people needed to be, they ought to be, exposed to feeling great angst; and so come to elect to strive to make a leap beyond the distractions of the material world. Leaving behind being in thrall to the aesthetic they might become more ethical; but that was still to fall short of what was necessary for true faith. Adopting reasoned seriousness and consistency of moral choices, to have an ethics of duty, to choose to have an opinion on right and wrong rather than judge according to what was fun or boring, was not enough. The further leap beyond that was to become truly religious; to jump into the abyss, choosing faith rather than the false comforts of pleasure or reason.

In his time and context he was a scorned outcast of his own society, an enemy of the people he criticised as believers with a non-committal approach. The underlying idea was to express a view about soteriology that would in other guises recur. This was that coming to know that other people's views of objective truth could be irrelevant to shaping a person's life. And that the things knowable through reason are relatively, to a committed believer, unimportant. Instead, people needed to find truth for themselves in acts and choices in their brief existence; and the really important truths are to be approached through faith, despite what others think or feel. For some, echoes of this analysis would be revisited and adapted as forms of existentialism. For others, it would be in the positive thinking, self-improvement allied with spiritual development philosophies. These can be seen to share the core idea that people create their own natures, and these are not fixed in advance. An encounter with alienation, despair, boredom, nausea and absurdity,[1] some kind of crisis, will be a crucial formative experience, in the philosophical traditions associated with sensing and responding to the idea that 'God is dead', or more pragmatically, in the self-improvement tradition, encountering a low point, loneliness, failure. In responding to the experience of angst and dread, or that sense of failure and loneliness, people could retreat into a metaphysics of false comfort, or accept being alone and free and make choices: to be responsible, to live authentically and truly, to take control and improve.

These themes were interwoven by Tillich into a pro-soteriological but non-aesthetic analysis. He believed that modern humanism offered a new variation on self-affirmation, and a kind of neo-stoicism, which pervades subjects like HRD: that what threatens the self, and self-esteem, needs to be overcome. That, rather than the way of salvation, is attractive; salvation is more neglected, rarer, and it is more difficult to persuade people of its significance. Yet anxiety and a bondage to fear do not disappear in the age of self-affirmation. Indeed, self-affirmation becomes part of the more and more industrious and manically playful and dynamic; people need to stop and let the stillness impact upon them. For without stopping, at least on occasion, and developing the more complete understanding that can only come with stepping outside of the dynamic frenzy, any understanding is going to be warped, biased and inadequate. And the arts may play a role in promoting the dynamic frenzy, not allowing mediation free of it.

Tillich discussed these issues in the course of revitalising the concept that the virtue of courage could help provide a focus. Courage was a virtue with larger meanings about what was noble and worthy of sacrifices. The aristocratic and military version of courage had been about manly strength in contests. The Christian and humanistic variation had been to promote courage in seeking wisdom, knowing good and evil, being rational and democratic. This bequeathed two split concepts of courage, one of a meaningless vitality and one of a bloodless intellect. The unity of courage should be restored. To do this meant revisiting how Christianity had emerged as triumphant against the stoics. The stoics believed in cosmic resignation, and a personal courage for managing that. A central part of the Christian metaphysic was, in contrast, to believe in cosmic salvation. For stoics this belief reflected people in conflict with their rationality: such beliefs are reason undermined. Yet the Christian message of hope through salvation, rather than authenticity in enduring, came to prevail for a considerable period of time. For Tillich this was because Christianity better addressed human psychology; working with a sense of guilt and a need for salvation fits with human nature.

With the decline of organised religion, faith had again become associated with a belief in the unbelievable. Its proponents either have to accommodate credibility issues and engage with rational objections, and change, or go down the more emotional and fundamentalist path to resisting change. Each still tries to speak to the human condition as one of estrangement, awareness of separation: we are lonely and do not deserve love. But being accepted by something greater than ourselves is still desired. The positive option is to be accepted despite being unacceptable: that is the religious option. The other option is to be cynical and negative, refusing to follow anyone or anything, holding to no values or truths, having no answer to the question of meaning, and undermining anyone who believes otherwise. The result is a culture of compulsive self-affirmation, and ultimately either unabashed narcissism or self-surrender, a culture that produces Postrel's homage to beach volleyball and Starbucks coffee.

But being embedded in an age of aesthetics, in a creative class, is not to dispel the three primary anxieties that have existed with the decline of faith. These are an anxiety about an absence of meaning and purpose, anxiety about the intractability of guilt and a need for forgiveness, and anxiety about death as the vanishing point of existence and being. For Tillich, people are just as concerned with these as they have ever been, and with seeking to make a life that includes failure and loss, not just making a living with denial of those things. They are concerned to be self-affirming but not just shallow, ego-boosting, to mask low self-esteem. People would prefer to have constructive human relations rather than coping with estranged relations. They seek meaning in being, despite circumstances undermining that rather than confirming it.

The courage to overcome these kinds of anxieties is different from that needed to deal with fears. Fears have an object, a face, can be analysed and attacked, or endured and struggled with. Anxiety is rooted in an awareness, coming and going, of the possibility of non-being, the latent awareness of having to die, of universal transitions. This anxiety cannot fix on an object, so we are helpless to struggle with it. The threat is nothingness, an unknown of a special type. There is a reciprocity; the sting of fear is anxiety, and anxiety strives towards fear. That is, we wish to turn all that we may have to struggle with into fear, which can be met by courage. But there is that before which we cannot stand for more than a second, and that cannot be eliminated or turned into fear. To experience this is existential: that is, it belongs to existence, it is not abnormal.

Stereotypically, the USA, Tillich's home context, affirms the creative development of mankind, the capability to overcome failures and catastrophes. The productive act itself is the whole reason; to be part of the creative process of history is felt to be divine. Beyond this kind of economic participation in creativity one response can be to become very creative, to invest in constructing imaginary worlds. The bearer of creativity is the individual; they hope to find in beauty some core of meaning, in imagination a legitimacy to spirituality, and in being creative something to overcome the anxiety of emptiness and meaninglessness. To participate meaningfully in art, as in science or politics, is to participate in meaning and affirming the spiritual life. These all provide an answer to the meaning of existence, at however symbolic or practical a level. They also seem to offer a place to replace the loss of a spiritual centre, but the craving and searching will be unfulfilled.

Thus creativity may represent a non-pathological striving for security, to contain the fear of fate and death. This can, though, become another prison; people may have unrealistic goals for security, moralistic perfection and certitude. People may 'escape' into neuroses, and avoid the problems of threats of non-being by avoiding real 'being' in the first place; they may affirm a reduced self. What is left becomes a refuge, a reduced self to defend within an imaginary world. The danger inherent in such a strategy is that of the unrealistic reduced self being displaced by nothing; neurotic anxiety has the power to break the walls of reduced self-affirmation. Then the fragmentary courage with which a person has mastered accustomed objects of fear, and acted creatively, can be itself threatened. In response, such people may become fanatical defenders of existing symbolic and social orders. This, according to Tillich, is why mass neuroses appear at the end of historical eras and accompanying transitions into new eras; this is a dramatic social version of a commonplace individual response.

Critical theory

An associated spiritual home for this line of analysis and set of concerns has been that of critical theory, whose proponents considered matters of aesthetics (Habermas 1984; Marcuse 1979). The analysis for such critical theorists was that ordinary people had been reduced to lives dominated by consumerism, and had been seduced into passivity rather than political activity. This was the downside of rational progress. To remedy this passivity the answer was 'critical theory': the act of taking on and critiquing ideologies, and advancing via critical reflection against those who sought to restrain dissent. For them all knowledge, including their own, was guided by interests – different kinds of interest. There was an instrumental interest in facts and exploiting them. There was a practical interest in communication. But despite the appearance of investigation and communication, in fact only that which is functional, consumable, rationalised was legitimate. There was a need to subvert the one dimensional ideology of technical rationality, containing human needs in the limits of a consumer culture. There was also an interest in emancipation, critical self-reflection, autonomy, responsibility, justice. This meant seeking to transcend the great refusal to think critically for themselves. So activists should seek to reappropriate not only the economic means of production but also the cultural means of experience and expression.. The critical potential of the creative imagination was essential, vital; the aesthetic dimension mattered as a forerunner, a trigger, a charge.

The main features of capitalism require the bondage of existential life: the erosion of a personal sphere of critical experience. Instead of personal authenticity, inclinations to love, friendship, community are denied and limited and displaced by consumption.

There is, though, an irreducible human disposition towards freedom, to consciousness to transcend these conditions – not class consciousness but an existential consciousness, that can be nurtured within the aesthetic imagination, which capitalism still values. That which is conserved and protected by being aesthetic retains some ideals that offer a critical refuge from the otherwise repressive, utilitarian, reality-principle-fixated practices of bourgeois society, seedbeds for cultivating new utopianism. For art can take on the dragons of reification by making the petrified world speak, sing, even dance; it spurs the drive for the conquest of suffering and the permanence of joy.

The major events of the twentieth century, including the rise of fascism and the failure of communism, convince them of the analysis. There is a complicity of positivism and authoritarianism, and uncritical compliance with the 'objective'. Even worse, following these is the strength of view that says 'leave everything as it is'. For this denies Eros, the creative life-instinct. Not to be denied, Eros seeks refuge in the unreal, the imaginary world of dream, art, myth, the culture that ensures people engage with the creative life instinct via the strange truths which imagination keeps alive in folklore and fairy tale, in literature and art. Eros as the bedrock of civilisation splinters. In fragments people seek to recover past utopian aspirations as a foretaste of potentials of liberation. The desire for unproductive and useless play is meant to cancel out the exploitation of labour. Yet instead, people have abundance, but still fabricate new needs to keep them busy. The repressive manipulation of the private sphere continues apace. The economy delivers the goods, providing satisfying sexual things to love and outlets for aggressive energies and things to hate. A question then permeates everything: how is it that the subjective needs of happiness and freedom are becoming increasingly repressed in every modern civilisation which offers the most advanced objective conditions for their fulfilment?

The initial critical theorists looked to the refugee of defamed humanity to be those who would have an interest in emancipation, and be receptive to critical theory, and therefore provide the starting point for turning back the consumerist, rationalist tide: those involved in third-world struggles, intellectual dissidents and students. Following disappointments with that, they returned to the aesthetic project, and to the business of finding existential peace in critical refusal. Art should protest at the way things are. The aesthetic dimension offers an opportunity for formal autonomy, to experience rather than to analyse, and an opportunity for spiritual inwardness, a private sphere.

Conclusion

One of the bigger and deeper questions that creativity poses for HRD is the extent to which belonging to the creative class brings with it an expectation of contributing to the expression of human vitality, and substitutes for those belief systems that in the past promised the hope of ultimate deliverance. If aesthetics is about finding meaning and affirmation for purpose beyond artfulness at a moral level, HRD involves an telling affirmation around the question 'What have you made of yourself?'

Aspiring to improve human beings, individually and collectively, rather than accumulating and applying scientific, objective and disembodied theoretical knowledge, is for some the essence of HRD. Being of the creative class does matter to those directly concerned with HRD and raises some thorny and difficult issues for them. The interest here is to directly address rather than understate these issues. The aesthetic and the soteriological traditions may either converge and interact or conflict. These aspects of HRD are a difficult and problematic area to identify and explore.

The dangers of becoming entangled in mysticism are ever present, but HRD could be further vitalised by engaging with the sources of interest in such metaphysics. And to reintroduce terms like 'vitality' and 'spirit', and the metaphysics they entail, to HRD may be regressive. Discontent arising from dividing man into two halves, mind and matter, or self and brain, has not abated. The 'spirit' may be approached via a materialist metaphysic, with the core idea that processes of development accompany and assure the replication of a complex and interacting ecology of life; it may be the vitality of genetic replication and evolutionary psychology. Alternatively there is also the idealist metaphysic, the core idea that there is nothing but ideas, or mind, or spirit. Development in that context, then, has to be explained with regard to seeing and interpreting experiences of growth as connected with approaching unity with the 'ultimate' or absolute, however that may be conceptualised. Those who do endorse such idealist metaphysics, faiths, may or may not hold also that either science or the good of humanity will be forces for progress and change.

Part III

Opportunities

9 Developing strategies for creativity

Introduction

The first and most obvious focus function for HRD in making the creative future and creative class is to nurture creativity itself (Johnson 2002; Robinson and Stern 1997). There are a range of development strategies available for nurturing creativity (see Table 9.1). They are considered and analysed in turn.

Can we instruct our way to increasing creativity? In corporate training learning design, where the corporate curriculum is the subject of learning design, and performance improvement rather than accreditation is the object, design is commonly identified as a stage in the systematic training cycle, prior to the production of learning materials or management of learning experiences. The question is where creativity fits in this. In the practice and theory of instruction, a concern with the design of processes has always been more evident (Heap 1996). The development of concepts for thinking about the learning process, and 'learning about learning', derived primarily from the human sciences, offered a metalanguage. This can be applied to design and construct a learning experience. The concepts and theories used here have been diverse, from the establishment of a tripartite division of what is being learned in terms of 'knowledge', 'skill' and 'attributes' to discussions of learning styles. In addition to these typical concerns, contemporary concerns with 'employability', core competency or 'transferable' skills now present themselves.

The professional development of trainers, the training of trainers, is an issue. Professional instructors understand and use the principles of structured and programmed instruction in design and delivery. They are to encourage creativity. But what about the best creators, the artists and others whose business is creativity? Being the best performer is not a sufficient condition for being an effective instructor. Some of the best performers are unable to engage with supporting the learning of others, and cannot perform well as instructors. The best instructors may rather be those who best grasp the 'business' of learning, even though they themselves are not from the ranks of the top performers, in this case creativity. Being, or having been, an

Table 9.1 HRD for creativity

HRD *strategies*	*Sources*	*Forms*	*Issues*
Instruction How training should be done	Integrate with workforce training	Instructional design objectives Trainer-led delivery	Identifying needs Telling Transfer to performance
Facilitation What learners can do to construct understanding	Experiential learning	Small group work Coaching Mentoring	Learner resistance to doing the 'work' of creativity Coaches and mentors to nurture creativity
Andragogy Adult learning	Education Development to adulthood Adult learning	Curricula content Courses Classrooms Resources	Motivation to be creative Meanings of creativity in practice Beyond surface learning to deep learning about creativity
Play Fit with what engages people	Organic and natural forms e.g. Arts, Computer games	e.g. Computer games User engagement Goals Decision making Gameplay	Digital natives (youth) and digital immigrants (educators) Don't suck the fun out of learning about creativity
Dialogue and community Encourage relations	Social construction Making sense in creative communities	Bringing people together Allowing exchanges Building with each other Open spaces	How do we design such creative communities?

excellent conductor, an excellent artist or an excellent creative scientist is not any guarantee of being able to coach others in a sport, develop others' artistic talents or develop other managers.

Facilitation

Can we facilitate our way to increasing creativity? Partly because of the nature of adult learners, and partly because of the kinds of learning and development (L&D) required, methods other than instruction have evolved and are in use to deliver L&D at work. In determining what is needed to provide an effective learning experience, Kolb (1984), Lave and Wenger (1991) and Schön (1995) provide important reference points. Facilitation is the use of methods which require the participation of learners, and which enable 'constructive learning' through discovery. Facilitation is explained with reference to the operation of an 'experiential cycle' of learning rather than an instructional model to develop cognition, capability and behaviour.

The connection between these ideas about facilitating learning and broader issues with creativity are evident. It is often the case that analysing specific problems with managing learning escalates to a broader and bigger analysis of wider issues, such as Rogers' seeing the causes of problems with learning as being part of broader problems of alienation (Rogers 1969). Rogers' conclusion was that the design issue was a need to create communities of learners, where the educator is facilitating change and learning, not instructing learners. They needed therefore to construct learning by dealing with real problems, provide resources, and use 'learning contracts' to organise groups and stimulate inquiry. Facilitators would set the mood, enable learning, moving away from 'formal' teaching roles to being in learning relationships.

Andragogy

In the field of learning the act of design has its origins and evolution in andragogy. As Knowles emphasised (1998), responsibility for adult learning, from decisions about what should be learned, how it should be learned, when it should be learned, and whether it had been learned, lies with the learner, not the teacher. While a pedagogue is a strict or pedantic teacher, excessively concerned with details and rules and displaying their learning, an andragogue is a flexible and learner-centred supporter of development.

The theory and practice of the still predominant pedagogy is one that includes standard design elements: the design of specialist institutions with defined curricula, set courses, classrooms and activity, with formal testing for grading and qualifications. Applying these to creativity would be the kiss of death. Knowles proposed a model of 'andragogy' to initially replace this, but then came to accept that it should complement pedagogy; it was not either–or but both, as appropriate to the situation.

The design challenge is that the content of creativity be fully identified and properly articulated at the right level. Learning will be subject based, and will include differentiation in progress from the simple and surface level to the complex and 'deep'. The determination of a curriculum that accurately and comprehensively maps a subject area has been, and arguably remains, the key design challenge. What is the curriculum for creativity?

Play

Can we encourage greater creativity through play? Play includes relaxation, a buzz, degrees of hilarity, some kind of euphoria. But can the feast, the dance, the masque, the costume ball be foundations for learning and development? Play is a category that can include many practices; these include games, outdoor experiential learning, and the use of theatre. The perceived leading edge of play, which can be explored more closely, is the use of computer games. Prensky (2003) identifies the norms and expectations of 'digital natives' and 'digital immigrants' (see Table 9.2). Digital natives, who have grown up with computer games, provide the primary audience for much learning design, a generation who have grown up with communications technology such as mobile phones as the norm. But at the moment design is in the hands of the digital immigrants.

This generation encounters, like all others, a system that requires them to learn things that they do not want to bother learning; but that system is now also using methods which they think and feel to be outdated. That further demotivates them. For proponents of play and games, the solution is obvious; if the methods were changed then learners can be engaged. They will want to learn. Prensky believes that games embody the qualities that the digital generation are attuned to, and which they are fit for. And there is nothing to be ashamed about in this, for games are the most intellectually stimulating form of activity that people can engage with.

Powell (2003) explores how in the past few years there has been the emergence of three competing videogame console formats, obsessive online gaming communities and the capability to deliver games to almost any device with a screen and a few buttons. This is because of the nature of gaming: playing and competing are not just exciting and engaging, they are intellectually stimulating. Games are self-motivating and self-marketing. People now ask of HRD if it is going to be enjoyable and worth their time. Games address both questions by offering a pleasurable experience that engages the learner so that he or she wants to spend time playing them. A well-designed game strikes a balance between short-term and long-term goals and challenges, which creates a pattern of challenge and reward that pulls players towards completion. The challenge of getting high scores and online game play creates competition between users. Games create an engaging, emotion-creating buy-in from the participant. Elements of failure, indecision and excitement make people more attuned to what's being taught. Games don't have to be analogues of real-world experiences to create emotional buy-in from users; tension, elation, and disappointment can be conjured by even the simplest games. Games have the Generation Y factor.

Table 9.2 Prensky's digital immigrants and natives

	Digital immigrants	*Digital natives*
Speed of learning	slow	'twitch' speed
Processing skills	single	parallel
Search skills	linear	random
Mode of communication	text	graphic
Individuality?	stand alone	connected
Ethic	work ethic	play ethic

Aged from 6 to 25, Generation Y have an intimate grasp of technology and high expectations for technology-based learning. They're the first generation to be raised and educated in the presence of personal computers and videogame consoles. They've grown up with cutting-edge videogames and they're not going to be impressed unless they are engaged through game play. The depth of play found in videogames will always be greater, but other games to make the delivery of information fun and engaging can evolve. It is game play that keeps players excited. People will accept an application whose 'eye candy' is poor if the game play is good.

Dialogue and community

Can creativity be increased through developing creative communities of practice? Conversation and community are not only a means of learning, they are also an end of learning: what is sought and desired in wider life. The cultivation of dialogue itself is considered to be the high road to greater wisdom and learning. In modern cultures people are able to interact and converse with one another in many ways, with an infrastructure of communications technologies. But their ability to talk together about subjects that matter deeply to them is as flawed as ever, with dispute and division leading to conflict and the displacement of dialogue by force. Precisely because dialogue seems to fail in wider life, it is seen to be vital to nurture it in the design of development. Indeed, the burden in society on learning and development to be the agency by which the wider promulgation of dialogue is achieved is growing.

Dialogue also matters where knowledge is not a fixed thing or commodity to be grasped. It is not something 'out there', waiting to be discovered. Rather, it is an aspect of a process (Gadamer 1979). As agreement cannot be imposed but rests on common conviction, the concern is not to 'win an argument', but to advance understanding and human wellbeing. In this, the understanding we bring from the past is tested in encounters with the present and forms what we take into the future. People may experience a 'fusion of horizons'.

Indeed, what is required for a conversation, which is mutual trust, respect, a willingness to listen and risk one's opinions, represents an ideal: a situation where each has an effective equality of chances to take part in dialogue, where dialogue is unconstrained and not distorted. This does not require egalitarian relationships but it does entail some sort of reciprocity and symmetry. Encouraging creativity through dialogue and community then involves establishing the following:

- Concern: in being creative through dialogue there is more going on than talk about the overt topic. There is a social bond that entails interest in, and a commitment to the other.
- Trust: in being creative we have to take what others are saying on faith, and there can be some risk in this.

- Respect: while there may be large differences between partners in dialogue, the process can go on if there is mutual regard.
- Appreciation: linked to respect, this entails valuing the unique qualities that others bring.
- Affection: dialogue involves a feeling with, and for, our partners.
- Hope: we engage in creativity via dialogue even if it is not clear what we will gain or learn, with faith in the inherent value of dialogue.

The conversations we have or do not have establish the horizons of our current and potential learning. In dialogue we can all achieve more than is possible alone, and travel and explore further together than apart. So cultivating dialogue can be a central part of encouraging creativity. And it is not simply the form that learning design takes, but also part of its purpose. Through dialogue or conversation, testing out prejudices, searching out meaning, people learn and become more critical. We become better able to name our feelings and thoughts, and place ourselves in the world. We can develop a better language of critique and possibility which allows us to act more intelligently. To afford each other the opportunity to say things means being able through conversational inquiry to go where otherwise we would never have gone.

Conclusion

There is indeed now an industry of companies and consultants in creativity (Lucas 2004). They sell old techniques in new guises, like brainstorming. But the problem is that contrasting approaches may get the same results. An individual contemplating in a solitary and inward-looking way may be as creative as a set of people in groups competing to be clever, to parade their knowledge. Creativity requires questioning, uncertainty, risk-taking, living with uncertainty and ambiguity, admitting that we do not know, and resilience and perseverance to stick at it. It depends upon trust, respect, engaging communication, fruitful disorder. The problem is an environment with too many factors working in the other way: distractions of e-mail, fear-inducing managers, dependence on standard slide shows for presentations. Ultimately the concerns centre on the dilemma between freeing creativity requirements and the norms of the classic 'company way' requirements (see Table 9.3).

For strategic significance to be secured, the meanings of creativity in HRD can be clarified, and the strategies for HRD can be researched and evaluated as a means of supporting creativity. There remains a major issue which may yet undermine the engagement of HRD and creativity at a strategic level. This is the clash of value systems around connecting creativity with HRD. There has been a fragmented corporate interest in creativity since concepts like brainstorming were conceptualised by Osborn (1953, 1964), but as recently as the 1990s (Solomon 1990) scholars still had

Table 9.3: Freeing creativity versus the company way

Freeing creativity	The company way
Free rein to try new things	Control process, repeat the same things
Free to fail	Anticipate and avoid public failure
Please themselves	Please the boss
Eccentric, unconventional	Conformist
Iconoclastic	Adhering to order
Emotional, egotistical	Neutral (EI), company-focused
Excitement, go off on tangents	Calmness and stick to the target
Creative abrasion helps	Smooth running
Imagination overtime	Problem-solving capacity
Playful	Serious
Do not play by the rules	Play by rules
Adventurous, funny	Cautious, dour
Spontaneous, independent	Need a script, team players
Sensitive	Hard headed
Enthusiastic, idealistic	Calm and measured
Bold	Safe
Faith in the creative process	Faith in rationality

to challenge the view that people were either creative, and therefore naturally imaginative, wild, hard to manage, entrepreneurial, or not. He argued that creativity was a skill that could be taught or enhanced with practice. For him it was relevant, as it provided a plus in business, linked to improving the quality of products and services in an information-rich environment. Creativity was the best way to get more from your resources.

In its broadest terms, the domain of HRD is formed and contested by the values of either the economically driven or the socially driven interpretation of people's potential: that people's potential is developed either for the utility that it provides to the individual and the organisations they inhabit, or as a natural feature of the loving and caring relations people share in their families and communities. The beliefs associated with each, and resistance to the other, is a well-established part of the HRD area; indeed, the antagonism between them may be seen to enliven and indeed animate the whole subject.

If creativity is now more important, and is to be incorporated more into HRD, then this aesthetic value system, and its fit or conflict with other value systems in use in HRD, comes to some prominence, and people will either like and accept that or dislike and resist it. For example, in contrast to the economic type, the aesthetic type may see the processes of organisation and business, and associated image-related manipulations like advertising, as an affront to the values most important to them. There could be conflicts between aesthetically grounded and economically grounded views of what matters in HRD. And in contrast with socially embedded values, aesthetes may be said to be interested in 'humanity' as material for creativity but not for humanistic reasons; indeed, they, the aesthetes, may tend towards being individualistic and self-sufficient. In other words, the core of the values associated with making creativity central and strategic may conflict with the present core values of HRD as it is commonly understood and practised by those with other value systems.

Such conflict is not inevitable; there may be good points of connection. For the economic type, interested in what is useful and the practical affairs of business, creativity can be linked to wealth creation. The economic interpretation seeks to harness creativity to be practical, regarding unapplied creativity as wasteful. For the social paradigm the core values of altruism and philanthropic motivation and aims to be sympathetic and unselfish may link, through the form of Corporate Social Responsibility projects, to arts projects. They may look to arts forms, like theatre or musical groups, to illustrate and reinforce that message about the value of effective human relations.

10 Creative industries

> It is both liberating and profoundly unsettling to think that our livelihoods depend upon something as impalpable but as important as ideas.
>
> (Evans 2001)

Introduction

Beyond nurturing creativity HRD also becomes the engine of the culture of beauty and the economy of the imagination. Interest in the growth of cultural and creative industries has been evident for some time in government. For some the rise of cultural and creative industries in certain countries, advanced economies, is a harbinger of the final realisation of a leisure society, where work takes a lower priority and culture is more to be enjoyed for greater periods by larger numbers. HRD for work becomes less of an issue, and HRD for enjoying games, galleries and culture becomes more of an issue. Alternatively, it may be that the rise of the cultural and creative industries marked in the advanced economies represents the onset of a new economy, a new world of work, where these industries represent the wealth-generating and employment sectors of the future. For some the growth of the creative industries represented an onset not of the leisure age but of a new economy; the 'real' economy was becoming dependent on what came out of people's heads: imagination, talent and creativity, knowledge, skills. HRD then needs to be oriented on supporting and developing these. In either view HRD itself is in transition around the creative and cultural industries, in the advanced economies and elsewhere. The state has had to respond to this.

UK history and context

The rise of the cultural state in the UK is a phenomenon that has become established only since the mid-twentieth century.[1] The vibrant, innovative and respected state of the arts in the UK now would have been beyond the expectations of those who initiated the funding and institutional framework for culture and the arts in the post-Second World War era in the UK.

And in the period after the war some key figures, including John Maynard Keynes, took a strong interest in the arts and government support for them. This was when the Arts Council was established. In the UK Keynes' major interest was to grow the national opera company. Behind the more recent concerns with the economic value of the creative industries lies a history of argument and evolving policy reflecting the core issues of politics and the arts and the ambiguous status of the arts within government circles. The issues are intertwined: the role of the state, the need for subsidy, high versus low culture, the function of art, and art for art's sake.

This is the context within which cities take a keen interest in and compete for designations like 'European City of Culture'. The belief is that jobs, visitors and investment in regeneration are all at stake. Culture is the catalyst of these. Yet just prior to the Second World War there was no network at all to speak of, and art was seen as a privilege for a minority. Since then various arts czars and ministers have put their stamp on strategy, generating disagreements and disputes, championing either high culture or broader access and benefits, in the belief, after Ruskin, that there are only three forces, the economics, politics and culture; and only culture lasts and matters. On the other hand is popular opinion, as manifest in the tabloid press, which seems to hate the arts. So are people proud to be a nation of philistines or proud of their galleries, museums and orchestras as their greatest achievements? The UK is a culture in which only a minority of people attend cultural events (Table 10.1).

The seeds were sown for revamped galleries, theatres, festivals over sixty years ago, when there was little subsidy for the arts. Post-war there emerged movements to tour 'art for the people' to towns with no galleries, and for theatres to be subsidised, with Shakespeare rather than vaudeville. The leadership of the Arts Council was upper-class, progressive, Bohemian, and

Table 10.1 People attending events in the UK in the last twelve months and the last four weeks (2001)

Event	Last twelve months % of sample	Last four weeks % of sample	% of managerial sample	% of unskilled sample
Film	53	16	67	43
Live music	41	12	36	21
Art or other exhibition	24	6	33	8
Play or drama	21	6	41	15
Carnival, street arts, circus	18	3	24	21
Dance	10	3	15	9
Classical music	9	2	18	5
Cultural festival	5	1	15	7
Poetry, book reading	4	1	–	–

Source: Arts Council of England

worshipful of great art and artists, as a great civilising force. Other art was pretty worthless; they knew what was best, and everyone else ought to learn to love it.

On the political side, the first arts minister was Jenny Lee, mocked as a champagne socialist. She felt that the arts did not belong to Oxbridge, and people needed to be enticed into museums and galleries.

During the 1960s spending on the arts increased, and it was a flourishing time with a high profile. Alongside the white heat of technology the arts were to help boost the UK's self-image and PR image. They were connected with modernity, associated with the avant-garde. Through the 1970s times changed. There were incidents that brought the question of subsidies for art into question. Underlying issues about defending an artist's right to freedom of expression arose, and the questioning of 'But is it art?' that threatened politicians' popularity. The onset of the era of Modern Art controversies emerged. A cycle of 'shock, protest, defence, debate' that was to be repeated endlessly, providing much free publicity, and thus making such art more prevalent.

The other issue which emerged and which persists is that of subsidising the unaccountable elite, focused on spending on opera. This is a big and expensive art form for a small minority. The charge is elitism. Art is not for ordinary people, it is for 'toffs', experts on the obscure, with no sense of reality about life – a small group of the same people going to all the shows, a metropolitan elite. For everyone else art is entertainment, not something the state should subsidise. Commercial success is the key, not intellectual importance.

Subsidy has always been needed for serious art. It was historically provided by the church in the Middle Ages, Florentine bankers in the Renaissance, and royal families in emerging nations. Serious art has never stood on its own feet.

There remains a deep vein of scepticism, and a cringe factor about associating with art and the old and new elites who control it: the trendy people, the arty. They counter that they are not elitist, simply interested in the best. This was most evident during the 1980s, when there were public battles around public funding of the arts. The Conservative government pursued a policy of pruning support, believing that this medicine would help produce a stronger arts world, in tune with what audiences wanted, making the consumer the king. Companies should be able to stand on their own feet or find support elsewhere, from business, via business sponsorship. The Arts Council chairman was tasked with taking the system to pieces and contracting it out. People also perceived the government as being hostile to arts organisations and individuals who were not sympathetic with the government's aims. Indeed, the performing arts were seen by some in that world as being one of the few forces to offer a critique of the government and its radical changes. There were then disputes and conflicts between arts organisations and their funding agents. The arts world was accused of being made up of left-wing agitators with a begging bowl, while the government was lambasted as philistine and divisive.

Winning over the business community became a concern. Aside from the obvious concerns about control and direction of arts work, one problem was that many people were seeking to draw from the same, limited sources of benefaction. Business faces came to feature on trustee boards, and brought with them fresh views and challenging assumptions. At the same time new concerns around multi-cultural and social justice issues came more to the fore, rather than traditional high versus low culture issues. By the end of the decade the old guard of left-leaning figures had given way to a new generation that knew and accepted a role for business, internally and as a source of revenue. The 'subsidy junkie' era was over, and the arts had to partner with companies, not just the state.

In the late 1990s, with the election of a Labour government, a Creative Industries Task Force was established. The aim was to map an area whose scale and scope was unknown. The conclusion was that the creative industries were a major source of economic activity and growth, and were major employers. These were, indeed, astonishing figures, seeming to indicate that they were more important than manufacturing industries. This strong interest, though, came at a price. It represented an interaction with the economic and political value systems, at the expense of art for art's sake. The creative industries had to serve economic and political purposes, to fit in with the way government thought. But the extent to which partners, either economic or political, would be effective had to be questioned.

The economics of subsidising the arts entered a new era with National Lottery funding providing funds on a scale unseen before. Major building projects as well as institutional support for national and regional bodies were increased. The minister with responsibility had a seat in cabinet, but all were keen to avoid what were seen as the negative overtones of having a culture ministry: that is to say, a manipulative, ideological control of the production and use of arts for the support of the existing regime. Politicians were attracted by the glamour and sexiness of culture and the arts. But, on the other hand, the arts were never discussed at cabinet meetings. Government members were rarely personally interested in the arts, and their interest was viewed cynically by an arts world that feared censorship from too close a relationship.

It was acknowledged that the economic concerns had imbalanced the analysis; support for art for art's sake returned. Institutionally, government remained at arm's length, subsiding intermediary bodies, the Arts Council, to distribute funds and liaise with the arts world. Politicians fear being embroiled in controversy and scandal emerging from subsidised arts activities. The fact is that no prime minister has ever attended an Arts Council event, despite many invitations. The talk is now of supporting 'complex culture' rather than forms of culture concerned with entertainment: that is, culture which challenges, has impact and affects people. That this means subsidising high culture, perceived by some as for the elite and elitist, resurrects the eternal arguments about high versus low culture. High culture, however else defined, is usually expensive and for a minority who could not support it on their own. Low culture, in contrast, is usually cheap, for the mass, and paid for by the consumers. Clearly opera is the prime example of the high and television-watching of soaps is the prime example of the low. Opera is highly subsidised; soap operas attract advertising income as they gather huge audiences. The ideology of the arts world, and its hope for leadership, is that people appreciate that the arts' role is to make people better human beings; it has that ameliorative role, and that is why it should be subsidised. How classical opera fulfils that role but soap operas do not is open to question. What is beyond doubt is that, for many, great operas are the apex of culture, the highest of the high, and that its consumption is limited to a few. In contrast, the soap operas are one measure of the extent to which dumbing down rather than smartening up has been the primary trend over recent times. Thus the economic interplays, and their political contexts, never disappear, though their forms will vary as times change.

Spelling out the practical benefits that culture brings to society in financial, human and social terms, and identifying the obstacles that public sector cultural institutions face in fulfilling a potentially far more significant role in society, was the challenge taken up by Evans in his analysis of the economy of the imagination (2001). He considered three claims that culture and cultural institutions have an impact which should lead to an increased recognition of their value in HRD terms. These are that they demand and supply skilled individuals, they encourage creative problem-solving, and they can create social capital in run-down communities. In the first instance the creative industries represent 5 per cent of GDP in the UK (see Table 10.2) and a sizeable proportion of employment now and in the future. Second, it is desirable that there are in the workforce people who can generate and apply novel and distinctive ideas, work in teams, think laterally, mix the new and old. Engaging with culture and the arts helps produce the creative outlook. Finally, culture and the arts help to construct and reconstruct social capital: that is, to generate shared commitment and social inclusion, promoting trust and a shared perspective. Museums, galleries and libraries have a role in that. Creative problem-solving issues were considered in the previous chapter, so the other two are considered in turn below.

Demand and supply of skilled individuals: are creative industries a critical foundation of the 'new economy'?

SCMS (2001) defined what counts as 'Creative Industries' in their mapping document (See Table 10.3). These represent a range of industries whose inclusion under one umbrella as creative industries is an issue, as the extent

Table 10.2 Total business investment by art form, 2001, made up of sponsorship (50 per cent), membership (15 per cent), capital projects (15 per cent), sponsorship-in-kind (15 per cent), donations, awards and prizes

Artform	Amount (£ millions)
Museums and galleries	25.4
Drama/theatre	10.9
Music	9.4
Opera	8.5
Film/video	7.5
Visual arts	6.4
Festivals	6.3
Arts centres	3.2
Community arts	3.2
Heritage	2.2
Dance	1.9
Literature/poetry	1.3
Total	86.2

Source: A&B (2002) Arts and culture in the UK, Arts and Business policy and information unit

Table 10.3 Creative industries

	Revenue (£ billions)	Employment total	Exports (£ millions)
Software and computer services	36.4	555,000	2,761
Design	26.7	76,000	1,000
Publishing	18.5	141,000	1,654
TV and radio	12.1	102,000	440
Music	4.6	122,000	1,300
Film and video	3.6	45,000	653
Art and antiques	3.5	37,000	629
Advertising	3.0	93,000	774
Architecture	1.7	21,000	68
Interactive leisure software	1.0	21,000	503
Designer fashion	0.6	12,000	350
Performing arts	0.5	74,000	80
Crafts	0.4	24,000	40

Source: SCMS, Creative Industries Mapping Document, 2001

to which their workforces use 'creativity' and have in their employ 'creatives' varies widely. What is clear is that the creative industries range well beyond the activities of the stereotypical geniuses or 'struggling artists', and advanced societies and economies are both heavily dependent on them. The struggling artists should not, though, be forgotten (see Box 10.1).

Box 10.1 Making Their Mark

Studies of artists commonly show that they exist in a pragmatic, mixed economy where opportunities to exhibit and sell work are crucial. To be an artist is to be a dedicated, underpaid professional. In one study 45% of artists under 35 years of age made work that generated no income. Gross incomes for others are low, with only 17% earning more than £10,000 a year from their artistic practice. Rather than artists teaching business they themselves seem to have basic business and professional development needs; in marketing and promotion.

Source: Making Their Mark. Available at http://www.scottisharts.org.uk accessed 14th September 2004

The industries included in the UK mapping of creative industries included the following, considered in descending rank of revenues:

Software and computer services This includes software development, systems integration, analysis and design, project management, infrastructure design. Around 555,000 people are employed, including 114,000 programmers and 129,000 engineers. The UK is the second largest software market in Europe after Germany. Many have sector-specific skills, for example IT in banking and finance.

Design This sector includes various services, components of an industry, interior and environment design. It is integral to most economic activities. There are 4,000 design consultancies in the UK, 73 per cent employing fewer than twenty people, plus freelancers and designers in commerce. There are some world-class design businesses in graphics, product and interior design. The UK is a top exporter of design, and has a very good design education system. There is, though, no overarching industry body.

Publishing This includes books, journals (from library subscriptions), newspapers, magazines, digital. Books produce £3.8 billion of revenue, with 15,000 publishers. Mergers and acquisitions have been prominent, as has the growth of electronic publishing.

TV and radio This sector includes production, programme and packaging, broadcasting, transmission. In this sector, 54 per cent of all employment is London-based. There are around 74,000 employees and a further 40,900 freelance staff. The major areas of employment within TV and radio are:

- TV 20 per cent.
- Radio 20 per cent.

- New media 17 per cent.
- Facilities 11 per cent.
- Independent production 10 per cent.
- Commercials 10 per cent.

Audiences are increasing, and it is a dynamic industry. The impact of digital technology, the internet and telecoms innovation is a strong factor. Regulation of cross-media ownership is an issue, as is regulation of converging markets.

Music   This sector includes production, administration, live performance, management and song writing. In 1997 there were 8,700 concerts, to audiences of less than 500 mainly, and 89 outdoor events. It employs a total of around 122,000 people. The major areas of employment in music are:

- Live performance 46,000.
- Retail 4,000.
- Record companies 7,128.
- Manufacturers 3,000.
- Education and training 31,353.

Only 10 per cent of musicians are full-time employees. The UK has the third largest market for sales in the world. Online music sales are a controversial issue.

Film and video   This includes screenwriting, production, distribution (US majors) and exhibition (cinemas). The sector has around 4,400 firms, employing 20,500 production staff and 12,500 in distribution and projection. Around 100 films are produced a year. UK companies win awards for films but distribution is dominated by US firms. There are few integrated companies.

Art and antiques market   This involves the trade in arts and antiques of all forms and retailing via auctions, galleries and so on. In the UK there are 754 auction houses and around 9,400 dealers. In terms of revenue the UK is second only to the USA, which earns around £6.7 billion. It is a sector that is London-dominated, with Sotheby's and Christie's at the forefront. The British Council helps expose arts abroad.

Tourists to the UK consider art markets important. They support ancillary industries.

Advertising   This is an important sector in its own right, and also provides the primary revenue stream for other creative industries and external suppliers. It entails consumer research, client marketing, identifying consumer tastes, creating advertising and promotions, PR campaigns, media planning and producing advertising materials. The workforce is one where of the total employed 6 per cent are copywriters, 8.5 per cent work in creative services, and 9 per cent are art directors. In the UK, London is one of three main global centres for the advertising industry. The industry needs more skilled people, better training methods, and to nurture more small and medium-sized enterprises (SMEs).

Architecture   This includes building design, planning approval and production information. It is a sector dominated by small firms; 26 per cent of architects work in practices with only one or two staff, and only 39 per cent in offices with eleven or more staff. Practices are partnership structures (30 per cent), with associates (11 per cent) state/internal (21 per cent), sole principals (20 per cent). There was a rise in commissions and major projects throughout 1990s as a result of National Lottery funding. It could be exported more proactively, and involve more women and ethnic minorities.

Interactive leisure software   This sector includes games development, publishing, distribution, retail, and console and PC games. In development around 5,900 are employed and in publishing/distribution another 3,600. Retailing includes a further 8,346. The UK is the third largest market for consumption, after the USA and Japan. There are subsidiaries of major game publishers in the UK, but most studios are small, employing five to fifteen people. The industry is one with periods of famine and feast.

Designer fashion   This sector includes clothing design, manufacture for exhibition, consultancy and diffusion lines. In the UK this is mainly small companies rather than large multinational brands such as Calvin Klein, Gucci, Chanel. Concerns exist around improving business skills, relations with manufacturers, retailing outside London.

Performing arts   This includes content origination, performance production, live performance, touring, costume, lighting. There are 800 theatre venues, 500 companies, 550 festivals, 2,750 amateur companies. Many are supported by subsidy, via the Arts Council, local government, business sponsorship and the National Lottery. They employ around 32,00 people, with a further 42,000 self-employed. It is a sector with accumulated deficits, despite 110,000 tickets a day sold. The Edinburgh International is the largest festival. Attendances are static, with skills and facilities not being well used.

Crafts   This is the sector of people producing textiles, ceramics, jewellery, and metal and glass products. It is a sector needing better training opportunities and better-quality trade fairs. Many sell direct to the public; 48 per cent are self-employed. A distinct business model applies, with supply chain issues.

Does the pursuit of cultural capital help build social capital?

Does the pursuit of cultural capital help to build social capital, a sense of shared commitment and inclusion which, many economists argue, binds a society together, promotes trust, provides a sense of shared perspective? In a world in which many people fear that social bonds are fragmenting, culture still provides many of our most important shared experiences. Museums, galleries and libraries may play a role in social regeneration. In both the East End of London and Silicon Alley in New York, art galleries and artists were the precursors for the creation of clusters of new media and digital businesses. As new galleries in Walsall and Newcastle, Glasgow and Liverpool testify, cultural institutions can have an inspirational effect on how a town or neighbourhood is seen and sees itself. Culture can give access to hidden depths of self-confidence and vitality in communities. Cities may seek to structure their regeneration, and their rebranding, around creative industries and cultural institutions. Economists and policy-makers looking upon dead industries, dilapidated warehouses and abandoned factories had to think through new solutions. Pride in industrial strength was displaced by competition for branding as cities of culture, places of vibrant arts and entertainment.

The example of one city, Glasgow, is illustrative (McDermott 2004). This is a city of once strong manufacturing and heavy industry, now a shrinking city, with record poor health, yet with credible claims to be one of the most creative in the world, producing a vibrant music scene with internationally acclaimed artists. While the city had been 1990 European City of Culture, that was just a blip which gave some temporary extra funding. The background to this success has been attributed to the following factors. First, size matters: the city is big enough to support a strong cultural sector, but small enough for artists to network easily compared to other metropolitan areas. There is a closeness between the music scene and the art scene. The chances for collaboration are magnified. Second, there have been creative bursts: the music scene was driven by a series of successful bands and clubs. Key figures at the heart of these anchor activity. These occurred within a context of an independent spirit, self-contained but not parochial, with people defiant about identity, on division between high and low culture. There was an institutional centre, a school of art, as a centre of cross-pollination. The creatives were not stuck with a 'great' history; unlike other centres where much art history forms their identity, places like Glasgow turn to music and film. They were free of the pressures of the spotlight and hyped scenes, were not being constantly judged, and flourished deprived of attention. The economics were harsh: artists were not able to make a living at one thing, so there was cross-over. The roots of the recent success lay elsewhere: in dilapidated warehouses taken over and exploited as an exhibition area on one floor and a concert room on another. Attempts to ride on the back of this, with PR campaigns geared at tourists selling Glasgow as Scotland with Style, representing the city as hip and happening, cool and modern, seem shallow. And there is an awareness that the whole design community is 'fragile', not a robust centre of design excellence, even with current and growing interest and respect.

Reflections

While more than three-quarters of a million Britons describe themselves as working in the creative industries, the significance of these sectors and other creative/cultural industries reaches beyond that. The UK, thanks in part to the role of English as a global language, has an enormously strong position in some of the world's fastest growing cultural industries. Music and computer games industries are as large as steel and textiles. Publicly funded cultural institutions play a role in supporting these industries, turning out film-makers, animators, designers, architects, musicians, performers and visual artists. So these cultural and educational institutions are a part of modern industrial and economic policy, because they produce the specific and often highly technical skills that are transferable and used in the high-growth private sector industries.

But to reinvigorate and reform the framework for publicly funded cultural institutions for the future as an economic policy is a leap. It is difficult to measure, describe, value and mobilise this economy. The UK may now have a strong position in creative industries with a growing global outreach, from media and fashion to music and computer games; but is that sustainable? Would altering the nature of central government's relationship with the institutions that it funds change that? The sector feels over-regulated, inhibiting the very creativity and innovation for which it should be known. It feels the legitimate need for accountability is not correctly weighed against the need to promote initiative, innovation, risk-taking, diversity and creativity

If wealth is increasingly derived from generating and applying novel and distinctive ideas then having more creative people is sensible. But believing that children should be more encouraged to enjoy cultural experiences, through drama, art, music-making, to acquire a creative outlook for economic purposes is to confuse value systems. Cultural institutions can and should widen and deepen their role in education to help provide the context and background for creative education for its own sake. Business sponsorship has a role in that, but the kinds of companies involved are few and the amounts they invest tend to be small (see Table 10.4).

This over-selling of creativity is similar to the over-selling of the creative industries. The over-inflation in the 1990s of 'Cool Britannia', and the subsequent bursting of that bubble, contains lessons. There is also a problem

Table 10.4 Business and arts levels of sponsorship

Business organisations involved (approximately)	800
Total investment	£110 million
Investing <10K	400 companies
Investing 10–100K	240 companies
Investing >500K	40 companies

Source: A&B (2002) Arts and culture in the UK, Arts and Business policy and information unit

Table 10.5 Major cultural attractions in the UK

Attractions	Location	Visitors (millions)
National Gallery	London	5.0
British Museum	London	4.8
Tate Modern	London	3.5
Tower of London	London	2.0
Eden Project	St Austell	1.7
York Minster	York	1.6
Victoria and Albert Museum	London	1.4
Science Museum	London	1.4
Edinburgh Castle	Edinburgh	1.1
Kew Gardens	London	1.0
Kelvingrove Art Gallery and Museum	Glasgow	1.0
Tate Britain	London	1.0
Westminster Abbey	London	1.0

Source: A&B (2002) Arts and culture in the UK, Arts and Business policy and information unit

of measurement. While there may be much creative talent, that does not mean there are equally strong creative industries. The UK lacks a domestic film industry capable of building on this talent. Accounting is ill-equipped to tell us the value of ideas, brands, creativity and innovation. The shift to an economy of the imagination challenges deep-seated assumptions about identity. There needs to be a shift in imagination about how we make our living and what we are known for in the world, prior to reforming policy to support an economy of the imagination.

There are a set of important issues in the UK which reflect more general concerns. There is the regional bias of the culture industries around a major metropolitan centre: in the UK that is London and the South East (see Table 10.5). There is a problematic link to regional development and retaining talent in the regions rather than seeing them drained away. There is the impact of e-commerce on these services and information. There is the issue of export potential in the global economy; increasing demand. The evolution of partnerships and industry forums to help deal with all these issues is important.

Conclusions

The opportunities for growing the creative industries and depending upon them for jobs, wealth and a secure identity in the global economy are evident. The implications are clear:

- stimulating creativity and innovation in young people to ensure we have a long-term supply of creative talent;
- ensuring that at primary and secondary school and tertiary education levels it is possible to identify and develop new talent;

- ensuring that people have both the creative and the business skills to succeed;
- ensuring access to financial support, and making the financial sector aware of investment opportunities;
- responding to global opportunities, promoting UK creativity, removing obstacles to free trade or preventing the introduction of measures that harm UK competitiveness.

These are aligned with broader concerns about exploiting e-commerce; ensuring wider public awareness of the importance of intellectual property rights (downloading and pirating); lightening the regulatory burden; recognising the interlocking relations between the subsidised and commercial sectors, and the broader cultural sectors.

The extent to which this growth can be done successfully in all these creative industry sectors is questionable. On the one hand there is an interconnection and synergy between all these sectors. On the other hand there are problems of each being overshadowed by bigger players: for example, in film by companies based in the USA, in fashion by the major global brands. There is also the problem of being seduced into subsidising activities that are not economic otherwise, such as opera and other performing arts, in the name of economic growth. The prescription that all culture industries can be subsidised and sustained as a central part of economic success is hard to sustain.

Determining the interrelationship between financial capital, social capital and cultural capital remains a vexed question. That possible synergies exist is undeniable, but there are also possible illusions and delusions about what each can do for the other. More, it may be that they are contradictory; pursuing social capital, for Florida (2002), means compromising the creation of cultural capital. This interface between the long-reigning force of financial capital and the organisational forms it favours, with the newer reconceptualisations of social capital, cannot be analysed any longer without taking into account cultural capital as well.

11 Taking it seriously
Subverting double standards

> The metaphysical always appears at the point of greatest contrast between desire and impossibility ... the desirability of a desire we cannot renounce and the impossibility of that desire's fulfilment.
>
> (Kirwin 1999, p. 43)

Now that these constituent themes around creativity, beauty and imagination have been applied to both aspects of the interaction of aesthetics and HRD, it is possible to revisit the whole concept of the creative class, and the HRD interaction with it, more reflexively. Reflections on Florida and a counter-analysis are outlined. The central reflective point is that double standards exist around creativity, aesthetics, beauty and the imagination. These are the double standards of the still dominant ideas of the middle class which are, on the one hand, to regale, treasure and venerate creativity; but on the other hand it is as much traduced, disregarded and hounded. As long as these double standards prevail the impact of creativity on HRD, and vice versa, will be limited and compromised. Transcending these double standards means exploring more honestly what aesthetics can do for HRD, and what HRD needs to do for the age of aesthetics. This can be done by reviewing what three major thinkers, Marx, Nietzsche and Freud, contributed to understanding the double standards of the middle classes.

Questioning Florida

Reflections on this analysis may be either primarily economic or social. On the economic side the definition of creativity is loose and obscure. Creativity is essential; it is multifaceted; it is in tension with 'organisation' which will stifle it. But what exactly creativity is, among other kinds of economic activity or processes, remains unoperationalised. What Florida mainly discusses in practice are varying forms of organisation. (See Florida 2002, on which the following discussion is based.) He cites the 'Hollywood model' of organisation, for example, as representing what creativity means. In times past the Hollywood model for making movies was the studio system, consisting of large, permanent organisations with fixed staff. Now there is a different Hollywood model and system: a producer takes an idea to a group of investors and pulls together an ad hoc team to make it; then they dissolve to reform elsewhere. This system is about small, flexible networks with ever changing talents. So the economics of creativity are the economics of small, flexible networks in transition. That change may be worth identifying, but the underlying point surely is that Hollywood in essence is still Hollywood, no matter the model. If Hollywood had not existed in the past, and had just come into being now, then that would be a significant sign of the rise of the creative impulse and an expansion of the creative class. It is still doing the same thing now as it always has. And in that sense there is no greater or lesser role for creativity, no greater or lesser dependence on creativity now compared with the past.

There are also issues around socio-economic trends and realities. The biggest class, which is continuing to grow, is not the creative class: it is the low-paid service class. For most of these people, what makes a place attractive or not is the extent to which general policies, sound local governance and a balancing of many different groups' interests are found. The kinds of playgrounds they want are generally for their children. Florida is clearly ambivalent about the idea of community, wanting it in some defined form but aware that his analysis essentially characterises community as inhibiting. Hollywood is again a popular reference point; it is considered to be a place, an industry, where social ties are tenuous and contingent, a place where rats hug and kiss each other prior to backstabbing each other. The characterisation of community, and strong ties, as the only other alternative to this but repressive, is false and dangerous. A society of weak ties may rather suit a much more repressive form of governance; totalitarians much prefer it if people's personal ties are displaced by commitments to abstract ideals. For Florida the benign purpose is of supporting those who are deemed creative, but for others the same environment can be desirable for quite opposite reasons.

That many people live quasi-anonymously, with weak ties and contingent commitments, may appeal at some points in life but not at others. Those points where this environment can present serious problems would include the point of being a teenager, having a family of your own, retiring from work, and being elderly having lost a partner. Either these people are to be excluded from the places where the creative class wants to prevail, or they need to be incorporated, challenging the creative class mix as Florida presents it. Many people may not be choosing the 'weak ties' way of life and work; they may feel that it is alienating and miserable, but they have no alternative. They may then rationalise this as being what they want, at least for a while. But the evidence is that many actually desire the exact opposite, to opt out of that kind of environment and live in small, more intimate communities, where their existence is noticed, known and meaningful. This opting out into the intimate may be into the home and the family, or indeed to start a family of their own, or it may be in some other form. The attractiveness of cults and New Religious Movements (NRMs), the desire to leave jobs, sell up and move to new locations, and other phenomena reflect this.

Florida backs down from following through on critical issues, particularly the subversion issue. The subversion issue is simple; many creative people are iconoclastic, taking on the prevailing order, rejecting things as they are, opposing the essence of the economic system. Florida appreciates that, but his creative class is not a revolutionary class. For the subversion of a creative class that he endorses is tame and lame: the subversion of creating a new look for a car, a new look for buildings, a new trend in fashion. Any subversion that might challenge the broader and deeper order of private company profit-making as the central dynamic is containable.

Yet creativity is hard to contain; it has elements of the wild, and may be a genie out of the bottle, able to turn on those considering themselves its masters. Florida begins to make distinctions: between the mercurial and methodical, the radical big idea or tinkering with things creative, the team player and the solitary creative. But he fails to follow this through, defining only a single kind of environment to nurture all kinds of creativity: valuing creativity, positive challenge, providing resources, and being receptive to creative work.

His identification and defence of people's 'desire' for quasi-anonymity is most worrying. He argues that the people he talks to do not want community connectedness; they want to get away from that. Yet if weak ties are so crucial to the ideal environment, then he ought to have such an index and measure places with weak ties. Even though he has indices for everything else he has none for this, for the valuing of 'weak ties'. Might that show that places where weak ties are predominant are not places of economic success at all? Weak ties, he argues, are not restrictive, and this is good for growth. Indeed, strong communities are 'exclusionary' and negative, so good riddance to all that. It never was, despite the veneration of the Christmas classic movie and homage to small-town existence, 'a wonderful life'. The veneration of ordinariness is to be opposed.

The ambivalence leads him ultimately to compromise, concluding that it is wise to maintain a core of strong ties with significant others, but not to be dominated by them as was the case in the past. Significant others can be accommodated as long as they do not actually encumber or restrict how the creative classes live – the lives, for example, of those who inhabit research universities, like himself. This extension of mythologising the milieux of the research university as a role model for a whole place is ludicrous. There are some who want to bring back 'restrictive', fundamentalist communities; they are a minority. But people who seek to support diversity, research universities, film industries, sunrise industries, can also want to protect the integrity of the individual, value strong ties and belong to a community. And that comes at a cost; it requires commitments other than aberrations of narcissistic self-fixation dressed up as self-fulfilment. Commitments are to be recognised for what they are: the very stuff of life, not restrictive and encumbering. The problems that breakdowns in belonging bring with them can otherwise be serious, as people seek and find something else to belong to.

Reality checks

The creative class is a platform for reversing the decline of cities. Using a recipe including an old ideal, that of building a people climate not just a business climate, produces this analysis for the creative class. Florida concludes that we need to invest more in creativity, to overcome the new class divides for economic and moral reasons, and build new kinds of social cohesion without conventional agencies like the family or church. Research universities can be the creative hub of these, containing as they do technology, talent and tolerance, and being open to diversity, cultivating it, investing in lifestyle amenities that people want and use, not just retail complexes, to attract immigrants, Bohemians, young people. But do research universities foster these qualities and provide models of creativity? Does promoting diversity produce all these things? If it did, the most tolerant places would thrive and the most oppressive wither – but it is not so. There was plenty of creativity in Stalin's Russia and Hitler's Nazi Germany, two of the most intolerant totalitarian regimes ever. Of course many artistic, and some scientific creatives did flee these regimes, to escape suppression or worse, as these regimes oppresed on a scale previously unknown. In them creativity still existed and was channelled by and through agencies for causes which, for example, generated the knowledge and technology that would help produce travel into space. These were exceptionally intolerant places that nonetheless still proved able to nurture some kinds of creativity. They were ultimately defeated by cultures which could be seen, in Florida's terms, as equally hamstrung as they were founded on strong-tie communities; Britain and the use in the 1930s and 1940s.

Dysfunctions relating to marriage, having children, family relations – these are all a potential encumbrance on the freedom of the creative or, to look at it a different way, on the psychically undeveloped, the ineffectively socialised, those stuck in narcissism. From strong ties to weak ties may be a long-term trend, and creativity as an economic force may give it impetus. But these issues of personal growth, lifespan development and the difficulty of making choices have always been with us. Justifying the unencumbered life, the narcissistic life, the psychologically dysfunctional life, by claiming it enables creativity and in turn economic success, is to have allowed economic values to outstrip reason and twist culture into such distorted knots.

The counter-argument to this is to be found in Fukuyama (1995). He asserts that many of the differences that used to exist between countries in the past have gone; advanced countries adopt liberal democratic institutions and market-oriented economies, and are interlocked in the global division of labour. For him, the challenge is that 'now that the question of ideology and institutions has been settled, the preservation and accumulation of social capital will occupy centre stage' (p. 362). The enormous prosperity we have created enables a regime of universal and equal rights to be a feasible goal. Governments cannot realise this by legislating for further improvements through social engineering and government programmes. Rather, they must depend on a healthy civic society for the realisation of these goals. This is founded upon a strong and stable family structure, vibrant sectors in businesses, voluntary associations, educational institutions, clubs, unions, charities and churches. Government can only nourish the conditions for these, not bring them into being; so the right culture matters.

In neoclassical economics it is assumed to be self-interested, rational behaviour that provides the dynamic for economic activity. This is true for much economic behaviour, but there is more: there is the influence of culture, though that is often missing. Culture shapes economic activity. The single most important and pervasive cultural characteristic for developing all these sectors is the level of trust in a society. Utility, the pursuit of pleasure and the avoidance of pain, matters; but there are also other goals, ideas and other choices. These are seen to be revealed in preferences: what people feel to be useful is revealed by the choices they make. And in making these choices people are embedded in groups: they are not lone, selfish maximisers making cost–benefit calculations. Reciprocity, moral obligations, community duty and trust are all grounded in the habit of groups, not individual rational calculation.

There are still two great forces affecting humanity: one of rational desire, seeking wealth, and one of being a moral being and having one's worth recognised. It is the desire for recognition that can lead passions to overcome rationality; if people are neglected they get angry, or if they fail they feel shame. Conversely, if they receive attention they feel pride. People are selfish creatures and at the same time have a social side that shuns isolation. There is a systemic balance between these in, respectively, capitalist economics and liberal democracy; together they co-determine, rather than one causing the other.

In the contemporary world people invest economic activity with many of the moral values of their broader social lives, and so entrepreneurship is an outlet for the energies of ambitious people. Alongside this is the need for people to work together for common purposes in groups and organisations. This is why social capital matters, producing High Trust and group-oriented cultures in which entrepreneurs can flourish. These cultures, for Fukuyama, include the USA. His concern was that in the USA there seemed to be a decline of sociability and social capital. As governments could not easily build this up, such a decline was significant and serious.

The middle classes and creativity

All the above reflections on the rise and role of the creative class are far from new; they are part of a long line of questioning contradictions about valuing creativity, art and aesthetics (Eagleton 1990). That had been resurrected to a place of prominence in contemporary thinking before and alongside the growth of interest in the creative class. And that was because of an evident and increasingly important double standard: that the aesthetic is that which is of the highest value but of the lowest priority. Understanding why this double standard should exist, what purpose it serves, is essential to connecting aesthetics with HRD, as part of the critique of middle-class hegemony in modern societies.

On the one hand the aesthetic capacity serves the interest of staying alive, alongside reason and rationality. The pursuit of pleasure and avoidance of the disgusting is hard-wired into human beings. There is no need to develop it at all. But on the other hand the aesthetic represents an alternative to reason and rationality, a cultivated capacity that is learned. And that competes with reason and rationality. For some, cultivated aesthetic valuing is an inferior capacity that may undermine reason and rationality. For others, it is a superior and greater capacity, deserving of greater recognition and indeed reverence than it receives. For Eagleton the interest and significance of natural and cultivated aesthetics is now arising in a specific historical context, one in which the proponents of reason and rationality find the reincarnation of sensibility to present a problem and a puzzle. But what is being witnessed now, in the name of exploring aesthetics, is an attempt to restore unity to answering the three 'great' questions of philosophy down the ages:

- What can we know?
- What ought we to do?
- What ought we to desire?

While answers to these questions were available as interlocking and internally consistent wholes, as they were in eras and cultures characterised by theologically grounded ways of sense-making there appeared to be little scope for significant 'double standards' to emerge. To breach one dimension was in effect to breach them all. According to Eagleton breaking a unified and interlocking framework of understanding, was part of the growth and rise of the modern middle classes. That introduces the possibility of double standards around sensibility and the problem of aesthetics. The middle class valuing of certain forms of sensuous pleasure sits alongside two contrasting and conflicting phenomena. On the one hand there is a denial of sensuous desire as a positive force, and an opposition to it in its many unsanctioned forms; from enjoying forms of 'low culture' to sexual 'deviance'. On the other hand the middle-classes themselves exhibit a continuing preference in practice for experiences other than sensuous fulfilment, even in high culture forms. In a culture, in other words, where it is possible that commitments to imagination, creativity and beauty might be expected to flourish and provide a critical frame of reference for ruling ideals there is instead a corralling of these into a restricted domain, the world of art. This is apart from life, and life outside art proceeds as a mundane, routine and frequently dull or ugly affair.

That provides the central analysis about why double standards about knowledge, morality and pleasure arose, then became overshadowed, but have more recently returned. Many major thinkers over the last period, like Marx, Nietzsche and Freud, whose ideas have shaped how we think about society and mankind, were always considering aesthetic concepts and matters as integral to their influential interpretations of man and society. They were questioning why and how double standards about knowledge, morality and pleasure were an integral part of the existence of the middle classes as the dominant force in capitalist economies and democratic societies; and how that presented problems for people.

While there are always many more pressing things on the political and social agendas, exploring and exploiting double standards about pleasure as problems with knowledge and morality take precedence, working through similar problems with aesthetic valuing is still essential for the continued dominance of the middle class, including their dominance around HRD. How the middle classes define and legitimise pleasure, or do not, and how they control and police its meaning is at the heart of both their general success and their vulnerability, their potential failures: the accurate reflections and distortions of what HRD can be. It is at the heart of their confusion about the value of the vocational and the academic, the defence of elitism in education and the democratisation of education, the significance of the arts and their worthlessness.

The middle class

Eagleton (1990) considers the possibility of the hegemonic rise of the middle class to have been founded on rendering the three great questions separate. For alongside political battles, social change, technological invention and moral force, indeed enabling all of these, was the rupturing of thought from feeling. Knowledge, politics and desire were to be split from each other; the cognitive, the ethico-political and the libidinal-aesthetic would become detached and separate subjects. Each could then go their own way, independent of the others. This freed knowledge from ethics; ideas could be developed without ethical constraints, as their creators were split from concerns about moral value. It was all right to press on to do whatever was possible, whatever the ethical objections might be, as nothing was taboo. The ethical was confined to the religious; and with that the seeds of secularisation were sown, and the freedom of belief to splinter into many variegated forms. And art too was freed: freed from the ecclesiastical and the interests of powerful patrons. The downside was, for both the ethical and the aesthetic, that they were also free to cease having any wider effect. They were no longer to be so intimately associated with the centres of power, the people within them and the rituals they enacted. Art became a commodity, freed of its functions within church, court and state. It existed as its creators pleased, according to their own lights only; just like knowledge it could take any form as it was for nothing and nobody in particular.

This rupturing brought with it advantages: the unprecedented growth of knowledge and science, at the expense of ideological aspects of morality. The iconic example remains Darwin's discoveries about evolution and the devastation of Christian metaphysics this entailed. It enabled the flourishing of many styles and schools of art. But it also brought problems and difficulties, and produced a new zone of messiness, the messiness of pleasure and the problem of the body. For, alienated from a unity of view, in an era of knowledge expansion and economic change, what was pleasure for? The aesthetic had become disassociated from any other sphere of determination; it had to stand alone and isolated, set apart from the other primary questions. This independence then produces the double standard. On the one hand the aesthetic, and pleasure, might come to matter more as it provides a measure. Anything now might become aestheticised; truth could be that which satisfied the mind, morality could be a matter of merely what was in style or pleasurable, and to live properly could be to turn oneself and one's life into a thing of art, an artefact. On the other hand the aesthetic was also much more politicised. What was to be deemed pleasurable, beautiful, what was to be imagined and created, was now an open and sensitive matter, intertwined with the politics of who was to control and exercise power and about what. This made the aesthetic seemingly dangerous, volatile, a source of potential upset and contest.

Intellectually the double standard was framed as exploring the difficulties proposed as philosophy had 'awakened' to the fact of the body: the gaze, the gut, the gross and the palpable. Philosophers sought to understand how the sensible life existed alongside reason, and vice versa. In this context aesthetic valuing was then seen as a kind and form of reason: a sister of logic. There was an inner, but inferior, logic; aesthetic sensibility was a cognitive 'unskilled labourer'; things were attractive because they were pleasurable and beautiful or repulsive because they were dangerous. This mere sister of logic provided little more than an intuitive pre-given structure for the perceptive body in its primordial physicality. Attention to surfaces was all that was necessary to satisfy the aesthetic sense. The presence of the aesthetic did not inspire, or require, higher analysis as reason and rationality did. This basic faculty was superseded – by reasoning, by culture, by civilisation and by wisdom. Culminating in the Enlightenment, humanity was big with wisdom about reality, but for others it was also deaf, dumb, blind and empty-handed before the real world.

The crisis of reason

At the time when the middle class was emerging there was a perceived crisis of reason, the threat of appeals to feeling and passions having the capacity to inflame discontent. The powers of art to elicit and direct emotion, allied with utopianism and republican rationalism, also influenced a re-evaluation of matters aesthetic. The left-wing critique of the rise of the middle classes evolved to include aesthetic matters in various ways, with the central thrust becoming that art could and should be a party to smashing illusions, lies and falsehoods. Having and using creative and artistic powers became a central part of a critique of alienation and a seedbed of potential change; this is represented in the thinking of Schiller through Morris and Marcuse. Sticking with organic craftsmanship, one response to the machine and industrial age, still appeals to this day as a way to take on and beat the system, albeit it a personal and secret subversion of it, a kind of refusal to be co-opted.

A right-wing critique also evolved. There were various expressions, but the major stream was to equate high culture with national culture and then venerate these, while belittling middle-class and low-brow popular culture. Great art was a sign of national significance, and in a world of much change and uncertainty all classes could agree with that, and take pride in it. This was a variation on the unitarist world view, seeing society as an organism, with its parts in harmony, without serious internal conflict. This is what great art both reflected and stimulated. In more extreme nationalistic versions this would became part of the cultural mix of 'thinking with the blood', of believing in and defending cultural traditions, real or imagined, as a secure foundation of national identity and justification for feelings of superiority. This sense of coming from a superior tradition was a better cultural foundation for modern man than anything offered by the contemporary individual artists or movements which had flourished. These were movements peopled with vain, narcissistic and egoistic creators whose warped imaginations could produce nothing of beauty. This line of thinking was associated with thinkers like Burke, through Coleridge, to Yeats and Eliot.

For both the left or the right, the freeing of art with the rise of the middle classes was a kind of triumph but also a defeat. Art in the industrialised, machine-dominated, commodified world was useless. It might represent a kind of non-reified, non-instrumental form of activity for those whose lives were otherwise permeated by commodification. It offered people the best chance they had to get a glimpse outside the prison and cage of their alienated existence as mere objects among objects, part of a system of exchangeable commodities. This could seem a positive role, a sanctuary for sustaining a human identity in an inhumane world, one in which no one cared about people's whole lives and individuality. That is so; but this is also a potentially negative function for art as well. For if fulfilment through art reconciles people, in some way, to things as they are, to the status quo, then that is systemically bad. Artists should not help build and protect this sanctuary; they should help tear it down, in the name of pursuing real change. These are the roots of an art that rejected the conventional aesthetic. The hope of a revolutionary avant-garde, turning art against the established order, becomes the issue. Pleasurable aesthetic experience has become part of the problem, not the partial and temporary solution that some would cling to. And so are brought into being artists whose aim is producing an art which is not art.

An alternative for some was to sustain art, but to seek to subvert the co-option of aesthetic value to serving power by developing a certain kind of aesthetic content through the form of harsh realism. Showing people how things really were through art forms and triggering the right affective reactions, could elicit people's support for change and progress. But the problem encountered is that as this follows aesthetic principles the artist is always encountering a paradox: feeding the middle-class appetite for the real rather than challenging it. Ultimately this ends up fuelling the source of the problem in the first place – the power of markets – as the market in works of realist art is stimulated. The way to respond to that is then to leave content behind altogether and go for form alone, for abstraction rather than realism. But then a market and an affirmative culture co-opts even this and embraces these works as marketable commodities. Continuing rather than giving up means the next logical extension: even form must go, leading to anti-art. Anti-art cannot be appropriated, and sold, as it is not art at all. Meaninglessness cannot be bought and sold for show in corporate boardrooms. And so is brought into being the negative avant-garde, avoiding absorption by not producing an object at all; they only make gestures, happenings, disruptions.

Either the positive or negative versions of the avant-garde encounter the question of connections with broader political movements. Their success in change or failure and absorption stands or falls with the destiny of broader political movements. It is historical record that neither the positive or the negative avant-garde helped to contend with either Stalinism or fascism, or even to form a substantial and critical element of the movements that ultimately did. Indeed, fascism arguably entailed a form of wholesale aestheticisation of society as a means to and an end of its ideology: fascism still stands, aside from its militaristic garb, in myths, symbols, orgiastic spectacles, appeals to passion, racial intuition, the pulse of blood rather than reason (Paxton 2004). This raw emotionalism and passion was about form as much as content: crowds intoxicated by emotion, rallies rather than dull meetings, the romance of destiny, the abuse of methods of mass communication. And Hitler, the failed painter, is in some accounts depicted as, at the end, preoccupied with architectural plans and models of monuments for the Reich as Berlin was occupied and devastated.

The degradation of avant-garde attitudes towards truth, morality and beauty makes sense in the run up to and the fallout from that context, the growth of fascism. The libidinal body is rediscovered, but only to be used as a means to horrendous ends, and post fascism even more firmly yoked to the imperatives of profit, to the tune of the legitimations of those like Postrel and Florida. If artists cannot bring regimes down with organic craftsmanship, they may try the silent scream. Secret subversion, silent resistance, stubborn refusal. They may dance on the grave of narrative, semantics and representation. More positive versions seek to be part of mass movements, and win and appropriate or lose and be incorporated anyway. But, as Eagleton (1990) puts it, truth, morality and beauty are too important to be handed contemptuously over to the 'other side'. The iconoclastic avant-garde turns on itself, with self-reflexive subversion, or consumerist hedonism and loss of self in a world of weak, quasi-anonymous relations in the metropolis. There must be more than a fetishism of style and the superficial, a cult of hedonism, the displacement of sustained relations and meaning with random intensities. History progressed, as ever, by its bad side. Adorno's view is that after Auschwitz all culture is rubbish (Spivey 2004). The body and its pleasures as an affirmative category are tainted by fascism in the first instance and then mass society thereafter. Rationality was instrumental in both of these, and the violations and victimisations they afforded. Art is an alternative, but complicit with capitalism and commodity culture. On the side of autonomous social relations, freedom; on the side of the futile, subversive but pointless and impotent. Art can only hope to be valid if it provides an implicit critique of the conditions which produced it.

See evil, hear evil, talk evil: Marx, Nietzsche, Freud

The broad picture outlined above, and its implications for HRD, can be filled out and interpreted by considering how three major thinkers came to explore the aesthetic. The aesthetic is a compact with failure: be poor but honest, as the hidden irrationality is brought to light, rather than rich but inauthentic. The worse things become, for some, the more this is a sign of immanent transcendence, and is therefore to be welcomed. But we need more sober and systematic analysis. Start with new bad things: structure of commodity, death of storytelling, vacancy of historical time, technology of capitalism – the very new and the very old together – shocking.

For Marx the point of aesthetics was to critique how capitalism reduced workers to being a body with minimum needs, with people stripped of their senses in the fullest meaning. The middle classes sought to contain their own senses of pleasure and gratification, as they ought to save rather than spend on gratification. For others, with the denuded and estranged lives that went with labouring, the escape into gratification, the short-term pleasures and long-term harm of drink and substance abuse, were ever-present. There was a dialectic of brute materialism and capricious idealism, and the contradictions of being beset by the attractions on one hand of the ascetics of bare necessity and on the narcissism of gross indulgence. To overcome property relations, to alter productive relations, would be to restore to people their natural senses and satisfactions through seeing, feeling, tasting and touching fully. This exercise of the senses would be an end in itself, not to serve the forces of production and consumption.

There is a view here that human capabilities are spontaneously positive. If human powers are spontaneously positive then their emancipation requires no careful discrimination: actualise all with abandon, allow people to express themselves. Others would qualify this, as not all human capabilities are positive. The principle would be only allowing realisation of the self which favours similar expression in others: emancipate in yourself as you would have others emancipate in themselves. Further, there is the problem of utopianism, of grasping too quickly for a future, by an act of will or imagination, beyond what is feasible. People desire uselessly that which is unattainable. Becoming ill with longing rather than considering clearly the potentialities of the present is a danger.

The materialist and radical is ever hopeful that oppressive orders generate forces that can overthrow them. The aesthetic is part of that: a system of value used to manage domination but also a vulnerability that permeates every object and relation. And it cannot be eradicated, having its irreducibility in the being of the body rather than the capriciousness of artists. A more pessimistic view is that aesthetics cannot help undo the nightmare bequeathed by history. It is not the beautiful and the imaginative that history furnishes for change: it is the powerless and the brutalised, products of a long and repeated pattern of defeat. That a work of art could function as a radical civiliser, a rescuer of those vulnerable to brutalised, powerless existence, seems a feeble case. Yet, in the absence of social change to realise their dreams, people could make do with art.

With Nietzsche there is more interest in drawing attention to the myth of the ascetic, among adherents of science, religion, philosophy. Theirs was a sensibility that turned if it could away from the blood and toil in which consciousness was embedded. The human animal has to be degutted and debilitated to be fit for civilisation. For Nietzsche, the Warriors who used despotic powers on humbled populations, and hammered them into shape with an artist's egoism, had no need for such ascetic mythologising; they were brutal subjugators, and they acknowledged it. In his contemporary times, with the decline of faith, people were exposed again to fresh possibilities, experiment and adventure. But rather than take these they preferred to seek culture to fill the void. In the face of the godless indifference of the universe to their human fate, they sought via the aesthetic the solace of the civilising, the educational and the therapeutic. For Nietzsche, who believed that art should tell the truth that there is no truth, this was a dismal emasculation of art's amoral power.

For him, art should be strenuous, muscular, productive and mendacious. Making art required people to master themselves, but only in order to then be able to live mischievously. It could produce people who could halt at the sensuous surface and accept that was all there is, rather than hunting for illusory depths beneath. As there was nothing but surface there were no metaphysical grounds for any benefits to moral behaviour. People ought to just accept violence and domination as the way things are, and celebrate power as an end in itself. If art sought to avoid that it was corrupted.

With this interpretation of the beautiful as superficial, the aesthetic was, like all else, shallow; all except the will to power. Nietzsche in undermining conventional views, undoing ethics and epistemology, also shattered not just the supernatural consolations and scientific totems but their aesthetics as well. The dynamism of the 'overman' should terrify the stout citizen. Yet these stout citizens are also resourceful self-improvisers in the market place. The middle class seek to be free and unconstrained, but to be protected from others like that. That is their dilemma, that they are a self-thwarting subject, restless and never at peace.

For Freud, also, the middle classes were never at peace, but for other reasons. The conventional interpretation of aesthetics also had to be challenged. The ideal of a unity of spirit and sense, reason and spontaneity, with the body judiciously re-inserted into a rational discourse, was a false one. Instead the theatre of the sensational, life was to be revealed in all its sexuality-grounded hedonism, egoism and murderous aggressiveness. The alienated subject was to be rescued not from the reign of commodities or the death of God but by unmasking the libidinal, reconnecting it with the questions of life via the medical model of therapy. The rich, potent, serenely balanced subject (harmonious) was a myth; certainly the presenting problems of otherwise healthy patients showed that. Rather, there were people with drives in contradiction, faculties in state of war, fulfilments fleeting and tainted. The human subject was fissured and unfinished. The highest had its basis in the lowest.

He sought to demystify aesthetic disinterestedness. Idealists saw the sensuous without desire, and this had to be unmasked as pious naivety, for all was libidinal in origin. Psycho-social views were to be more dry-eyed and hard-headed about the corollaries of heady instinct, intuition and spontaneity, for these could be odious as well as great. And be sceptical of the compensating role of the aesthetic. Pleasure and reality are intermeshed; reality becomes a disguise for pleasure. Desire is sublime, defeating attempts at representation – giving voice to it is only displacing it.

The history of desire in its debate with authority: it is helpless and protected while dependent and submissive. Individuals and civilisations sought to temper the sadistic brutality of law, where to fall outside the law is to be sick. For the individual superego control is the law; but double binds means that the law cannot always be obeyed. It is the source of both idealism and guilt. Sublimating narcissism and aggression are also tied together; the more civilised we become the more internal guilt we contain, and are then subject to the authority of the discontented superego. There needs to be a balance of expression and control, mutual and reciprocal: man's turbulent constitution, arousing what it interdicts, provoking and containing revolt. The more Eros is sublimated the more vulnerable people are to Thanatos. Law abidance and impulses struggle, neither ever gaining final victory or defeat, both valued and resented, chronically inclined to abstract idealism. We can free arrested energies for other ends; but what other ends? The superego, grotesque suffering and high-mindedness, is counterbalanced by the comic.

Freud was, in this view, a pessimistic, conservative authoritarian, suspicious of the masses, supporting strong and charismatic leadership. Affectionate gratitude for the care of elders was the source of morality; learning to love is bound up with authority reverence and aggressive impulses. Seek rather an egalitarian style of loving, with reciprocity. That is the goal of psychoanalysis. People should not continue to pretend that the old vigorous, individualist ego is an adequate model. Instead they ought to look for deeper controlling structures, necessary forces and processes opaque to everyday consciousness, in the concepts of the unconscious, of being, the role of language and archetypes, covert and true determinants of identity which are inscrutable, logical in their operations but indifferent to people. In the idea of myth and eternal recurrence, the familiar returns with slight variation.

So, mirroring the trinity of the split of the cognitive, the ethico-political and the libidinal-aesthetic, there is the trinity of Marx, Nietzsche and Freud. Politics, knowledge and desire are uncoupled and become specialised. Knowledge as science is not linked to values. Why be moral? Just do what feels good. And art becomes an end in itself, as it has no other purpose: perhaps a safety valve or sublimation of dangerous aspects of the psyche. There is just a mess of marginalised pleasure, reified reason and empty morality. That is liberating; art is not constrained by church, court or state, just the market place and taste and style. So it exists for itself. So aesthetics is born at the moment of art's demise. It is aesthetics which holds out a hub for reuniting the three realms, by eating them up; everything becomes aesthetic. Truth is what satisfies the mind; morality is style. Politics takes an aesthetic twist. It can go leftward towards seeing 'play' and creativity as good means and ends, the Bohemian turn. Or it may go rightwards, towards the aesthetics of nation myth-making, nationalism and destiny.

The biggest picture within which to interpret the significance of aesthetics, the historical picture, is one of a progressive conflict between systems and humanity. By 'system' is meant the power of a partnership between economic agencies and the state, penetrating all areas of life and reorganising all else to suit themselves. This, rather than rationality founded on human, moral agency, or subject to genuine democratic and participatory processes, prevails. The instrumentalisation and remorseless systematisation of all forms of human activity ensue, and concerns with the aesthetic emerge as a counterpoint to this, if not an opposition. It raises issues about values other than those of concern to the economic and the state, and values of emancipation, of a cultural life free from labouring, or a culture manipulated to support elites in power. It represents the hope of pleasurable creativity available to all instead of a world in which the only purpose is to work, and keep working, and keep working; and on occasion fight.

Conclusion

The middle classes care both hugely and little about creativity, aesthetics and the rest; as long as their working lives are, for them, balanced, and their children obtain superior schooling and have professional career paths to give meaning and structure to their lifespans. They are happy with that, as long as they have values of a vaguely humanistic nature. As long as people are accepting of hierarchy, distinction and unique personal identity they can accommodate as much postmodernism as their colour supplements might care to cover. What actually threaten their hegemony is not coherent political movements but the continuing, ceaseless, relentless whirlwinds of the rule of dynamism, of commodification undermining what they actually value, taking away their professions, their work–life balance, their structures of meaning. The ways of the commodity bring potential disruption, the ruin of hierarchy, distinction and personal identity; cash prevails over vague humanism. The era may be replete with high-sounding metaphysics about the spiritual, about God, freedom and family, but its advocates keep getting caught with their fingers in the till, and they have no shame about that but can always excuse themselves as some kind of victim. Or appear a fool or a hypocrite: that is preferable to taking any blame and shame.

So it is that capitalism continues to subvert the middle classes' comfortable aesthetics, not letting the double standards rest. Is pleasure important or not, are the desires of the body to be accommodated or not? The middle classes continue to rate culture as highly as ever, and to express love for the arts, but to have no time for them. As truth is no longer in fashion, and gross deception, cover-up and lying are permanent and structural features of the culture, this may seem small beer. But actually it matters; all kinds of things may become potentially explosive. This is what continues to embolden the artists, and give them treacherous hope. Artists turn from avant-garde diversions back to their art forms, to making dramas of things which should be trivial by now, but which may yet have power. The system is not too powerful to be broken; the system is a web of aesthetic valuing that is continuously open to contest and change; those who control the means of aesthetic valuing can engage with interests, desires and beliefs.

What began centuries ago with an interest in the aesthetic as a modest assertion of the body against the tyranny of abstract reason becomes a source of a radical critique of contemporary capitalism. For as a systematising administrative rationality rules over all else, including the moral and democratic, it also erodes its own resources. It undermines aesthetic consensus, upsetting the double standards and exposing people to pleasure, the libidinal, the desirable. People who have sought to defend the lived against the logical, and defend what was immanent in arts against the functional demands of economic systems, sense a turn of the screw. For some there has been a deep mistrust of all and any aesthetic value, what it represented and what it could be used for. Alternatively, aesthetics provided a retreat from the nightmare of history and dealing with the demands of reality. The retreat into the aesthetic, once as a kind of resolution, is now, though, an impossibility.

12 Ending the silence aesthetically

> The abandonment of utopia is just as treacherous as the hope for it, the negations of the actual are as indispensable as they are ineffectual, [and] art is at once precious and worthless.
>
> (Eagleton 1990, p. 357)

Introduction

Through all the analysis that has gone before is a sustained confrontation with several powerful beliefs. These are: that people are just individuals whose ultimate value is purely a function of their place in society; that material standards of living provide the ultimate criterion of 'the good life'; that science as the means of raising the standard of living is the ultimate to value. In this context the aesthetic is merely gloss added to the substance of material wealth to make it shine more brightly. The only serious questions are how to keep increasing and effectively distributing the world's wealth, and these are not questions aesthetic analysis is competent to address. While all those powerful beliefs have been challenged by aesthetic analysts, it remains the case that aesthetic analysis can be its own worst enemy.

In conclusion, some problems around seeking to understand the greater interaction of HRD and aesthetics in the context of meanings, membership of the creative class and its manufacture are explored with reference to the values system model. The issue is how the values underlying the aesthetic framework impact on other stakeholders in HRD, the sceptical economists, the committed social campaigners, the critical positivist scientists or the pragmatic politicians, and how aesthetics may offer a value system for understanding and interpreting HRD. The challenge is to make as clear a case as can be made that understanding the totality of realising people's potential is enriched by acknowledging that the aesthetic exists and matters. That gestalt can help to counteract the imbalances produced by other frameworks: the utilitarian imbalances of impractical measurement ambitions, the social imbalance of seeking through HRD to remedy problems whose roots are elsewhere, the political imbalance of the right and the left in co-opting HRD to their causes, and the theoretic distortions of objectivism. There is also an imbalance, a shadow side, to the aesthetic way of making sense of HRD.

This can be understood via the imbalance it introduces with regard to each of the other value systems. These would include being anti-economic, by valuing 'higher' things and artfulness, making HRD ineffectual, not more effective; by being in effect anti-social, and accommodating mysticism, the irrational and the Bohemian instead of concentrating on pressing social issues; by being anti-truth, offering a refuge to any fantasy, falsehood or ideology as long as it looks right and is fashionable, as long as it makes the right impression; by being anti-political, offering an excuse to substitute personal creativity for collective action, living inside the belly of the whale; and by being anti-spiritual, affording the sensual and the passionate precedence over the moral. These are all issues which can impede the acknowledgement and development of an aesthetic analysis appropriate for an era in which creativity and the creative class do offer real and significant challenges.

Two faces of aesthetics: sense and nonsense

Take it, then, that everywhere – from the grand scale of the physical environment inhabited, the buildings and homes, the furniture and products people use, to the detail of the food they require for nourishment – everything is now much more consciously and explicitly informed by aesthetics, by look and feel issues and how that shapes the choices people make. Yet sense and nonsense in HRD discourses does not yet appear to be be affected by that; it is still centred around utilitarian, ameliorative, strategy, performance and conventional policy reform discourses: there seems to be little scope for the 'philosophical' and 'academic' language of aesthetics to be adopted.

Yet in HRD there are also emerging attempts to connect social issues with the economic, to understand the psychology of informal learning, to re-introduce spirituality as a dimension to organisational analysis. These all represent attempts to unsettle the prevailing hierarchy of values and restore a fuller view of sense in HRD. Of course this brings with it threats of new kinds of nonsense, to add to those that already prevail The desire to now research 'informal learning', learning careers, community learning and experiential learning recognises how much of an error past limited and narrow views of training and learning have been. But in researching these the same mistakes may be made if a broader but still partial and limited set of value systems and participants are engaged. To better make sense of people making sense of HRD, the need is to seek out the sensational, the passionate, the human, to find the attractive and the repulsive. There are fears that expanding values, and including in HRD concerns about aesthetics, will produce distortions of understanding HRD (see Table 12.1).

It is possible to connect aesthetics with HRD, as a long marginalised source of sense-making based on values which stand alongside the economic,

Table 12.1 Concerns about the impact of aesthetic valuing

	Core value	Creative class distortions
Economic	HRD as means to an end	Beautifying HRD as an end in itself
Social	Family and community matter most	Look and feel of specialist institutions and professionals takes precedence
Theoretic	Rigorous system-building	Attractive accounts are preferred
Political	Emancipating concerns Inter-subjective and mutual reflection and critique	Consuming concerns displace change, interests masked
Spiritual	Human potential development is a sacred duty	Narcissism of self-affirmation

social, political and theoretic as ways of understanding HRD. How this impact from aesthetics into HRD, via exploring developing potential as an art rather than a science, was explored. How HRD also provides the base of the infrastructure of the aesthetic age, enabling the creation of the creative class, was also explored.

There are objections to proposing an aesthetic and HRD interdependency and the lines of inquiry associated with it. These include objecting to the 'superficiality' of concerns with look and feel, with style; the negative or ideological aspects of dealing in constructs of beauty; and the objection that effective HRD is to be based on the 'success' of psychological models of learning. These last do not require an understanding of the nebulous unities of mind, body and sensibility. Overall, the objection is that engaging with the problems of 'continental philosophy' in which the contemporary study of the aesthetic is seen to be entangled constitutes a diversion from the real tasks faced (for example, Gross and Levitt 1994).

Aesthetics can be seen to matter for practice in and perceptions of HRD in both directions. In one way they suggest a need for creativity, innovation and imagination to be taken more to heart in the world of HRD; there ought to be some explicit discussion of them in major HRD texts. In another way they express a critique of the physical, cultural and pedagogic facilities, relations and institutions that embody design methodologies, and approaches to education, training and development, or managing and organising, that can be perceived to be inadequate in the learning societies, knowledge economies and global culture we are currently meant to be constructing. The emerging infrastructure needs to be questioned, and aesthetic sense-making offers one way of doing that. Is the existing infrastructure up to the job, is it in the right physical and cultural places and is it a socio-technical system allowing us to do the right things? Some worry that it is not: that the whole edifice of the infrastructure, the buildings, professions, technologies, systems and processes of education, training and development are part of the problem (Laurillard 2002).

The legitimacy, or otherwise, of exploring these connections depends on seeing HRD as involving an aesthetic, as well as a social, economic, political and scientific, enterprise. But suggesting that understanding aesthetic value is central to HRD, in the senses cited above, rather than either materialistic questions associated with 'economic models' of human capital or phenomenological questions about constructing better learning organisations, raises further questions. Better understanding aesthetic value can be a means to a desired end: more people involved in better HRD. And it is an end whose pursuit in itself can make overcoming trials and troubles, the vicissitudes, easier rather than harder.

The case against aesthetic values

To take up arms against the aesthetic imperative, and oppose it, is of obvious appeal to all opposing value systems in some way. A brief recall of the harsh realities of shareholder judgements about company performance, or the merest visiting of the facts of life which afflict the poorest nations and peoples of the world, would provide justification enough for many. Equally the lack of immediate pragmatic policy change in what the aesthetic entails, and a long tradition of narrow-minded critical realism in management studies, would equally dismiss the potential of the aesthetic. The look and feel of HRD where even basic education is a struggle against the odds seems strange, if not even an obscene, concern. It would be tempting to dismiss Postrel's paeans to dynamism, and Florida's prescriptions for weak social ties as being only too typical of the denuded, class-bound and socially bereft view of human sensibility prevailing among some populisers of an aesthetic imperative era view.

That would be a mistake. There are in the analysis of aesthetics ideas and outcomes of significance across the board; this is not a creed for the elite, advanced, affluent, Western ears and eyes alone. The more academically robust approaches (Carr and Hancock 2003), disinterring the work of the Frankfurt School to take up arms against an unbridled hedonism around consumption, represent one strand of that, though they also display the contrasting difficulty. Being essentially philosophical in their analyses, they are in danger of not connecting with anyone much beyond fellow travellers and the already converted. To address the aesthetic is to seek to address a real issue of substance, the interest in the aesthetic imperative, that should not be easily driven back to the sidelines. The proponents of the idea of a strong aesthetics imperative may be overselling something as new that has always been around. It may have been overshadowed in recent history, but the aesthetic imperative as a construct of interest, import and impact has been an abiding source of value that civilised humanity has held fast to. It has been reinvented, along with morality and metaphysics, to help inform and shape our behaviours, our identities, our cultures and our lives from the cradle to the grave. Or, perhaps more to the point, informed and shaped our behaviours from perceiving the attractions of a potential partner to the defence mechanism that consciousness employs once our loved ones die.

So HRD is something that is produced and consumed, and it may be seen to be connected with aesthetic imperatives, rather than being an 'aesthetics free' subject. This may involve connecting practice in and perceptions of HRD with various concepts associated with aesthetics; such as ideas about creativity, drawing on personal and cultural judgements about the beautiful, and the role of human imagination. It extends more broadly to connecting aesthetics-based analyses with better understanding of human nature and identity and the strengths and weaknesses of investing in HRD among people who exist as agents, blessed and cursed, with a mind–body sensibility complex. At one level the culmination of all this is simply to identify the general, ideal properties involved in creating pleasing and delightful experiences, a universalistic template of what looks and feels right in different circumstances, and it is of value aesthetically to engage people in HRD. In contrast, the notion of a clear, normative culmination to this analysis may be seen as doomed; at best there may be reference to 'fit', that what is of value aesthetically is to be determined in terms of a fit with different kinds of people in different kinds of situations. Theories about these, not a single universal standard, are the eventual outcome. Do we seek rigid, geometric forms and structures, or looser and wild forms and structures? Do we seek to nurture harmonious people, or do we seek the conditions in which optimum conflict drives the desire for future fulfilment from current discontent?

For either the positivist or the naturalist conception of HRD the idea that creativity, beauty and imagination matter, and with them the engagement of mind, body and sensibilities, is not then alien. But exploring what is and what might be using concepts that are aesthetically warranted and in ways that are derived from understanding aesthetics, rather than those offered by science, is different in each case. For one it is about operationalising what creativity, beauty and imagination mean, and why they matter and have a legitimate role to play in understanding, studying and practising HRD. For the other it is about importing debates about contemporary art into discussing organisation and management to better inform better HRD.

In the positivistic tradition the aesthetic can be discerned to be a concern or perspective already in use, even if disguised, in the direct and explicit discussion of design in HRD. The preparation of blueprints, a design activity, has always been seen to follow on after an analysis stage. This is the case in the modelling of the classic training cycle, for those who see HRD as training-oriented, or in terms of organisation design for those who adopt a broader definition (Piskurich *et al.* 2000). This introduces, but also at the same time relegates, questions of aesthetics: introducing a narrow conception of design, relegating it to the technical preparation of blueprints for best practice training programmes. In fields of design outside HRD, for example in graphic, building or product design, the use of this concept of design is sometimes similarly narrow, but it can also be much broader and significant. In a narrow sense, blueprints for, respectively, an act of communication, a building or a product are needed to guide their actual construction.

Designing is, in this sense, a technical process of creating the abstract, two-dimensional using drawings or three-dimensional using scale models, to pre-figure the construction of actual, material, objects. But design is also about ideas being articulated and appraised, and about creative and aesthetically pleasing solutions being made manifest. This is not a stage encountered after analysis; it is a stage encountered from the very outset. It requires the use of the imagination, creativity and a sense of beauty informing decisions and judgements from the beginning. In these areas, creativity is inherent in any design, which is an activity driven by reaction: reaction against an established set of standards, a look, a prevailing fashion. These dynamics of prevailing fashion and reaction require imagination and creativity at the heart of such activities, not as an afterthought. In producing beautiful as well as functional HRD objects and experiences, this is inevitable.

The equivocation about accepting aesthetic imperatives in either the positivist or naturalist perspective is also philosophical; it confronts some cherished beliefs about HRD, hardened in the pursuit of a more serious and strategic role for HRD in modern business and management. The apparent advantages of scientific research, and the pressures to be seen as being 'of value' in business, have become apparently inseparable and highly satisfied bedfellows. One consequence of this is to exclude considerations of aesthetics and beauty as relevant or sensible in the 'real world' of practising or improving HRD, in developing better-quality HRD or structuring change in or through HRD. Beauty is not utilitarian. Imagination is not strategic. Creativity is not the key to change. Aesthetes may be right to seek out or to create beauty, but this has no social or moral purpose which serves the interests of organisations. And HRD is not for aesthetes, it is too concerned with the functional. What matters is what works, not how it looks or appears.

Conclusion

Aesthetic valuing ultimately matters at all only in as much as it affects conduct. The culture of HRD is one that is too strongly influenced by the economic, social, political and theoretic and not enough by the aesthetic and the spiritual. Rather than continuing to extend HRD and affecting conduct by producing objective theory, HRD has become bogged down in utilitarian and scientific rationalism. HRD needs to become better connected with conduct that fits with aesthetic valuing: being creative, exploring beauty, exciting and enacting the imagination. This is not to be overly prescriptive, for when debates that resurrect the spiritual and/or the aesthetic emerge, curious variations arise. Florida considers the creative class and contends with social capital prescriptions for the quasi-anonymous lifestyle. Postrel considers this an age of aesthetics more than any other, a new dividing line between forces for and against capitalism formed around matters of style.

For both of these, though, it is the old vigorous individualist ego that is still an adequate base for understanding. The potential roles of the unconscious, of language, of archetypes in determining identity, and along with these the sense of what HRD could be, are to be considered, not ignored. In this context the issue of the artful versus the industrial arises.

For the aesthete, the artful, the principle of art matters more than anything else, and the freedom to be artful has to prevail above all else. In this context artfulness means being autonomous of social relations, free to do what the artful choose to do. On the other hand, in such circumstances the artful is in effect ignored, as it is no longer an integral part of social relations. Neutralisation was the price of autonomous artfulness, with artists free to be as openly subversive as they wanted to be, and nobody much caring. That is why for Eagleton creativity, beauty, imagination and aesthetics are at once precious and worthless. This is the dilemma the aesthete has to live with, and which is to be replicated in HRD as that is aestheticised.

For as art is both precious and worthless, then if HRD is artful it too encounters that bind. The problem is traceable back to the big split, to the differentiation of the domains that had been intermeshed: the cognitive (knowing), the ethico-political (acting) and the libidinal-aesthetic (desiring). Each was linked with the other; knowing constrained by the moral, acting not existential but centered on clear roles, art not separate. Then these three great areas of history and life, knowledge, politics and desire were uncoupled and became specialised. Knowledge was to be scientific, and not linked to values. There was no need to be moral, just to do what felt good. Art became an end in itself, as it had no other purpose, except for the creator as a safety valve or sublimation of aspects of the psyche. The aesthetic became an environment in which this split has been glimpsed, analysed and struggled with. Every domain that seeks to appropriate the aesthetic invariably has to engage with these issues. So it is for HRD. It is another arena where the conflict between being free to do what is creative and imaginative is in tension with seeking to embed the subject back in a unified form; where knowledge, politics and desire are recoupled, and make sense in wider social relations. That kind of embeddedness is the only path through HRD to the ends desired, not the free agency and imaginative creativity of the independent aesthete: the ends of a better world, a place of solidarity, mutual affinity, peace, security, fruitful communication.

So the essential argument comes down to this: in pursuit of change and progress the role of the aesthetic is to offer an alternative to a world seemingly founded on or shaped by science and technology, over-dependence on science and technology tends to exclude or trivialise the aesthetic. People do not sense that they depend upon the aesthetic, they sense that they depend upon science and technology. The aesthetic is reduced to a secondary role, a diversion or entertainment. The attendant confusion of art and entertainment that this produces causes a further difficulty. This is the contest between those concerned about the triumph of pop culture and the attack on high standards of aesthetic achievement and those for the democratisation of culture and its humanisation.

There is though, an agreement that aesthetics, and aesthetic analysis, provides people with moral challenge and insight. Scientific rationalism is not a moral resource; it only helps us decide how best to do things that have already been decided upon. HRD, is not about the science of skills development in isolation, but about how to think about people and their potential.

The continuing successes of science and technology render culture, the arts and humanities, the aesthetic, both more precarious and more precious. They are more precarious because they seem of such little economic, social, political and theoretic value. They are more precious as the preservation of culture, the arts and the aesthetic as more than entertainment and diversion, as a source of making sense of conduct, is as essential as ever. As the potentials of science and technology present more moral challenges, from the prospects of genetic engineering to the assumption that every problem facing mankind is susceptible to technological intervention and control, the troubled voices of those concerned with aesthetics need to be heard more strongly and loudly. Exploring aesthetics in HRD is not an excuse to be diverted from appreciating the role and function of developing people's potential: it is an invitation to confront current and future dilemmas face on.

Notes

1 Pretty smart

1 In England only.

3 Valuing aesthetics

1 The term at the root of all this, 'values', is complex and is often used interchangeably with the term 'belief'. Another concern is the emphasis on 'humanism'. However warranted a humanist approach to any aspect of human science may seem to be, humanism is itself a form of belief, a form of satisfactory truth, and cannot be assumed to be a transcendental framework. To pursue the study of values or beliefs in human systems should not mean having to subscribe to cultural or political versions of humanism, making the debate one between humanists and their opponents rather than being about analysing beliefs. Certainly in the development of social psychology and phenomenological sociology, where beliefs have been a central concern, there appears to be a strong humanist tradition. The extent to which any values-based approach, given its commitments to fidelity with human experience while ostensibly 'bracketing' all assumptions, will inevitably lead to a humanist interpretation of truth, is an area to explore later.

2 For instance, some individuals may hold right goals and consider right behaviours regarding always being practical and of utility. That will be central to their identity and sense of what is ethical for them and others; consequently they will have goals associated with being of use, and these will mean most and will be most important to them. They will then hold values that illustrate this; they will value hard work, commitment to work, useful employment of time and resources. They may feel that spending time on work is far more important than being with their friends or family, and they may perceive individuals whom they see as having an alternative, perhaps more family-oriented value system, as being weak, inadequate and soft, as this precludes them being practical and useful.

3 The issue here is accepting or rejecting the idea that human sciences are required to emulate the processes of the natural sciences rather than the processes of the humanities. The former entails formulating hypotheses within theoretical frameworks, defining relationships between variables, and using objective and reliable measurements and observations. This provides explanations based on statistics, universal laws and processes. But along with this 'reality' is fragmented; research is limited to parts, details and elements, and not the study of the whole person. The individual, in whom all these fragmented parts are amalgamated in a meaningful way, is a mystery to science. The historical and continuing appeal of developmental psychologists such as Freud and Piaget, who still feature in rankings of the top psychologists, is that they sought such gestalts, merging cognitive, emotional, personal, motivational, perceptual and physical development into a complete picture.

4   Spranger defined them as the theoretic, the economic, the aesthetic, the social, the political and the religious. They accord, respectively, with giving precedence to the ethics of legality, utilitarianism, form and harmony, loving and caring, a will to power, or adherence to faith-based codes.
5   The existence of faith-based schools in the UK is evidence to some extent of a continuing spiritual value system participant influence, but this is not the norm; the norm is professional, neutral, state or privately funded development, aside from religious values.

4 The illusion of potential

1   The late twentieth-century fad of aiming to discover the 'child within' as a healing and therapeutic process revisited this Romantic ideal.

5 Caring about beauty

1   It is intriguing to see that these reflect the varieties of value system adopted for this text; with economic, political, spiritual and social versions alongside the aesthetic as ways of coping with status anxiety.

8 Beyond artfulness

1   Often behind the attempt to shock, to render reality absurd, is a motive to prompt people to seek a truer life rather than just laconically accept the absurd.

10 Creative industries

1   This outline of the history and context was informed by the excellent Radio 4 series *The Cultural State*, broadcast in the UK in 2004, presented by Tony Wilson.

References

Allen, A. (2003) Out of the Ordinary, *People Management*, 4 December; online journal, available at http://peoplemanagement.co.uk.

Allport, G. W., Vernon, P. E., Lindzey, G. (1970) *Manual: Study of Values*, third edition, revised, Boston: Houghton Mifflin.

Amabile, T. M. (1998) How to Kill Creativity, *Harvard Business Review*, Vol. 76, No. 5, pp. 76–88.

Austin, R., Devin, L. (2003) *Artful Making: What Managers Need to Know about How Artists Work*, New Jersey: FT Prentice Hall.

Averett, S., Korenman, S. (1996) The Economic Reality of the Beauty Myth, *Journal of Human Resources*, Vol. 31, No. 2, Spring, pp. 304–30.

Baer, M., Oldham, G. R., Cummings, A. (2003) Rewarding Creativity: When Does It Really Matter? *Leadership Quarterly*, Vol. 14, No. 5, pp. 569–86.

Balakrishnan, V. (2004) *Remaking Singapore*. Online. Available http://www.remakingsinga-pore.gov.sg (accessed 11 September 2004).

Beardsley, M. (1966) *Aesthetics from Classical Greece to the Present: A Short History*, New York: Macmillan.

Berger, P., Luckman, T. (1979) *The Social Construction of Reality*, Harmondsworth: Penguin.

Berger, R. (2003) *An Ethic of Excellence: Building a Culture of Craftsmanship with Students*, Portsmouth, NH: Heinemann, 2003.

Boud, D., Miller, M. (eds) (1996) *Working with Experience: Animating Learning*, London: Routledge.

Bredeson, P. V. (2003) *Designs for Learning*, Thousand Oaks, CA: Corwin Press.

Burke, E. (1998) *A Philosophical Enquiry into the Origins of our Ideas of the Sublime and the Beautiful*, Oxford: Oxford University Press.

Carr, A., Hancock, P. (2003) *Art and Aesthetics At Work*, Basingstoke: Palgrave Macmillan.

Caudron, S. (1994) Strategies for Managing Creative Workers, *Personnel Journal*, Vol. 73, No. 12, pp. 104–11.

Cazeaux, C. (2000) *The Continental Aesthetics Reader*. London: Routledge.

Coleman, E. (2004) *The Pedagogy of Making, Cultural Comment*. Available http://www.cultural-commons.org (accessed 16 October 2004).

Cowling, P. (2004) *The Arts and Organisational Change*, IPPR seminar summary. Available http://www.ippr.org/culture (accessed 16 October 2004).

Darso, L. (2004) *Artful Creation: Learning-Tales of Arts-In-Business*, Gylling, Denmark: Narayana Press.

Darso, L., Dawids, M. (2002) Arts in Business: Proposing a Theoretical Framework, paper given at the conference of the European Academy of Management, Stockholm, Sweden.

Davies, I. (1975) *Objectives in Curriculum Design*, London: McGraw Hill.

De Botton, A. (2004) *Status Anxiety*, London: Hamish Hamilton.

Eagleton, T. (1990) *The Ideology of the Aesthetic*, Oxford: Blackwell.

Earl, T. (1987) *The Art and Craft of Course Design*, London: Kogan Page.

Eco, U. (2004) *Beauty: A History of a Western Idea*, London: Secker and Warburg.

Egan, K. (1992) *Imagination in Teaching and Learning*, London: Routledge.

Eisner, E. (2002) *The Arts and the Creation of Mind*, New Haven, CT: Yale University Press.

Etcoff, N. (1999) *Survival of the Prettiest: The Science of Beauty*, London: Little, Brown.

Evans, M. (2001) The Economy of the Imagination, The *New Statesman* Arts Lecture, *New Statesman*, 2 July, available at http://www.mla.gov.uk/information/policy/newstat01.asp (accessed February 2005).

Florida, R. (2002) *The Rise of the Creative Class*, New York: Basic Books.

Fukuyama, F. (1995) *Trust: The Social Virtues and the Creation of Prosperity*, London: Penguin.

Gadamer, H.-G. (1979) *Truth and Method*, London: Sheed Ward.

Gagne, R., Perkins Driscoll, M. (1988) *Essentials of Learning for Instruction*, Englewood Cliffs, NJ: Prentice Hall.

Gallwey, T. (1986) *The Inner Game of Golf*, London: Pan Books.

Gardner, H. (1982) *Art, Mind, and Brain*, New York: Basic Books.

Gilley, A., Callahan, J., Bierma, L. (2003) *Critical Issues in HRD*, Cambridge: Perseus.

GLRA (Global Renaissance Alliance, now the Peace Alliance Foundation) (2004) website, available at http://www.renaissancealliance.org/.

Goguen, J. A. (1999) Art and the Brain, *Journal of Consciousness Studies*, Vol. 6, No. 6/7, June/July, special feature.

Gross, P., Levitt, N. (1994) *Higher Superstition: The Academic Left and Its Quarrels with Science*, Baltimore, MD: Johns Hopkins University Press.

Grossman, D., DeGaetano, D. (1999) *Stop Teaching Our Kids to Kill: A Call to Action Against TV, Movie and Video Game Violence*, New York: Crown Publishers.

Habermas, J. (1984) *The Theory of Communicative Action, Volume 1*, Cambridge: Polity Press.

Hamermesh, D., Biddle, J. E. (1994) Beauty and the Labor Market, *American Economic Review*, Vol. 84, December, pp. 1174–94.

Heap, N. (1996) The Design of Learning Events, *Industrial and Commercial Training*, Vol. 28, No. 10, pp. 10–14.

Henneman, T. (2004) A New Approach to Faith at Work, *Workforce Management*, October, pp. 76–7.

Henry, J. (ed.) (1991) *Creative Management*, London: Sage.

Howard, V. A. (1992) *Learning by All Means: Lessons from the Arts*, New York: Peter Lang Publishing.

Huizinga, J. (1938/1971) *Homo ludens. Proeve eener bepaling van het spelelement der cultuur*, translated as *Homo Ludens: A Study in the Play-Elements in Culture*, trans. R. F. C. Hull, Boston: Beacon Press.

Jaccaci, A. T. (1989) The Social Architecture of a Learning Culture, *Training and Development Journal*, Vol. 43, No. 11, pp. 49–51.

Johnson, S. D. (1992) HRD and Corporate Creativity – Reaction, *Human Resource Development Quarterly*, Vol. 3, pp. 239–42.

Kao, J. (1996) The Heart of Creativity, *Across the Board*, Vol. 33, No. 8, pp. 23–8.

King, L. (2002) *Game On: The History and Culture of Videogames*, London: Laurence King Publishing.

Kingdon, P. (2002) *Sticky Wisdom: How to Start a Creative Revolution at Work*, London: Capstone.

Kirwin, J. (1999) *Beauty*, Manchester: Manchester University Press.

Klein, N. (2000) *No Logo,* London: Flamingo.

Knowles, M. S. (1984) *Andragogy in Action; Applying Modern Principles of Adult Learning*, San Francisco: Jossey Bass.

—— (1998) *The Adult Learner: The Definitive Classic in Adult Education and Human Resource Development*, fifth edition, Woburn: Butterworth Heinemann.

Kolb, D. (1984) *Experiential Learning: Experience as the Source of Learning and Development*, Englewood Cliffs, NJ: Prentice-Hall.

Krohe, J. (1996) Managing Creativity, *Across the Board,* Vol. 33, No. 8, pp. 16–21.

Langlois, L., Kalankanis, L., Rubenstein, A., Larson, A., Hallam, M., Smoot, M. (2000) Maxims or Myths of Beauty: A Meta-Analytical and Theoretical Review, *Psychological Bulletin*, Vol. 126, No. 3, pp. 390–423.

Laurillard, D. (2002) *Re-thinking University Teaching.* London: Routledge Falmer.

Lave, J., Wenger, E. (1991) *Situated Learning: Legitimate Peripheral Participation*, Cambridge: Cambridge University Press.

Lawson, B. (1997) *How Designers Think: The Design Process Demystified*, Oxford: Architectural Press.

Lieberman, J. N. (1977) *Playfulness: Its Relationship to Imagination and Creativity*, New York: Academic Press.

Lucas, B. (2004) Think Again, *People Management*, 29 January; online journal, available at http://peoplemanagement.co.uk

Lyman, D. H. (1989) Being Creative, *Training and Development Journal*, Vol. 43, No. 4, pp. 45–9.

Lyotard, J. (1994) *Lessons on the Analytic of the Sublime*, Stanford, CA: Stanford University Press.

McDermott, L. (2004) The Empire Strikes Back, *Sunday Herald,* 4 April.

McGoldrick, J., Stewart, J., Watson, S. (2002) *Understanding HRD: A Research Based Approach*, London: Routledge.

Marcuse, H. (1979) *Aesthetic Dimension: Toward a Critique of Marxist Aesthetics*, Boston: Beacon Press.

Marquardt, M., Berger, N., Loan, P. (2004) *HRD in the Age of Globalization*, Cambridge: Perseus.

Mellander, K. (2001) Engaging the Human Spirit: A Knowledge Evolution Demands the Right Conditions for Learning, *Journal of Intellectual Capital*, Vol. 2, No. 2, pp. 165–71.

Mole, G. (1996) The Management Training Industry in the UK: An HRD Director's Critique, *Human Resource Management Journal*, Vol. 6, No. 1, pp. 19–26.

NACCE (1999) *All Our Futures: Creativity, Culture and Education*, London: DfEE.

Nicholls, S., Nicholls, A. (1975) *Creative Teaching: An Approach to the Achievement of Educational Objectives*, London: George Allen and Unwin.

Norman, D. (2001) *The Design of Everyday Things*, London: MIT Press.

Oldham, G. R., Cummings, A. (1996) Employee Creativity: Personal and Contextual Factors at Work, *Academy of Management Journal*, Vol. 39, No 3, pp. 607–35.

Osborn, A. F. (1953) *Applied Imagination*, New York: Charles Scribner's Sons.

—— (1964) *How to Become More Creative*, New York: Charles Scribner's Sons.

Page, C. (2004) Wife's Sex Trauma Highlights Offshore Safety, *Press and Journal*, 29 June, p. 7.

Paxton, R. O. (2004) *The Anatomy of Fascism*, London: Allen Lane.

Phillips, D., Soltis, J. (1998) *Perspectives on Learning*, New York: Teachers College.

Phipps, M., Trezona, M. (2001) *Did It Deliver? Evaluating Arts-Based Training Inside Business*, London: A&B.

Piskurich, G. M., Beckschi, P., Hall, B. (eds) (2000) *The ASTD Handbook of Training Design and Delivery*, New York: McGraw-Hill.

Pollock, L. (2000) That's Infotainment, *People Management*, 28 December.

Postrel, V. (1999) *The Future and Its Enemies; The Growing Conflict over Creativity, Enteprise and Progress*, New York: Touchstone.

—— (2003) *The Substance of Style*, New York: HarperCollins.

Powell, W. (2003) *Little Fun Goes a Long Way*, online. Available at http://www.learningcircuits.org/NR/exeres/88B0DE45–05FB-4B20–94EA-10C12B0F4D19.htm (accessed 12 October 2004).

Prensky, M. (2003) *Digital Game-Based Learning*, San Franciso: McGraw Hill.

Ramachandran, V. S., Hirstein, W. (2000) The Science of Art: A Neurological Theory of Aesthetic Experience, *Journal of Consciousness Studies*, Vol. 7, No. 8–9, pp. 15–51.

Robinson, A. G., Stern, S., (1997) *Corporate Creativity: How Innovation and Improvement Actually Happen*, San Francisco: Berrett-Koehler Publishers.

Rogers, Carl (1969) *Freedom to Learn*, Columbus, OH: Merrill.

Rokeach, M. (1960) *The Open and Closed Mind: Investigations into the Nature of Belief Systems and Personality Systems*, New York: Basic Books.

—— (1970) *Beliefs, Attitudes, and Values: A Theory of Organization and Change*, San Francisco: Jossey-Bass.

—— (1973) *The Nature of Human Values*, New York: Free Press.

SCANS (2004) *Secretary's Commission on Achieving Necessary Skills*. Online. Available http://wdr.doleta.gov/SCANS/ (accessed 13 October 2004).

Schön, D. (1995) *The Reflective Practitioner: How Professionals Think in Action*, Aldershot: Arena.

Schram, J. (2002) *How Do People Learn? The Change Agenda*, London: CIPD.

SCMS (2001) *Creative Industries Mapping Document 2001*, London: Department for Culture, Media and Sport.

Shalley, C. E., Gilson, L. L. (2004) What Leaders Need to Know: A Review of Social and Contextual Factors that can Foster or Hinder Creativity, *Leadership Quarterly*, Vol. 15, No. 1, pp. 33–53.

Shani, A. B., Docherty, P. (2003) *Learning by Design*, London: Blackwell.

Simpson, L. (2001) Fostering Creativity, *Training*, Vol. 38, No. 2, pp. 54–8.

Solomon, C. (1990) What An Idea: Creative Training, *Personnel Journal*, Vol. 69, No. 5, pp. 64–71.

Spivey, N. (2004) *Enduring Creation; Art, Pain and Fortitude*, London: Thames and Hudson.

Spranger, E. (1928) *Types of Men: The Psychology and Ethics of Personality*, trans. P. J. W. Pigors, Halle: Max Niemeyer. (Original work published 1914 under the title *Lebensformen: Geisteswissenschaftliche Psychologie und Ethik der Persönlichkeit*.)

Stern, S. (1992) The Relationship between Human Resource Development and Corporate Creativity in Japan, *Human Resource Development Quarterly*, Vol. 3, pp. 215–34.

Strati, A., Guillet de Montoux, P. (2002) Organizing Aesthetics, *Human Relations*, Vol. 55, No. 7, pp. 755–66.

Swanson, R., Holton, E. (2001) *Foundations of Human Resource Development*, San Francisco: Berret-Koehler.

Teo, T. (2000) Eduard Spranger, in A. E. Kazdin (ed.), *Encyclopedia of Psychology*, New York: Oxford University Press, Vol. 7, pp. 458–9.

Tierney, P., Farmer, S. M. (2004) The Pygmalion Process and Employee Creativity, *Journal of Management*, Vol. 30, No. 3, pp. 413–32.

Tierney, P., Farmer, S. M., Graen, G. B. (1999) An Examination of Leadership and Employee Creativity: The Relevance of Traits and Relationships, *Personnel Psychology*, Vol. 53, No. 3, pp. 591–621.

Tillich, P. (2000) *The Courage To Be*, second edition, New Haven, CT: Yale University Press.

Tobin, P., Shrubshall, C. (2002) *How to Access and Manage Creativity in Organisations*, London: RSA.

Van Slyke, E. J. (1999) Resolve Conflict, Boost Creativity, *HR Magazine*, Vol. 44, No. 12, pp. 132–6.

Vickery, J. (2003) *Organising Art: Constructing Aesthetic Value*. Online. Available http://www.essex.ac.uk/AFM/emc/tamara_call.htm (accessed 21 August 2003).

White, C. (2003) *I Love the Middle Mind: Why Americans Don't Think for Themselves*, London: Allen Lane.

Wilkinson, P., Foster, L. (2003) *New Partners; Evaluation, a Guide and Workbook*, London: A&B.

Williams, S. D. (2001) Increasing Employees' Creativity by Training their Managers, *Industrial and Commercial Training*, Vol. 33, No. 2, pp. 63–72.

—— (2002) Self-Esteem and the Self-Censorship of Creative Ideas, *Personnel Review*, Vol. 31, No. 4, pp. 495–501.

Winch, C. (1998) *The Philosophy of Human Learning*, London: Routledge.

Yell (2004) *A Nation of Shopkeepers No Longer: Welcome to Body Beautiful UK plc*. Online. Available at www.yellgroup.com/pages/pressreleases-anationofshopkeepersnolongerwelcom.html (accessed 13 October 2004).

Index